VOLUME 585

JANUARY 2003

THE ANNALS

of The American Academy of Political
and Social Science

ROBERT W. PEARSON, *Executive Editor*
ALAN W. HESTON, *Editor*

Higher Education in the Twenty-First Century

Special Editors of this Volume

PAUL RICH
*Policy Studies Organization and
University of the Americas–Puebla, Mexico*

DAVID MERCHANT
University of the Americas–Puebla, Mexico

SAGE Publications Ⓢ Thousand Oaks · London · New Delhi

Origin and Purpose. The Academy was organized December 14, 1889, to promote the progress of political and social science, especially through publications and meetings. The Academy does not take sides in controverted questions, but seeks to gather and present reliable information to assist the public in forming an intelligent and accurate judgment.

Meetings. The Academy occasionally holds a meeting in the spring extending over two days.

Publications. THE ANNALS of The American Academy of Political and Social Science is the bimonthly publication of the Academy. Each issue contains articles on some prominent social or political problem, written at the invitation of the editors. Also, monographs are published from time to time, numbers of which are distributed to pertinent professional organizations. These volumes constitute important reference works on the topics with which they deal, and they are extensively cited by authorities throughout the United States and abroad. The papers presented at the meetings of the Academy are included in THE ANNALS.

Membership. Each member of the Academy receives THE ANNALS and may attend the meetings of the Academy. Membership is open only to individuals. Annual dues: $71.00 for the regular paperbound edition (clothbound, $108.00). For members outside the U.S.A., add $24.00 for shipping of your subscription. Members may also purchase single issues of THE ANNALS for $21.00 each (clothbound, $29.00). Student memberships are available for $49.00.

Subscriptions. THE ANNALS of The American Academy of Political and Social Science (ISSN 0002-7162) is published six times annually—in January, March, May, July, September, and November— by Sage Publications, 2455 Teller Road, Thousand Oaks, CA 91320. Telephone: (800) 818-SAGE (7243) and (805) 499-9774; FAX/Order line: (805) 499-0871. Copyright © 2003 by The American Academy of Political and Social Science. Institutions may subscribe to THE ANNALS at the annual rate: $454.00 (clothbound, $513.00). Add $24.00 per year for subscriptions outside the U.S.A. Institutional rates for single issues: $88.00 each (clothbound, $98.00).

Periodicals postage paid at Thousand Oaks, California, and at additional mailing offices.

Single issues of THE ANNALS may be obtained by individuals who are not members of the Academy for $33.00 each (clothbound, $46.00). Single issues of THE ANNALS have proven to be excellent supplementary texts for classroom use. Direct inquiries regarding adoptions to THE ANNALS c/o Sage Publications (address below).

All correspondence concerning membership in the Academy, dues renewals, inquiries about membership status, and/or purchase of single issues of THE ANNALS should be sent to THE ANNALS c/o Sage Publications, 2455 Teller Road, Thousand Oaks, CA 91320. Telephone: (800) 818-SAGE (7243) and (805) 499-9774; FAX/Order line: (805) 499-0871. *Please note that orders under $30 must be prepaid.* Sage affiliates in London and India will assist institutional subscribers abroad with regard to orders, claims, and inquiries for both subscriptions and single issues.

Printed on recycled, acid-free paper

THE ANNALS

© 2003 by The American Academy of Political and Social Science

Editorial Office: 3814 Walnut Street, Fels Institute for Government, University of Pennsylvania, Philadelphia, PA 19104-6197.

For information about membership° (individuals only) and subscriptions (institutions), address:
Sage Publications
2455 Teller Road
Thousand Oaks, CA 91320

Sage Production Staff: Paul Reis, Barbara Corrigan, and Paul Doebler

From India and South Asia,
write to:
SAGE PUBLICATIONS INDIA Pvt Ltd
B-42 Panchsheel Enclave, P.O. Box 4109
New Delhi 110 017
INDIA

From Europe, the Middle East,
and Africa, write to:
SAGE PUBLICATIONS LTD
6 Bonhill Street
London EC2A 4PU
UNITED KINGDOM

°Please note that members of the Academy receive THE ANNALS with their membership.
International Standard Serial Number ISSN 0002-7162
International Standard Book Number ISBN 0-7619-2842-1 (Vol. 585, 2003 paper)
International Standard Book Number ISBN 0-7619-2843-X (Vol. 585, 2003 cloth)
Manufactured in the United States of America. First printing, January 2003.

The articles appearing in *The Annals* are abstracted or indexed in Academic Abstracts, Academic Search, America: History and Life, Asia Pacific Database, Book Review Index, CAB Abstracts Database, Central Asia: Abstracts & Index, Communication Abstracts, Corporate ResourceNET, Criminal Justice Abstracts, Current Citations Express, Current Contents: Social & Behavioral Sciences, e-JEL, EconLit, Expanded Academic Index, Guide to Social Science & Religion in Periodical Literature, Health Business FullTEXT, HealthSTAR FullTEXT, Historical Abstracts, International Bibliography of the Social Sciences, International Political Science Abstracts, ISI Basic Social Sciences Index, Journal of Economic Literature on CD, LEXIS-NEXIS, MasterFILE FullTEXT, Middle East: Abstracts & Index, North Africa: Abstracts & Index, PAIS International, Periodical Abstracts, Political Science Abstracts, Sage Public Administration Abstracts, Social Science Source, Social Sciences Citation Index, Social Sciences Index Full Text, Social Services Abstracts, Social Work Abstracts, Sociological Abstracts, Southeast Asia: Abstracts & Index, Standard Periodical Directory (SPD), TOPICsearch, Wilson OmniFile V, and Wilson Social Sciences Index/Abstracts, and are available on microfilm from University Microfilms, Ann Arbor, Michigan.

Information about membership rates, institutional subscriptions, and back issue prices may be found on the facing page.

Advertising. Current rates and specifications may be obtained by writing to *The Annals* Advertising and Promotion Manager at the Thousand Oaks office (address above).

Claims. Claims for undelivered copies must be made no later than six months following month of publication. The publisher will supply missing copies when losses have been sustained in transit and when the reserve stock will permit.

Change of Address. Six weeks' advance notice must be given when notifying of change of address to ensure proper identification. Please specify name of journal. POSTMASTER: Send address changes to: *The Annals* of The American Academy of Political and Social Science, c/o Sage Publications, 2455 Teller Road, Thousand Oaks, CA 91320.

THE ANNALS
OF THE AMERICAN ACADEMY OF POLITICAL AND SOCIAL SCIENCE

Volume 585   January 2003

IN THIS ISSUE:

Higher Education in the Twenty-First Century

Special Editors: PAUL RICH
DAVID MERCHANT

FORTHCOMING

*Community Colleges at a
Crossroads: Emerging Issues*

Special Editors: JERRY JACOBS
KATHLEEN SHAW

Volume 586, March 2003

*Assessing Systematic Evidence
in Crime and Justice: Methodological
Concerns and Empirical Outcomes*

Special Editors: DAVID WEISBURD
CYNTHIA LUM
ANTHONY PETROSINO

Volume 587, May 2003

Islam

Special Editor: ASLAM SYED

Volume 588, July 2003

A New Look at The American Academy of Political and Social Science

Institutions can be slow to change, especially venerable ones like The American Academy of Political and Social Science and its bimonthly publication, *The Annals*. There is comfort in traditions, anchors to the past that help define and communicate what an institution is about. Amid a sea of change in nearly every aspect of our lives, it is reassuring to know that some things remain the same. Continuous quality improvement notions to the contrary, many of us also often work as if governed by the old adage "If it ain't broke, don't fix it."

The cover of a journal like *The Annals* invariably sends a message about its contents and the character of the organization that produces it. The admonition not to judge something by its cover is a powerful reminder of just how much it actually conveys, whether intended or not.

As you can readily see, *The Annals* has a new cover and a new layout. We have made these changes for several reasons: some pragmatic, others symbolic. On the more practical side, we believe the changes make the volume more user friendly. We intend these changes to make it easier to learn what is inside and easier to read the articles that each volume carries between its covers. The contents are communicated more clearly and easily: first, by a black-and-white photograph that represents the theme of the volume and second, by a list of the articles and authors on the back cover. Indeed, we believe you can tell a lot by this new cover.

On the more symbolic side, we have retained elements of the color by which *The Annals* has been identified for decades, the orange that evokes so many vivid reactions. We want to convey in retaining this element our intention to improve the journal and better serve the members of the Academy and the institutions that subscribe to *The Annals* while preserving a tradition of quality. Few interdisciplinary journals can rival the authors and special editors who have graced its pages, which have included dis-

DOI: 10.1177/0002716202238563

ANNALS, *AAPSS*, 585, January 2003

tinguished scholars such as W. E. B. DuBois, Harold Lasswell, and Margaret Mead as well as important public figures such as Eleanor Roosevelt, Mahatma Gandhi, and Francis Perkins. Few interdisciplinary journals are as widely cited or as broadly indexed as *The Annals*.

The broader symbolic meaning of these changes concerns the Academy itself, the organization that produces *The Annals* (along with its publisher, Sage Publications). The Academy is in the midst of several changes that its officers, staff, and board believe will renew and reinvigorate its commitment—as its 1891 charter proclaims—to "promote the progress of the political and social sciences" and to provide a forum in which the well-informed and intellectually curious can satisfy their interest in understanding contemporary issues that cut across the boundaries of academic disciplines.

Clearly, the Academy will continue to serve its mission by publishing *The Annals* and by convening conferences and symposia that bring the best available social science to shine its light on issues of major public concern.

But the Academy will also move in the months and years ahead to broaden and renew its efforts to promote the progress of the social sciences by launching a series of programs organized around four themes:

- Speaking Truth to Power: using the best social science understanding of contemporary problems to help inform efforts to address them.
- Fueling the Pipeline for Talent: helping to attract and retain talented individuals to pursue research and teaching careers in the social sciences.
- Strengthening Bridges across Disciplines: fostering an understanding of important issues from multiple disciplinary perspectives.
- Better Managing Social Information and Knowledge: helping social scientists and the policy community better manage the increasing volume of data and information about social phenomena.

The Academy has already begun these efforts. Three years ago, for example, it began a program for the selection and installation of Fellows of the Academy. In doing so, the Academy recognizes social scientists who have made outstanding contributions to the progress of the social sciences while communicating their research beyond the confines of narrow disciplinary pursuits. More recently, the Academy has redesigned its Web site, including more information services helpful to its members. Recent issues of *The Annals* are now accessible in digital format, and we are seeking to have issues from 1890 to 1997 made available in an online archive. And much more.

The Annals has a new cover, symbolizing The Academy of Political and Social Science's renewed commitment to its long-standing mission. We are excited by the opportunities and challenges we face in achieving that mission and welcome others to become a part of that future.

ROBERT W. PEARSON
Executive Director
The American Academy of
Political and Social Science

The Environment of American Higher Education: A Constellation of Changes

By
ROGER BENJAMIN

The American university is one of society's key institutions, perhaps the lead institution available today to respond to changing societal imperatives. However, for the university to continue to play a leading role, it is important to match the functions of the institution with the societal imperatives presented by a changed environment. In short, for purposeful, intelligent redesign of the university to take place, new blueprints for changes in the role of the university must be constructed. This article aims at such a blueprint. A heterogeneous set of changes in the environment—globalization, immigration, rising social-economic inequality, centrality of the knowledge economy, and issues surrounding cultural identity—are the new changes that will transform the American university in coming decades. The implications of each of the challenges, particularly the recognition that the university must take a stronger responsibility to improve the nation's human capital, are discussed.

The following excerpt is from Felix Frankfurter's (1948) letter to the editor of *The New York Times*, 8 January 1948, in appreciation of Alfred North Whitehead shortly after his death.

To dwell, however inadequately, on the qualities of a teacher like Alfred North Whitehead is important if our universities are important. They are important if the institutions specially charged with the accumulation of the intellectual capital of the world are important to a society. Who will deny that Professor Whitehead was right in his belief that the fate of the intellectual civilization of the world today is to no inconsiderable extent in the keeping of our universities? "The Aegean Coastline had its chance and made use of it; Italy had its chance and made use of it; France, England, Germany had their chance and made use of it. Today the Eastern American universities have their chance. What use will they make of it? That question has two answers. Once Babylon had its

Roger Benjamin is president of RAND's Council for Aid to Education.

NOTE: The opinions expressed are solely the author's and do not represent those of RAND or its sponsors.

DOI: 10.1177/0002716202238564

chance, and produced the Tower of Babel. The University of Paris fashioned the intellect of the Middle Ages."

The awful question that confronts American universities is, What are they doing with their power and their duty?

The argument

A constellation of changes in the environment of American higher education adds up to a new landscape of constraints and opportunities that higher education leaders, both faculty and administrators, will need to address in the coming decades. The changes, which become new policy imperatives that will lead to a transformation of the University, are

1. globalization,
2. immigration,
3. rising social-economic inequality,
4. the knowledge economy, and
5. cultural identity.

All elements of these forces are of critical importance. However, abetted by new priorities of the state, the ultimate arbiter of what policy issues rise to the top of the public policy agenda, basic elements of these five changes suggest that a strategic repositioning of the mission and incentive system, accompanied by new ways to calibrate the repositioning, is in order for postsecondary teaching institutions. Because of the emerging Internet-based knowledge economy, the university faces multiple public claims that others can provide appropriate higher education better and cheaper than private or public higher education. These claims, now being tested in the marketplace, suggest the need for a major assessment of the quality of undergraduate education.

Second, higher education must exhibit stronger leadership in setting curricula and pedagogical expectations and stands, especially in teacher education. K-12 education will take the cue if higher education, through its admissions and financial aid policies, demands higher standards, and to do that, higher education must first raise its own standards appreciably. Assessment of learning is thus a fundamental formative and summative feedback necessity for raising standards and setting criteria for evaluation of the entire K-16 system. The result is that the American university will have a redesigned mission, which focuses on improving the K-16 education system, the main lever for human capital development that will be a top nation-state priority in the next several decades.

The university in its American form (the mix of public land-grant and private independent colleges) that emerged out of the nineteenth century is one of the two most successful institutional innovations (the other being the modern corporation) that should be acknowledged as the primary engines of American economic and social progress. In addition to being a fulcrum for economic growth, the higher education sector has been responsible for intergenerational social mobility for most citizens (Native Americans and many African Americans). But just now the leadership of the American university is not engaged with the fundamental issues that will demand attention during the next several decades.

University leaders do not understand their obligation to take a leadership role in human capital development (the economic term for education),[1] in particular, leadership of the K-16 educational continuum, which is the key to continued social mobility and economic growth. Nor does there appear to be much engagement in the academy with the major challenges and opportunities a series of fundamental economic and social transformation poses to the university. The reason for this situation may well be the rapidity with which a constellation of forces is sweeping over the university (cf. Hirsch and Weber 1999). The following discussion justifies this assessment.

The role of the university

The university has always been in a patron-client relationship, first with the church, then with the state, and now also with industry. However, at critical historical junctures, the university has also become the primary venue, the transforming element in human development (i.e., the Renaissance and the invention and impact of the land-grant university in late-nineteenth- and early- to mid-twentieth-century America). But the role of the university must be understood within the forces of economic and social change itself that in turn compose the context within which the university operates. The university has never stood completely outside society. Rather, it must be understood as a major institution of society. The argument of this article is that we are now well into another of these critical historical junctures, a set of threshold changes in the society, economy, and political landscapes that present a novel set of challenges and opportunities that the university must respond to during the next several decades. The goal of the article is to lay out these challenges, which become policy imperatives on which the American university must focus as central demands in the coming decades. First, however, a word about the structuring assumption underlying this article.

In times of rapid change, the best social science becomes policy-relevant architecture based on an understanding of the emergent properties of economic and social trends that humanity must grapple with in the future. Such work presents blueprints for institutional responses to these projected trends (Benjamin 1982). This is so because institutions are designs in the most basic sense—human artifacts created for social purpose. As such, they can and are changed in a variety of ways over time. The university is one of society's key institutions, perhaps the lead institution available today to respond to changing societal imperatives. But for intelligent redesign of the university to take place, new blueprints for changes in the role of the university need to be constructed. This statement aims at such a blueprint.[2]

The New Policy Environment

Economic transformation to the knowledge economy:
Gaining and losing comparative advantage

The measures of GNP, formulated by S. Kusnet in the 1930s when the American economy was primarily industrial in nature, remains biased toward the production and consumption of material goods. Although it is still not clear how information-sensitive goods should be measured, their increasing importance to the American economy became clear in the decade of the 1990s. Old economy stocks were discarded as part of the Dow 30 stocks used to benchmark the Dow Jones Industrial Average and were replaced by high-technology companies. Aided by the economies of scale brought by Internet-based companies, which allow additional layers of management to be discarded, the productivity of the U.S. economy has resumed levels thought impossible just a few years ago. Whether the current productivity growth will be sustained remains an open question. However, no one disputes the importance of the information economy as being the key to productivity and, hence, economic growth for the American economy.

Since the early 1990s, economic growth has been recognized as dependent on value added—to data, to existing information systems, and to increasingly complex organized structures of meanings sometimes called knowledge algorithms at their fullest development. Internet Web–based sites are now a principal venue for economic activity. For example, business-to-business sites can cut many layers of previously required bureaucracy. All this now firmly places the knowledge economy as the dominant sector of the economy. I will emphasize the importance of value added measures to improving student performance below.

Figure 1 shows the change over time and also suggests that the role of the knowledge part of the economy will become even more important during the next several decades (Benjamin 1980).

Agriculture, once the major engine of the American economy, declined to less than 5 percent of the economy by the late twentieth century. The role of industry is also declining—although it will probably bottom out at between 15 and 20 percent of the economy. Whereas the level of steel production used to be a measure of the economic development achieved in a country, arguments are made today for minimum levels of steel and other key industrial indicators. Even this argument is problematic. With the global trading system opening up, there is no real economic or even national security justification for subsidizing inefficient industries. Each country, each region within larger countries, should focus on its points of comparative advantage.[3]

Human capital as comparative advantage

Most political leaders in functioning nation-states understand the importance of human capital as the only primary asset a country has; it is no longer as important

FIGURE 1
KNOWLEDGE ECONOMY PROCESS—STATE

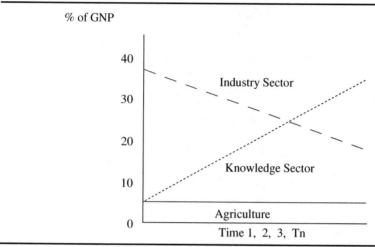

that a country has comparative advantage in land or labor defined in terms of numbers of people. This has meant an unprecedented focus on economic growth across the globe. Since most of the countries are at earlier stages of the product cycle, there continues to be an emphasis on the development of the manufacturing part of the economy. This, in turn, places additional pressure on the American economy to move up the product cycle (see Kurth 1979). Contrary to a political campaign slogan, it matters whether one produces computer chips or potato chips. In all likelihood, the U.S. economy will continue to lose its comparative manufacturing advantage to competitors abroad who produce manufactured goods of comparable or better quality at lower prices. Thus, individuals with increased human capital will be more successful as the American economy progressively puts a premium on high skills.

The New Policy Agenda

There are at least five major changes, which become new policy issue areas that taken together form a new context within which the university will operate during the next several decades. It is these policy areas that alone and in interaction, form a new set of imperatives for higher education. I will concentrate, particularly, on the implications of the first three policy imperatives here.

Globalization

After the end of the cold war, the world economy is accelerating, enabled by the Internet and advances in telecommunications. Globalization becomes a major challenge for all states because of the destabilizing nature of capital flows and loss of comparative advantage in whole economic sectors. Multinational corporations are not held captive to individual states; they invest where it is most profitable for them to do so. Increasingly, the main role of nation-states is to provide health, economic, and educational safety nets for their citizens who do not have the same luxury as corporations have to move around the globe.

Under such conditions, the main defense national leaders have is to enhance their human capital assets to ensure their nation is in the best possible position to compete in the world economy. Although every national leadership faces similar global challenges, each nation begins the twenty-first century with different assets and debits in their human capital structure. Education is a key to human capital development, and therefore a key goal national leaders will take on is how to improve their educational infrastructure. What role should universities take in designing responses to globalization? Should universities take a greater role in improving human capital, which, in turn, would mean an expanded K-16 role?

Because political leaders understand the importance of human capital to their national development, they are beginning to focus on ways to improve it. A typical strategy is for national leaders to make labor market projections, looking forward ten or fifteen years. This usually produces negative scenarios with too much of the future labor market employed in less desirable industries. The second task is to conduct an audit of all postsecondary education and training assets in the nation. Once this task is completed, the leaders compare the educational infrastructure to the labor market projections. They will find disconnects or an absence of alignment between where national leaders want their economies to go and what their postsecondary education and training systems are prepared to produce. Thus, course corrections can be made—new investments, say, in high-technology education.

Immigration

The immigration pressures in the United States are unlikely to abate. And because of the low level of educational investment present in many current and future immigrants, this presents critical policy issues for the United States. During the next fifty years, the world's population will grow, at a minimum, from 5 to 10 billion. Most of this growth will occur in areas of the world least likely to generate enough economic growth internally to absorb their population increase. Of course, it is always possible that the United States will adopt stringent immigration policies. However, based on America's history, it is more probable that immigrants will continue to come to the United States in substantial numbers. What role, if any, should the university play in response to the special needs of immigrants?

A doubling in the proportion of immigrants in the workforce since the 1970s (more than 10 percent of the workforce is now foreign born) and the lower educational level of more recent immigrants are additional factors in the growth of income disparity. In 1970, only 6 percent of the immigrant workforce came from Mexico or Central America, and 68 percent came from Europe. In 1995, 21 per-

FIGURE 2
LONG-TERM TRENDS IN FAMILY INCOME

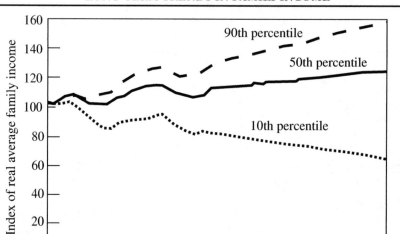

SOURCE: Prepared originally for Commission on National Investment in Higher Education (1997).

cent of the immigrant workforce came from Mexico or Central America, and only 34 percent from Europe. Because the educational level of Mexican and Central American immigrants is lower than that of many other immigrant groups, the earnings of more recent immigrants have deteriorated relative both to native workers and to earlier immigrants and are likely to remain low throughout these immigrants' working lives. If these trends hold, a growing proportion of workers will have less than a high school diploma and will face declining earnings during their lifetimes (see Schoeni, McCarthy, and Vernez 1996).

This point is critical because Hispanics will be the majority population in California, Texas, and New Mexico and the plurality in a number of other states in just a decade or less.

Rise of social-economic inequality

Wage and family income disparities have been growing during the past several decades. Figure 2 shows the distribution of family income in the United States in real terms, adjusted for inflations and indexed to 1976. (In other words, 1976 is shown as a base, and wages estimated for subsequent years are shown as a percentage of what they were in 1976.) As Figure 2 shows, families at the top of the scale will be earning about 50 percent more in 2015 than they did in 1976. This is not because men's wages are going up but because more women are working and families tend to be smaller than they used to be, creating more workers in the economy per family. Those in the middle of the income distribution scale will be a little bet-

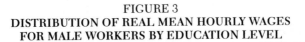

FIGURE 3
DISTRIBUTION OF REAL MEAN HOURLY WAGES
FOR MALE WORKERS BY EDUCATION LEVEL

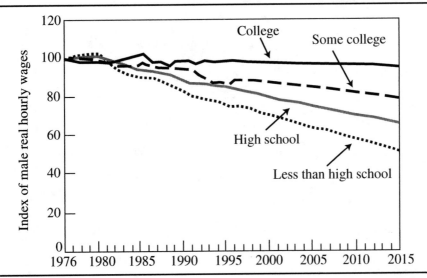

SOURCE: Prepared originally for Commission on National Investment in Higher Education (1997).

ter off, though not much. But for those in the bottom 10th percentile—consisting largely of single-parent families headed by women and families of low-education immigrant populations—we see a 36 percent fall in income compared to what families in that income bracket earned in 1976. In that year, families at the 90th percentile enjoyed income levels nine times greater than those of families at the 10th percentile. By 1993, the disparity was twelvefold. At this rate, the ratio will exceed sixteen to one by 2015.

Education and income: The intimate link

As noted above, the single most important factor in determining level of income is level of education.[4] Figure 3 shows the distribution of real hourly wages of male workers by education level. Men with a college education have kept pace with inflation during the twenty-year period, men with some college education have seen a decline in real income of 14 percent, and men with only a high school diploma have lost 18 percent. Meanwhile, real wages of high school dropouts have declined by 25 percent.

If these lines are drawn out another twenty years using the same rates, the result is devastating. By 2015, male workers with only a high school education will have lost 38 percent of what comparable male workers earned in 1976. And those without a high school diploma will have lost 52 percent in real earnings during the same period. If the U.S. economy continues to place a high value on a college-educated

FIGURE 4
RATE OF PARTICIPATION OF DIFFERENT
ETHNIC RACIAL GROUPS IN HIGHER EDUCATION

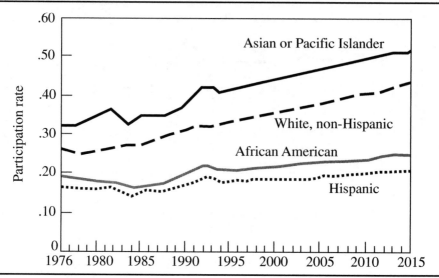

SOURCE: Prepared originally for Commission on National Investment in Higher Education (1997).

workforce, then only college graduates will be able to hold their own economically out to 2015. Those who attend some college will not do badly, but those who stop pursuing an education before or after graduating from high school will lose ground during their working lives (Benjamin and Carroll 1997).

Second, what is the relationship between race/ethnicity and education levels attained?

Like non-Hispanic whites, African Americans and Hispanics suffer economic consequences if they do not pursue higher education. Because larger proportions of these two groups fail to go beyond high school, larger proportions of these groups are among the poor. Figure 4 shows an index that conveys the ratio of the number of students in higher education for various ethnic/racial groups to the total number of eighteen- to twenty-nine-year-olds in those groups. The figure plot changes in that index over the twenty years and extrapolates the rates out to 2015.

As of 2000, Asians and Pacific Islanders scored 45 on this index, and non-Hispanic whites scored just less than 40. In contrast, African Americans and Hispanics scored about 22 and 18, respectively. Although participation rates are increasing for all groups, they are currently increasing more rapidly for whites and Asians than for African Americans and Hispanics. As a result, the gap could widen considerably by 2015. Only by increasing the proportion of African Americans and Hispanics going to college can the gap be stabilized or reduced (Benjamin and Carroll 1997).[5]

Finally, if we go to an example at the university-system level, the disparities between racial/ethnic groups are equally disturbing. A RAND report providing a statistical profile of City University of New York's (CUNY's) incoming freshmen presents information about the relationships among various test scores and grades at CUNY (Klein and Orlando 2000). CUNY is the third largest public university system in the United States (after California State University and the State University of New York). It also is the largest urban system. Consequently, findings regarding the characteristics of the students at this university are likely to be of interest to policy makers at other urban, public, higher education institutions across the United States.

The mean total SAT scores of the entering freshman at CUNY in 1997 were 817 for those entering community colleges and 910 for those entering senior four-year colleges. By comparison, the National Collegiate Athletic Association's eligibility requirements for athletic scholarships is an SAT level of 820. Overall, because the recentered SATs have a national mean of 1,000 for combined verbal and math scores, CUNY's scores place it in the bottom 10 percent of all higher education institutions. And, as is the case with tests using the SAT or similar tests around the country, Hispanic and African American entering students score significantly lower than non-Hispanic whites and Asian Americans. These figures continue to generate controversy at CUNY where they are used to argue for and against the use of SAT scores and whether and how remedial instruction should be delivered. But they are presented here for a different reason.

These figures suggest that remediation is the wrong issue to be concerned about. The figures indicate the effects of lack of progress throughout the K-12 system prior to coming to CUNY. Many of the students, as measured by the SAT scale, come to CUNY unequipped to do postsecondary education or training. More important, we know from recent progress in cognitive science that all racial/ethnic groups have the same innate cognitive abilities. Therefore, it is time to cease counterproductive assertions about the capacity of different ethnic groups to achieve and, instead, focus on removing the obstacles that stand in the way of underrepresented groups closing the gap with their Asian American and non-Hispanic white counterparts.

Social-economic inequality has clearly become a major issue. Policies and actions that reduce this inequality will be very high on the national political agenda in the future. If education is the fundamental solution to social-economic inequality, should the university accept the responsibility to take a more central role in dealing with this issue?

Two other macro forces, the knowledge economy and cultural identity, not immediately central to the growing importance of human capital, are presented in the appendix.

The state

If the nature and role of the state and the public policy issues it focuses on change, so do the challenges the university faces. This is so because the state is the venue through which new public policies are brought to the top of the policy agenda, and in turn, these new policy makers make these new policy issues a priority for the university. For example, most education policy studies do not question the role the state should play in forming education policy. Rather, this body of work typically seeks to corroborate more or less efficient existing systems, or new delivery systems, within the K-16 education system—for example, the effectiveness of class size reduction, curriculum, or governance reforms. But if one steps back and thinks about the state concept as having different roles in different contexts, the focus changes. I note the implications of two models of the state here.

The state as administrative order. This concept encompasses all the elements of the state as a coherent whole. Thus, bureaucratic agencies and personnel are elements that make up but do not define the state. Rather, attention is directed at the structuring principles that exist to aggregate discrete individual and institutional actors. Governmental institutions compete but also exist in discernible relation to one another. Authors in quite different schools of thought identify growth of the scope and penetration of governmental institutions across the full range of social and economic activities.

The state as institutional-legal order. This conceptualization is broader, with the state being conceived of as the "enduring structure of governance and rule in society" (Benjamin and Duvall 1985, 25; cf. Held 1989). This means the entire structure of law both in the de jure and de facto senses; thus, one visualizes the state as the institutional and legal order. It may be argued that the state as administrative order is derived from this deeper model. It is in this model that property rights, per se, should be defined as basic features of the state. It is the nature of property rights that determine what is considered public or private in society. What is viewed as private in one historical era may be seen as public in another era, for example, witness the rising claims of environmental groups in the late twentieth century who treat much more of what used to be considered private as part of the commons.

This model of the state places the focus on the legal system from which regulatory rules and procedures dealing with emerging systems of economic activity must come. The state as institutional-legal order becomes especially crucial during periods of threshold-type transition in the social and economical order at large. At later stages of social-economical development, new forms of property rights may be created in the form of entitlements as social payments or perhaps even public employment. Indeed, this is why we may expect education to increasingly be regarded as an entitlement in the future. Citizens will increasingly demand equality of opportunity in education as a right.

The point of this twofold model is that one derives different basic public policy foci depending on which model of the state one concentrates on. With regard to education policy, one concentrates on different issues entirely if one is concerned with the state as administrative order versus the deeper state as institutional-legal order.

TABLE 1
CHARACTERISTICS OF EDUCATION POLICY
IN KNOWLEDGE VERSUS INDUSTRIAL SOCIETIES

Order	Industrial Economy	Knowledge Economy
Administrative	Development of school districts Development of public post-secondary system Centralization of institutions and systems	Focus on assessment of quality, benchmarking of institutions Decentralization of institutions and systems
Institutional-legal	High school becomes entitlement, focus on greater opportunity—GI Bill, Pell Grants	Postsecondary education becomes entitlement, focus on equal access by all racial/ethnic groups, level playing field for all, equalization of school district funding within states

In knowledge economies, the primary elements of order and concentration on economic growth come under challenge as citizens begin to question the high level of social and economic inequalities generated in the earlier growth period when entrepreneurial freedom was emphasized. Justice becomes a more prevalent concern as groups and individuals become more attentive to the relative distribution of goods as compared to simply worrying about maintaining the order necessary to produce goods. In the phrase of those who analyze attitudinal data, "post-materialist" values come to the fore in the knowledge societies (Inglehart 1997).

Table 1 presents schematically the differences in education policy emphasis between industrial versus knowledge societies. One sees how the state in its context determines the kind of education issues that rise to the top of the public agenda.

The question is, What is the future role of the American university in the education or human capital policy equation? In the industrial phase of change, it was enough for the university to provide opportunities for social and economic mobility and be there for students prepared to respond to the demands of higher education. The high school was the market that provided the higher education sector with the material it desired at the quality level it needed. What if this is no longer the case? What if the university faces a very different kind of student?

Projections

The next two decades will be a time of dramatic change for the American university. The changes noted above will affect the way the university functions. Loss of the monopoly of production and consumption of knowledge will present new challenges and opportunities for faculty and administrators (see appendix). Because of Internet-based courseware and supporting archival material that will increasingly be available, university faculty will not need to be as focused on the development of their own courses, libraries, or physical plant. Markets will develop in which application service providers offer course material produced by the best academic minds available. Faculty and administrators will be able to focus on other ways to distinguish their college from others, for example, by a focus on a particular cultural identity or policy problem such as the environment.

Research will also be reorganized. The lesson of the Human Genome project is that private for-profits can pursue cutting-edge scientific challenges perhaps as well or better than the familiar nonprofit consortium of universities funded by the National Science Foundation. Universities will very likely enter into more partnerships with for-profit partners. Because of the Internet, higher education institutions are no longer remote. Faculties at the University of Texas at El Paso, for example, now routinely use the Stanford linear accelerator for their projects, something even three years ago they could not do.

It will no longer be necessary to build stand-alone research facilities. Indeed, this is fortuitous since big science R&D will eventually rule out all but the richest among universities as dominant research entities. R&D needs are becoming so large and complex that only twenty to thirty university centers of research may prosper in the coming decades.

In one sense, this coming change is an inevitable restructuring of the Vanevar Bush era during which the incentive system that governs the faculty, the research productivity matrix, dominated the reward structure of the academy.

Figure 5 shows the cumulative share of funding for federal R&D for higher education during a twenty-eight-year period.[6] The top fifty universities account for 63 percent of all federal R&D support. One hundred institutions account for 85 percent, and 650-plus institutions account for the rest. The fact that more than 650 institutions pursue the other 15 percent of federal research funding is due more to the absence of an alternative set of incentives to replace the research-based criteria for merit and promotion for these largely non-research-oriented universities. The implication of this is that calls for greater mission differentiation between research and teaching institutions will increase. While faculty in top universities will continue to focus on research, perhaps not teaching at all, student performance will become a greater focus for nonresearch universities. Fortunately, the need for a new set of incentives within the academy combines with the clear external imperative for the university to take on a much stronger leadership role for human capital development in society. The implication of both of these issues is to focus on improving student performance.

The outdated research-based metric

Although science confirms the equality of the innate cognitive abilities of racial/ ethnic groups, all ethnic/racial groups do not score the same on national tests. For a variety of cultural, social, and economic reasons, few believe that all races and ethnic groups will reach the same educational levels in the near future. Even among those who agree that all ethnic/racial groups are equally capable, there is no agree-

FIGURE 5
TOTAL FEDERAL R&D EXPENDITURES: FISCAL YEAR 1998

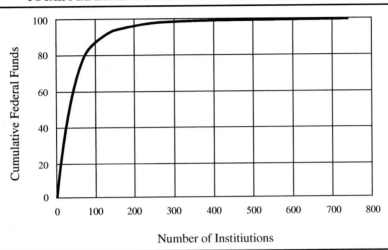

Number of Institiutions

ment about how a level playing field might be constructed. Moreover, there is no consensus that the playing field should be leveled or how it might be leveled. There is also no agreement that the state should take a stronger role in lowering social-economic inequality by ensuring human capital opportunities for all its citizens. In other words, we are not yet anywhere near the point where the state views human capital of such importance that K-16 institutions and other public institutions that play a supporting role are held accountable for ensuring equality of educational opportunity for everyone.

There is also no agreement among university faculty that the university as an institution should or could bear its assets more productively on improving human capital. There is little agreement also with the view that the university has a moral obligation to help level the playing field for all citizens. Instead, most faculty believe the role of the university in K-12 reform, if it is to have one at all, should be carried by the college of education—typically one of the weaker colleges in universities in status and resources. Arts and science faculties in nonresearch institutions continue to work under the research-based metric for their promotion and tenure and merit raises. Fortunately, there is an answer to the question of what might replace the research-based metric and lead the American university to respond to the set of twenty-first-century human capital policy demands from the state that will increasingly require the university to take a leading role in K-16 education.

The need for outcomes assessment[7]

I have described three trends—globalization, immigration, and rising social-economic inequality—that mediated through a nation-state that exhibits new priorities, places the future focus in higher education squarely on human capital development. The American university is not monolithic; this is an important point to remember. For example, even if human capital development becomes the top priority of the university, this does not mean all universities will focus on improving undergraduate education and taking the lead in raising quality throughout the K-16 education system. Research university faculty may increase their attention to research. And not all postsecondary institutions will need to produce B.A. degrees; many institutions and programs will be focused on providing certifications of skill sets. Among all of these postsecondary education and training institutions that focus primarily on teaching, there are enough commonalities among the problems and possibilities facing faculty and administrators to warrant a discussion of what needs to change among these institutions. I will discuss these changes and hold for another opportunity a more detailed discussion on the implications of the knowledge economy and new cultural identity questions.

There is a need, for both educational and public policy reasons, to assess the quality of undergraduate education. The increasing public cry for practical education; the advent of virtual education with its promises of better, cheaper, and faster; the ripple effects of the recent wave of high-stakes K-12 testing; and the concern over the perceived costs of higher education have caused serious questions to be raised about the quality of undergraduate education.

One result is that state legislatures are demanding better measures of quality as issues of access and accountability are increasingly dominating public policy discussion. In lieu of any systematic measure of quality by higher education itself, ranking systems such as those used by college guidebooks and *U.S. News & World Report* are being used as the surrogate measure of quality. The problem with all such rankings and comparisons is that they use input variables such as SAT scores, GPAs, rank in class, endowment dollars per student, and selectivity of admissions, none of which are measures of what students actually learn in college. Such rankings do a great injustice to the complexity and diversity of higher education in the United States.

Value added assessment: The only valid measure

Virtually everyone who has thought carefully about the question of assessing quality in higher education agrees that "value added" means the only valid approach. By value added, I mean the value that is added to students' capabilities or knowledge as a consequence of their education at a particular college or university. Measuring such value requires assessing what students know and can do as they begin college and assessing them again during and after they have had the full benefit of their college education. Value added is thus the difference between the measures of students' attainment as they enter college and measures of their attainment when they complete college. Value added is the difference a college makes in their education.

If value added is so obviously the best possible assessment, why is it not standard practice? Because value added is very difficult to measure for a number of important reasons.

Value has many dimensions. No college or university is trying to develop only a single capability in students. A campus may be doing a good job with one learning dimension but a mediocre one on another. And, of course, some dimensions are easier to measure than others.

Students are different. Everyone learns some subjects or capabilities more easily than others. Is a college or university doing a good job of educating some better than others because of this fact?

Institutions are different. Colleges and universities do not all seek to add the same kind of value to students' development. Their missions vary. How does one thus compare institutions for quality whose missions differ (e.g., a research university focused on graduate study compared to a small liberal arts college)?

Effects have many sources, and effects unfold. Even if students are full-time at a single institution, how can we tell what contributions that campus has made, as opposed, for example, to the contributions of a part-time job or their church? Moreover, the contributions to learning may not be realized in the short term; they may be felt only years later.

The most important effects are transformative. Because a liberal arts education seeks to develop a unique person, in command of all the capabilities within her or his potential, the most important effects may be uniquely combined and transformative of that person as a whole, a very difficult thing to capture on any measure.

Measurement of value added is expensive. Pretesting and posttesting, using writing samples rather than short-answer questions, and implementing tests that measure critical and imaginative thinking, for example, are far more costly than conventional testing in individual classrooms.[8]

Benefits of quality assessment

The quality assessment discussed here can have enormous educational value in that it can help

1. faculty and their students make better sense of the teaching and learning in which they are mutually engaged;
2. institutions of higher education measure the cumulative impact of their curricular programming;
3. higher education generally by providing benchmark data for comparisons by sector (e.g., community colleges, liberal arts colleges, research universities), as well as create the potential basis for an incentive system focused on student learning;
4. public policy decision makers concerned with issues of access, cost, accountability, and equity; and
5. the public make better decisions regarding selection of appropriate colleges and universities rather than relying on current invalid ranking systems.

In short, as we hear the chant for learning organizations in the twenty-first century, as we elevate the need to educate for an information-driven society, and as we are asked to make wiser use of scarce resources, such an assessment project has many benefits and has become an important national priority.

An important long-range rationale for measurement of quality defined in terms of value added to student performance is that it creates a marketlike mechanism through which policy makers, college administrators, faculty, parents, and students can compare institutions. Moreover, the measurement of value added to student performance is the missing necessary condition for attacking the "cost-disease problem" in higher education. Finally, it is the missing bridge between higher education and K-12 reform.

Higher education costs today increase at least a percentage above the consumer price index each year. This situation is very similar to the health sector's cost-disease problems that have become such a major issue at the start of this new century. Business leaders, of course, operating in a disciplined market understand this point very well—only when one has a quality metric that allows the assessment on student performance of the impact of productivity enhancements of alternative A compared to those of alternative B can one frame discussions of productivity in higher education in a meaningful way.

But there are several other reasons why the quality measurement movement will have strong effects.

With the existence of credible value-added measures on the effects of courses, majors, and total undergraduate experiences, faculty can engage in continuous improvement for the first time. We know from excellent case studies that faculty can and do teach for a decade or more with no apparent positive effect on the students in their classroom.

Internet-based distance learning is growing rapidly, from 300,000 to 3 million students being taught by this method during the next three years. The largest issue debated is whether these courses are inferior to the same courses taught on-site. With a value-added measurement strategy, we can compare the benefits of Internet-based distance learning courses with their on-site counterparts.

Are the more general structuring principles offered by liberal arts curriculum in student-centered learning environments superior to other forms of instruction in terms of value added to student performance? Does liberal arts learning produce graduates with stronger writing and reading skills and, in general, sharper cognitive skills? The value-added measurement of quality programs enables answers to these important questions.

The quality measure and K-16 education reform: The missing bridge

All but the top flagship public colleges and universities have open admissions. These same institutions do not have exit standards for their two-year certificates or four-year degrees. While they may have requirements of how many courses students must take to receive their undergraduate degrees, they do not set standards of performance in, say, writing, math, or reading levels that must be reached to graduate. Hence, there are no explicit standards for admissions or graduation for most American students (most European countries do have such standards).

While this may have been acceptable in an earlier period of American higher education when the number of students was much smaller and homogeneous—mainly white males from the middle and professional social classes—this is not acceptable today. Today's students are heterogeneous—female (more than 54 percent) as well as male and from diverse ethnic backgrounds and economic circumstances. It may have been reasonable in the past to assume that a smaller group of largely white males and their teachers and parents internalized what educational requirements were needed to become successful undergraduate students and successful graduates. One clearly cannot assume that this is true today. The development, implementation, and communication of transparent standards for both admission to and graduation from college are fundamental requirements of meaningful K-16 education reform. Standards must be raised throughout the K-16 system.

Parents, teachers, and students need to have as complete an idea of admissions standards as early as possible in the K-12 system. Only then can they effectively plan to meet the standards required.[9] Indeed, studies show that increased standards, carefully arrived at, improve performance. Students will improve to meet the new standards.

It is equally important to articulate standards for attainment of an undergraduate degree. Evidence of declining quality in undergraduate education is growing. We must reverse the decline by setting reasonable standards for B.A. and B.S. degrees. Knowledge of minimum requirements for an acceptable degree holder today is limited to families who understand the need to provide music, language, and basic mathematics, reading and writing building blocks for their children from a very early age. Unfortunately, if the previously cited CUNY study is representative of urban public colleges (see Gill 2000), the education level of a great proportion of our higher education graduates is becoming as unacceptable as the education level of high school graduates.

Faculty, like any group, respond to incentives that govern their performance. The existence of a viable set of measures of value added to student performance will provide an alternative set of incentives to the research productivity incentives that currently govern the academy.

Conclusion

If Justice Frankfurter were alive today, he might well answer his question in the negative. There are many good reasons why the university has not yet been transformed, but it is fair to conclude the following. Science and professional school faculties in the top research universities are in business for themselves. There is no core curriculum; the humanities are fragmented and demoralized and not ready to take on the challenges listed here. There are few if any higher education leaders taking a positive view of the challenges the university faces. Instead, the Internet and distance learning are viewed as a threat. The social-economic inequality problem, which may undermine democratic stability in the United States, is viewed as too challenging by many university leaders or as someone else's problem.

However, I have argued that a number of policy challenges combined with the need to develop a new incentive system to reward faculty performance in most four-year institutions and community colleges presents the need for institutional redesign of the American university. The policy issue that will be at the top of the agenda is the imperative for the university to take greater leadership of the education reform agenda. But as understanding grows concerning the fundamental importance of ensuring that all citizens are empowered to develop their innate cognitive skills to their fullest extent, so too will interest in addressing the other challenges noted here: (1) the collision between globalization, immigration, social-economic inequality and cultural identity; (2) restating what it means to be human in the age of technology; and (3) redesigning the university to take advantage of the opportunities offered by the Internet. And all of this transformation is occurring as the nature and the role of the state—in which the university lives in ambiguous relationship—is, itself, undergoing fundamental evolution.

A new agenda awaits those in academia who have the vision and courage to take it on. Equally, the changed context, especially the changed priorities of the state, will force responses to the new policy imperatives to the university noted here. And because of the urgency and importance of these challenges, we would be pleased if Justice Frankfurter delayed his return for a couple of decades; he then may be pleased with what the university is doing with its power and duty.

Appendix

The Knowledge Economy

The move to the Internet has major implications for the university that will reduce its monopoly on the production and consumption of knowledge.

The Role of the Internet

Internet-based application service providers will be the basis for the development of virtual libraries, specialized databases, and virtual researcher communities. All of this has the potential for extraordinary progress in knowledge development. For example, the implications of Moore's law suggests the social sciences are poised to make the same move from observation to the experimental that the physical and natural sciences did. One can envisage starting many research projects with the data needed for the project already present and even organized into a variety of useful sets of meaning. Under these conditions, the researcher starts the project at a much higher level of cognitive complexity and can spend much more time focusing on the implications of research results. Internet-based distance learning provided by for-profit and nonprofit postsecondary educational institutions is poised to erode the monopoly the university has held on the production and consumption of knowledge. How should the university adjust to these major challenges during the next several decades?

The Growth of Expertise as the Source of Authority

The complexities attached to issues such as whether Microsoft is a predator in the market, air transportation safety, health care regulation, child development, genetic engineering, the environment, and so forth are not amenable to ballot box solutions. Increasingly, the courts act as venues for scientific experts to debate and sort out answers to complex questions. The expert reigns under such conditions (Aronowitz 2000). At the start of a new century, Weber's famous predictions about the basis of authority resting in legal-rational bureaucracy appears to be confirmed. However, the seemingly limitless implications of technology also produce a strong reaction.

The Limits of Technology

The impact of technology on what it means to be human is another interesting development. If a tune whistled can be scored into a symphony composition by software designed for this purpose, what becomes the definition of creativity? If food can be genetically designed, are designer humans not far behind? Just as the last threshold set of social and economical changes created the industrial revolution (when there was an outburst of work in the arts and humanities that redefined much of the meaning of human in relation to industrialization), so too will there be a similar outpouring of fresh thinking about what it means to be human in the knowledge economy era.

Cultural Identity

If globalization is the wave of the future, it will produce a variety of counterreactions because human beings require community. Some (Huntington 1995) see clashes of civilizations looming between Islamic and Western societies. The Iranian revolution can be seen, for example, as a clash between the forces of economic modernity and traditional value systems. Tribal value clashes appear to be alive and well in the Balkans. We know that Eurocentric, white, and male images of what constitutes ideal citizenship in our K-16 educational institutions must be replaced, but with what? The themes of McGuffy's *Reader* and Henry Adams's *Education of Henry Adams* still reverberate in our cultural landscape. What should the role of the university be in forging new multicultural models of good citizenship in the future world where nation-states are no longer as sovereign as they once were? This is especially challenging for the American university, which will soon have 1 million international students in attendance in a society whose leaders presume to argue for an American version of universal values in a kind of twenty-first-century version of the manifest destiny. In other words, what value standards should the twenty-first-century American university aim for? This, of course, is a problem since the American university will presumably remain in a client relationship to state governments and the federal government. Can the American university develop such global norms and remain American? However, if the corporation of the future is to be increasingly multinational in design, perhaps corporate patrons will not be as nationalistic in the future. And private universities and colleges with significant endowments will have some degree of freedom of movement because they will control the use of the profits on those resources. There are thorny issues facing the university if universities are to once again take their role as fundamental critics of the existing society and cultural norms seriously. And if they do not, who will?

Notes

1. The economic term *human capital* is used because this article emphasizes the importance to society and to the individual of the economic returns to education argument. For a representative treatment of the concept human capital, see Hicks (1965). The availability of physical or human capital limits employment and economic growth. Capital shortages can develop if current capacity has become obsolescent in relation to technology, market demand, or input costs (e.g., energy intensive machinery can be priced out of the market when oil prices rise). In the knowledge economy, the importance of human capital, the skill level of personnel, begins to clearly take precedence over physical capital. And the human capital obtained through education investments can differ dramatically across nations and across racial/ethnic groups within a society. I employ human capital, in this article, as does the Chicago school of economists who have documented the returns to education; for example, the greater the amount of formal education, the greater the return to the individual in wages. See Hicks (1965) for the concept. Also, see Heller (2000) for illuminating essays on the relationship between access, cost, and accountability for a discussion of the "cost-disease" problem facing higher education. This article does not discuss the cost issue, which will become a more salient public policy issue itself in the coming decades in a way analogous to the health care cost debate. This article presents the case for measuring outcomes in undergraduate education. Without an understanding of the quality added by the instructor or the institution to student performance, one cannot assess the benefits and costs of productivity enhancements.

2. This statement has profited from a number of general assessments of the current and projected status of American higher education. Among the most useful were Duderstadt (2000); Bowen and Shapiro (1998); Bogue and Apter (2000); Levine (1999); Tierney (1999); Ehrlich (2000); Coady (2000); Altbach, Berdahl, and Gumport (1998); Cole, Barber, and Graubard (1994), Koblik and Graubard (2000); and Lucas (1996). As noted, the goal here is to make a set of projections about the American university's future based on assessment of the probable impact of the changed environment the university faces.

3. *Comparative advantage* refers to the unique characteristics that make an activity produced by group A of equal or greater value at a lower cost than the same activity produced by group B.

4. Of course, what determines the level of education is another matter. A central factor is the shift in family structure. The absence of one parent matters enormously, and today about 37 percent of American children live in single-parent households (see Keller 1999-2000).

5. Figures 2 through 4 present single point projections for the next fifteen years. However, in a just completed study of the Texas higher education system (Benjamin et al. 2000), the probability of a future dramatic participation gap in postsecondary education between Hispanics and African Americans versus non-Hispanic whites and Asian Americans is confirmed using a multidimensional modeling approach. See also Park and Lempert (1998) for further support of the participation gap thesis based on data from California analyzed with a multidimensional approach.

6. All the data come from the National Science Foundation's CASPAR database. These data reflect all awards of R&D funding to specific institutions by all federal agencies. The database includes only R&D funds; it excludes all funds for training, public service, demonstration projects, clinical trials, and departmen-

tal research not separately budgeted. In addition, the data are limited to the sciences and engineering. Thus, no data are collected on such fields as education, law, humanities, music, the arts, physical education, and library sciences.

The nine disciplines within the sciences and engineering for which the federal government has funded R&D during the twenty-eight-year period are as follows: engineering (includes aerospace, chemical, civil, electrical, mechanical, materials, industrial, and other engineering), geological sciences (includes atmospheric, earth, oceanography, and other sciences), interdisciplinary and other sciences, life sciences excluding medical sciences (includes agricultural, biological, and other life sciences), mathematics and computer sciences (includes mathematics and statistics, computer sciences), medical sciences, physical sciences (includes astronomy, chemistry, physics, and other physical sciences), psychology, social sciences (includes economics, political science and public administration, sociology, anthropology, linguistics, history of science, area and ethnic studies, and other social sciences) (Guess and Carroll 1997).

7. This section benefited from ideas developed with Richard Hersh and Stephen Klein. For a more complete application of these ideas, see the article by Benjamin et al. (2002) in *Peer Review*.

8. Because of the complexity surrounding the value-added concept, it is useful to identify the key terms, the frame of reference, and question. One further goal might be to compare the value added to students in institution A with similar students in institution B. One may focus on development of comparisons over time in which faculty can find useful cues for the improvement of their courses and academic programs within a particular institution. One further goal might be to compare the value added to students in institution A with similar students in institution B. Additional possible frames of reference are the individual student, the students aggregated in a class, a major, or an entire junior- or senior-year population. In every case, the answer to the question of what is the purpose of the measurement of value added is critical. The reason the frame of reference is critical is because the question to what use the tests should be put must be answered. These are questions that will require much attention by institutions (administration and faculty) participating in the research program envisaged.

9. Moreover, administering assessment tests on the Internet will give students, teachers, and parents real-time feedback on how well the student is doing—thus course corrections can be made to improve as soon as possible; assessment becomes diagnostic.

References

Altbach, Phillip G., Robert Berdahl, and Patricia Gumport, eds. 1998. *American higher education in the twenty-first century*. Baltimore: Johns Hopkins University Press.

Aronowitz, Stanley. 2000. *The knowledge factory: Dismantling the corporate university and creating true higher learning*. Boston: Beacon.

Benjamin, Roger. 1980. *The limits of politics: Collective goods and political change in postindustrial societies*. Chicago: University of Chicago Press.

———. 1982. The historical nature of social scientific knowledge: The case of comparative political inquiry. In *Strategies of political inquiry*, edited by Elinor Ostrom, 69-98. Beverly Hills, CA: Sage.

Benjamin, Roger, and Stephen J. Carroll. 1997. The challenge of the changed environment in higher education. In *The responsive university*, edited by William Tierney, 92-119. Baltimore: Johns Hopkins University Press.

Benjamin, Roger, Stephen Carroll, James Dewar, Robert Lempert, and Sue Stockly. 2000. *Achieving the Texas higher education vision*. DRU-2305-CAE. Santa Monica, CA: RAND.

Benjamin, Roger, Marc Chun, Richard H. Hersh, and Stephen Klein. 2002. Value added assessment of liberal education. *Peer Review* 4 (2/3).

Benjamin, Roger, and Raymond Duvall. 1985. The capitalist state in context. In *The democratic state*, edited by Roger Benjamin and Stephen Elkin, 19-58. Lawrence: University Press of Kansas.

Bogue, B. Grady, and Jeffrey Apter, eds. 2000. *Exploring the heritage of American higher education: The evolution of philosophy and policy*. Phoenix, AZ: Oryx.

Bowen, William G., and Harold T. Shapiro, eds. 1998. *Universities and their leadership*. Princeton, NJ: Princeton University Press.

Coady, Tony, ed. 2000. *Why universities matter: A conversation about values, means, and directions*. St. Leonards, Australia: Allen & Unwin.

Cole, Jonathan R., Elinor G. Barber, and Stephen R. Graubard, eds. 1994. *The research university in a time of discontent*. Baltimore: Johns Hopkins University Press.

Commission on National Investment in Higher Education. 1997. *Breaking the social contract: The fiscal crisis in higher education*. Washington, DC: Commission on National Investment in Higher Education.

Duderstadt, James J. 2000. *A university for the 21st century*. Ann Arbor: University of Michigan Press.

Ehrlich, Thomas. 2000. *Civic responsibility and higher education*. Phoenix, AZ: Oryx.

Frankfurter, Felix. 1948. In appreciation of Alfred North Whitehead. Letter to the editor. *New York Times*, 8 January.

Gill, Brian. 2000. *The governance of the City University of New York*. Santa Monica, CA: RAND.

Guess, Gretchen, and Stephen Carroll. 1997. *Patterns of federal support for R&D: 1973-1996*. DRU-1598-IET. Santa Monica, CA: RAND.

Held, David. 1989. *Political theory and the modern state*. Stanford, CA: Stanford University Press.

Heller, Donald, ed. 2000. *The states and public higher education policy*. Baltimore: Johns Hopkins University Press.

Hicks, J. R. 1965. *Capital and growth*. London: Oxford University Press.

Hirsch, Werner Z., and Luc Weber, eds. 1999. *Challenges facing higher education at the millennium*. Washington, DC: American Council on Education/Oryx Press Series on Higher Education.

Huntington, Samuel. 1995. *The clash of civilizations*. New York: Basic Books.

Inglehart, Ronald. 1997. *Modernization and post modernization: Cultural, economic, and political change in 43 societies*. Princeton, NJ: Princeton University Press.

Keller, George. 1999-2000. The emerging third stage. *Higher Education Planning* 28:1-7.

Klein, Stephen, and Marie Orlando. 2000. *CUNY's testing program: Characteristics, results, and implications for policy and research*. Santa Monica, CA: RAND.

Koblik, Steven, and Stephen R. Graubard, eds. 2000. *Distinctively American: The residential liberal arts colleges*. New Brunswick, NJ: Transaction Publishing.

Kurth, James. 1979. The political consequences of the product cycle: Industrial history and political outcomes. *International Organization* 33 (1): 1-34.

Levine, Arthur, ed. 1999. *Higher learning in America*. Baltimore: Johns Hopkins University Press.

Lucas, Christopher J. 1996. *Crisis in the academy: Rethinking higher education in America*. New York: St. Martin's.

Park, George, and Robert Lempert. 1998. *The class of 2014: Preserving access to California higher education*. MR-971-EDU. Santa Monica, CA: RAND.

Schoeni, Robert F., Kevin McCarthy, and George Vernez. 1996. *The mixed economic progress of immigrants*. MR-763-IF/FF. Santa Monica, CA: RAND.

Tierney, William G. 1999. *Building the responsive university*. Thousand Oaks, CA: Sage.

Engaged Universities: Lessons from the Land-Grant Universities and Extension

By
GEORGE R. MCDOWELL

Engagement is the vogue of relevant scholars into the twenty-first century. Yet there are concerns that scholarly objectivity requires detachment from society. The American experience with scholarly engagement comes from Land-Grant universities and extension. The Land-Grant principle emerged from the mandate to the Land-Grant colleges to improve the nation's agriculture. Agricultural science has been hugely productive because of the Land-Grant principle. The principle is general to all scholarship. The Land-Grant principle gives both intellectual and political power to engagement. Scholarship is made better substantially through the test of workability, a dimension of scholarly objectivity. The scholar is also made more skillful. The engagement making possible the test of workability makes the scholarship more relevant. Institutionalized access to the workable, relevant knowledge for those who need it generates substantial political power. At a time when universities, particularly public research universities, are seeking public support for more than their teaching, the strategies suggested by the Land-Grant principle are instructive.

A merican society is in peril, and its research universities have much to contribute to the society in the twenty-first century, wrote Derek Bok (1990), former president of Harvard University, in his book *Universities and the Future of America*. He explicitly identified the contributions universities can make to greater competitiveness, to a search for a better society, and to moral education. But he was also concerned to

George R. McDowell is a professor of agricultural and applied economics at Virginia Polytechnic Institute and State University, the 1862 Land-Grant university in Virginia. He has a twelve-month 100 percent extension appointment. His scholarship is primarily on issues of rural development, both internationally and in the United States (primarily in Virginia), and on the performance of the university and extension system. His book Land-Grant Universities and Extension into the 21st Century: Renegotiating or Abandoning a Social Contract *(2001) is one of the few books on Land-Grant universities and extension that is not primarily adulation. McDowell has lived and worked in agricultural and rural development for two years or more each in South Vietnam, Kenya, Malaysia, Zambia, and Albania and has worked and traveled in many other countries.*

DOI: 10.1177/0002716202238565

suggest ways and means whereby universities can organize themselves to engage the world and not "succumb to its blandishments, its distractions, its corrupting entanglements . . . [diminishing the] more profound obligation that every institution of learning owes to civilization to renew its culture, interpret its past, and expand our understanding of the human condition" (pp. 103-4). In contrast to Bok, the leadership of the Kellogg Commission on the Future of State and Land-Grant Universities is concerned that the universities themselves are in peril by failing to be sufficiently relevant to the society. The leadership of the Kellogg Commission stated at the inception of the commission,

> We are convinced that unless our institutions respond to the challenges and opportunities before them they risk being consigned to a sort of academic Jurassic Park—of great historic interest, fascinating places to visit, but increasingly irrelevant in a world that has passed them by. (Kellogg Presidents' Commission 1996)

To state the Kellogg Commission position in language Bok (1990) might have used, unless the universities engage the world more fully, they will not be able to contribute to the renewing of culture, provide an accurate interpretation of civilizations past, or provide relevant understandings of the human condition. The Kellogg Commission (1999) has codified its position on the university in society in its report *Returning to Our Roots: The Engaged Institution*, and that has started the discussion in higher education in America on engagement.

"Engagement" and "the engaged university" are phrases that derive directly from the deliberations of the Kellogg Commission and are formalized in its 1999 report (Graham Spanier, personal communication, February 2002). The concept is the newest expression of the university doing things in the society that houses it, whether the university is a public or a private institution. More than outreach, service, or extension, the connotation of engagement is explicitly a two-way street. Although newly coined, many involved with extension or public service had a two-way relationship in mind prior to the widespread use of "engagement." The tenth annual American Association for Higher Education Conference on Faculty Roles and Rewards, held 25-27 January 2002 in Phoenix, had as a theme "Knowledge for What? The Engaged Scholar" (American Association for Higher Education 2001).

Individual scholars'/professors' motivation to be involved in activities that constitute engagement, as opposed to consulting, stems from their own interests in scholarly relevance. Presumably that is what "Knowledge for What?" means at the 2002 American Association for Higher Education annual conference. For those academics primarily in teaching, engagement extends to the opportunity of exposing students to the realities of the real world for the sake of greater relevance in the teaching/learning experience. Sometimes, individual scholars make use of engagement activities to partially fund research or instructional activities through student projects used to solve someone's particular problem. For university administrators, the interest in engagement is quite different. University leaders' interest has explicitly to do with the opportunities to generate public and/or political goodwill that in the case of public institutions, may be exchanged for growth in budgets.

But academics and their administrators, particularly those in public institutions, should have a further, deeper interest in engagement. The Kellogg Commission's (1998) intention to assist America's public universities to return to our roots bespeaks more than effective and relevant teaching, more than a politically supportive public. Returning to roots speaks of the whole institution—the academy it houses and the scholarship it supports—being both better and more relevant in a rapidly changing society. The engaged institution is the American pragmatic answer to the elitism of Bok (1990). Although never made explicit in the Kellogg Commission reports, the language of returning to roots both begs and answers the question about who should control the scholarly agenda in higher education—in America they are the people's universities.

Unquestionably, the notion of engagement or public service is a characteristic that made public higher education in America unique in the world. That American style has had a major influence on the academy throughout the world. In describing the importance of the public service influence on American higher education, Stephen R. Graubard, editor of *Daedalus*, stated in the 1997 preface to a *Daedalus* edition devoted to the American academic profession,

> Without wishing to deny the importance of [the influences of the German and British universities], the uniqueness of the American system needs to be emphasized, and not only because of the Morrill Act and the innovations introduced by the land-grant principle, with its emphasis on research in agriculture and many other fields as well. The concept of "service" took on a wholly new meaning in state universities that pledged to assist their citizens in ways that had never previously been considered. (P. v)

Graubard (1997) correctly identified the origins of the service interest of the American academy with the Morrill Act of 1862, establishing the Land-Grant colleges of agriculture, and associated the land-grant principle with agricultural science. For many inside and outside Land-Grant universities, the Land-Grant principle, whatever it means, is explicitly agricultural. That misunderstanding of a principle central to the Land-Grant universities continues to mislead and confound the understanding of an insight significant to the future of the academy and higher education.

The Roots of Engagement

The Morrill Act was "the charter of America's quietest revolution" (Taylor 1981, 37). The 17,430,000 acres of land in the public domain committed to finance the Land-Grant colleges—30,000 acres per senator and congressman in each state—is not the thing to focus on in reflecting on the establishment of these institutions. Rather, the principle behind their establishment was without historical precedent. That principle asserted that no part of human life and labor is beneath the notice of the university or without its proper dignity. Both by virtue of the character of their scholarship and whom they would serve, the Land-Grant universities were established as people's universities.

Prior to the 1862 Land-Grant institutions, higher education was reserved for, and helped preserve, the aristocracy of the society. Being a university graduate was an imprimatur of high status in the society. The Land-Grant universities opened classrooms to young people whose previous experiences were primarily on farms, in machine shops, in bakeries, or in factories. Liberty Hyde Bailey, father of the discipline of horticulture in America, and dean of the New York State College of Agriculture at Cornell from 1903 to 1913, wrote that

> education was once exclusive: it is now in spirit inclusive. The agencies that have brought about this change of attitude are those associated with so-called industrial education, growing chiefly out of the forces set in motion by the Land Grant Act of 1862. This Land Grant is the Magna Charta of education: from it in this country we shall date our liberties. (Peters 1998, 53)

As America enters the twenty-first century, the national and individual ethic with respect to formal education is dominated by the expectation of access to higher education for all—attending college has become commonplace. Today, we expect all young Americans, who are able, to go to college. Many of them expect to go on to graduate school at least for a master's degree. Even though other developed nations have emulated the U.S. investment in higher education, still during the period from 1985 to 1991, the United States consistently reported the highest enrollment for eighteen- to twenty-one-year-olds in tertiary education of all developed countries, with U.S. rates between 33 and 38 percent (Perie et al. 1997).

An even more revolutionary idea than widespread access to higher education was embedded in the establishment and evolution of the Land-Grant universities. According to Taylor (1981), it was "that thought and action were indivorcible, that the place of the academy is in the world not beyond it, that it is the business of the university to demonstrate the connection of knowledge, art, and practice" (p. 37).

Prior to the Land-Grant universities, the aristocrats of the world, including Americans, were schooled in theology, the letters, and law and in some few institutions patterned after German universities like Johns Hopkins University, medicine. The Land-Grant view of scholarship directly challenged the prevailing norms of scholarship at the time of their inception by making the work of cow barns, kitchens, coke ovens, and forges the subject matter of their investigation (Eddy 1957). In 1890, the Babcock test for butterfat content of milk was both a scientific advancement and a political/economic act necessary to rationalize markets for fluid milk.

Access to classroom instruction is not, and has not been, the only way in which the Land-Grant universities fulfilled their contract with Americans regarding public access to the knowledge they create, although that was the initial effort. Around 1900, by which time agricultural scientists had demonstrated their ability to solve some of agriculture's practical problems, farmers clamored for access to the insights of the scientists. The claims on scientists' time became so great that the outreach function of the university was formalized as the Cooperative Extension

Service by the Smith-Lever Act of 1914. "Cooperative" referred to the partnership between the federal, state, and county governments in support of the extension program.

Smith-Lever provided for federal government funding to the universities in support of the extension outreach function, just as the Hatch Act of 1887 had funded agricultural research. Rainsford's (1972) research makes clear that the Smith-Lever Act was passed because the direct benefits to farming sought by agricultural interests in their support of both the Morrill Act and the Hatch Act had not been forthcoming. Most students in the Land-Grant colleges did not study agriculture and go back to the farm, even though they came from farm families; results of research and instruction did not reach farmers because they were not in college but on the farm.

Thus, the Land-Grant system was revolutionary in the history of higher education in three ways:

1. its classrooms and degrees were accessible to the working classes,
2. its agenda of scholarship considered no subject beneath its purview, and
3. it provided access to new knowledge to those who would never qualify, nor want, to be in its classrooms.

This system that integrated research and extension has been, and is, hugely successful. Agricultural productivity has grown enormously. American farmers who have survived the economic tests of global markets have prospered and have the most advanced means of production anywhere in the world, though many who failed to keep business and technological pace became obsolete. American society has continued to have an affordable, safe, and secure food system. The agricultural knowledge and information system (AKIS) itself has prospered with substantial support from both public and private sectors. The rate of return on investments in research and development and extension in agriculture are somewhere between 20 and 40 percent per annum (Alston and Pardey 1996). In a society whose long-term cost of government borrowing has seldom if ever been as high as 15 percent, arguably government should borrow at 15 percent and gain returns of 20 percent by investing in agricultural research and extension (Alston and Pardey 1996).

Evidence of the success of the system was made clear by the period from 1920 to the end of World War II, the "Transition to Science" era in American agriculture, according to Huffman and Evenson (1993). It was during this period that hybrid corn, among other science-based advances, was developed. However, the period of the 1950s and 1960s was the golden age for the Land-Grant agricultural research and extension system, according to Huffman and Evenson. By that time, the system was enabling U.S. farmers and the agricultural sector to successfully compete with producers anywhere in the world, as well as being judged as one of the most productive sectors of the U.S. economy (Huffman and Evenson 1993).

It will be argued here that part of the huge productivity of the agricultural science and information system derived from the engagement of campus-based science with the realities of agricultural problems at the farm level through extension. Busch and Lacy (1983) made clear in their *Science, Agriculture and the Politics of Agricultural Research* that most of the choice of research projects by agricultural scientists at that time was based on the personal preferences of the scientist. The only institutionalized link between the agricultural sector and the university, then and now, is through the extension function. Notwithstanding the low attention given to that activity by writers on the economics of the system (Huffman and Evenson 1993; Alston and Pardey 1996), the extension function is certainly a necessary if not sufficient condition to system success, and extension's influence on the research agenda may go a long way in explaining the high productivity of the system.

The early twenty-first century is a time when research universities, particularly public research universities, are struggling to persuade the people of America of the unique utility of such institutions, primarily in roles other than undergraduate instruction. The public support being sought is for both affirmation and funding. In that context, knowing that there was a time when the Cooperative Extension Services of the several states as arms of the Land-Grant universities were adjudged to be the most trusted source of new knowledge for ordinary Americans is instructive (Feller et al. 1984). According to Miller (2001), the Land-Grant universities that served to create and transfer science-based technology into use by agricultural producers is arguably ranked first of all the compelling scientific achievements contributing to human development and welfare from the United States in the twentieth century (McDowell 2001).

Engagement—Agricultural Scholarship Reconsidered

Scholarship Reconsidered—Priorities of the Professorate by Ernest Boyer (1990) is widely viewed as the contemporary manifesto of the dedicated and underappreciated undergraduate instructor. Boyer's work is heralded as a clarion cry for change in the academy on behalf of what many professors really do—teach undergraduates. While *Scholarship Reconsidered* nods deferentially to researchers and even acknowledges a preeminent role for research within the academy, Boyer argued persuasively that many in the academy are almost completely occupied by teaching. Faculty with those assignments, he asserted, should be evaluated for excellence in that function, and their scholarship should reflect that assignment.

Curiously, scholars heavily vested in research, many of whom view teaching as an unfortunate ancillary function of the academy that must be endured, commonly justify their relative priority setting on the two activities by arguing that excellence in research is a prerequisite of effective teaching. Unfortunately, empirical evidence does not support that claim. Involvement in research and research productivity is barely correlated with student evaluations of teaching effectiveness. It has a positive correlation in the range of .13 across multiple studies (Feldman 1987). The positive sign on the correlation coefficient is reassuring because it affirms that research activity by the professor does not harm students. But the statistic does not support much more of a conclusion about the relationship between research and teaching.

Academics and academic departments in the agricultural sciences have struggled with a different conflict than the one between teaching and research. In the agricultural sciences and in the departments and colleges that house them, the mandate to carry the results of scholarship to farms, fields, and barns and to have it work has created as great or even greater tension than that addressed by Boyer (1990). That tension is derived from the added institutionalized function and funding for extension/outreach imposed on those academics and academic departments associated with the early Land-Grant agenda and the federal advocate for that agenda—the U.S. Department of Agriculture. In some departments in colleges of agriculture, the extension obligation constitutes somewhere between a third and a half of the faculty full-time equivalents, with some faculty having partial appointments in all three missions—teaching, research, and extension.

Disagreements over evaluating and accrediting the extension function as legitimate scholarship is so great at some Land-Grant institutions that scholars with predominantly extension appointments are tenured under a different tenure system, and/or are housed in separate extension academic units. The analogy in the other part of the university would be to have two chemistry departments, one for chemistry teachers and the other for chemistry researchers. Such arrangements within the agricultural academic establishment are the result of great stridency and power struggles over the definitions of "rigor," the measurement and evaluation of scholarly output, and the nature and meaning of the Land-Grant principle and mission. The institutional responses such as separate tenure arrangements or separate extension departments to the stridency of the dialogue defeats the achievement of the Land-Grant principle.

So central is the ethic of carrying out extension, and so great is the debate over extension obligations and the reward and respect for them, that these issues within academic agricultural science constitute a major cultural difference between it and the rest of the university. When viewed positively, the cultural difference is described as a greater commitment to the Land-Grant principle and to the engagement it implies. At a large number of Land-Grant institutions, even the employment appointments for all academics within colleges associated with the original Land-Grant agenda are influenced by this functional and cultural difference. Twelve-month appointments are the norm within colleges of agriculture even where the remainder of the campus has ten-month academic-year appointments. It is not surprising then, given the strong association of this cultural difference with the agricultural sciences, that even Graubard (1997) might misunderstand and consider the Land-Grant principle to be agricultural-science specific. Indeed, many in colleges of agriculture and Cooperative Extension Services take a similar view.

The Land-Grant Principle—
The Power of Engagement

Engagement and the quality of science practiced

According to Blaug (1980), since the 1960s, great turmoil has occurred among those who philosophize about science and the scientific method. Among those challenging previously received theories of science were Sir Karl Popper and Thomas S. Kuhn. Both Popper and Kuhn agreed that most scientific advancement does not come about primarily by accretion but by the revolutionary overthrow of an accepted theory and its replacement by a better one. However, they disagreed substantially on whether the day-to-day work of scientists is revolutionary. They disagreed on when scientific tests are challenges of theory or tests of the ability of the scientist. They also disagreed on whether applications of science that are less than a test of fundamental theory are hack science or a necessary condition to generating revolutionary changes. Neither Popper nor Kuhn believed in induction as valid scientific method because there are no rules for inducing correct theories from facts—there is no logical basis for validation. Rather, both believed that the "falsification"—Popper's term—necessary to advancing knowledge is only possible from deductive reasoning—from hypothesizing, testing, and rejecting.

Kuhn (1970) asserted that the fundamental issue on which he and Popper agree is that an analysis of the development of scientific knowledge must take into account the way that science is actually practiced. Based on this insight from Kuhn about the importance of the behavior of scientists in the practice of their craft, the argument is made in this article that the engagement of scientists in solving real, practical problems via an involvement in public service activities contributes to the advancement of discovery scholarship and perhaps even the solving of theoretical problems.

Both Kuhn and Popper emphasize that scientific advances are made through the deductive process of repeated testing of scientific theories and the associated rejection or failure to reject the theories. Clearly, laboratory and experimental conditions and procedures prescribed by statistical analysis and the various scientific disciplines provide the most rigorous conditions for Popper's falsification. Kuhn, however, argued that Popper's emphasis on falsification in the advancement of knowledge gives too much emphasis to unusual and extraordinary research and too little emphasis to the day-to-day work in the practice of science. This day-to-day work, which is mostly solving puzzles rather than testing hypotheses, argued Kuhn (1970), hones the skill of the scientists such that on some occasions, some scientists actually are able to set forth hypotheses and perform experiments that test fundamental theories and advance scientific revolutions.

In describing his disagreement with Sir Karl Popper on scientific practice and the importance of solving puzzles, Thomas Kuhn (1970) wrote,

It is important to notice that when I describe the scientist as a puzzle solver and Sir Karl describes him as a problem solver, the similarity of our terms disguises a fundamental divergence. Sir Karl writes (the italics are his), "Admittedly, our expectations, and thus our theories, may precede, historically, even our problems. *Yet science starts only with problems*. Problems crop up especially when we are disappointed in our expectations, or when our theories involve us in difficulties, in contradictions." I use the term "puzzle" in order to emphasize that the difficulties which *ordinarily* confront even the very best scientists are, like crossword puzzles or chess puzzles, challenges only to his ingenuity. *He* is in difficulty, not current theory. (P. 5)

Kuhn (1970) further emphasized the importance of solving puzzles, in contrast to testing theories in scientific practice when discussing the practice of astrology. He said that astrology cannot be dismissed as unscientific on the basis of the vague and imprecise way that its practitioners couched their predictions, making refutation difficult, or on the way that they explained its failures. Even its limited success in prediction does not dismiss astrology as unscientific. Much of the same criticisms, he suggests, could have been levied at engineering, meteorology, and medicine of more than a century ago. Each of these respective fields, which were at the time more akin to craft than to a science, had shared theories and craft rules, which guided practice and established the plausibility of the discipline. And while practitioners had great desire for more powerful rules and more articulate theories, to have abandoned their practice simply because the desired new insights were not at hand would have been absurd. In the absence of a new set of rules of practice, neither medicine nor astrology could carry out research: "They had no puzzles to solve and therefore no science to practice" (Kuhn 1970, 9).

In comparing the early practice of astrology with that of astronomy, often practiced by the same people, Kuhn (1970) made the point that individual failures in prediction in astronomy would give rise to a host of calculation and instrumentation puzzles. The same was not true of astrology, which had too many possible sources of difficulty, most beyond the control of the astrologer. Thus, while individual failures could be explained, no one, no matter how skilled, could make use of them in a constructive way to revise the astrological traditions. "And without puzzles, able first to challenge and then to attest the ingenuity of the individual practitioner, astrology could not have become a science even if the stars had, in fact, controlled human destiny" (Kuhn 1970, 9-10).

Johnson and Zerby (1973) spoke of the distinction between practical and theoretical problems when discussing the way in which economists deal with values because, they asserted, addressing human problems without reference to values is impossible. The solution to practical problems—perhaps more akin to Kuhn's puzzles—Johnson and Zerby argued, result in action and require resolution. Theoretical problems, they asserted, are often never resolved—apparently consistent with Kuhn's disagreement with Popper that the testing of theories is not the usual, day-in-day-out work of scientists and are rare events.

To deal with values in the process of solving practical problems, Johnson and Zerby (1973) argue that scientists must engage both practical and theoretical beliefs. Practical beliefs can be either descriptive or prescriptive. They are beliefs about the nature of reality, both normative reality (what people believe) and nonnormative reality (what is), and about the rightness and wrongness of possible solutions to the practical problem at hand. Practical descriptive beliefs, whether about what people believe things to be or about what actually is, are only of practical value when combined with prescriptive theoretical knowledge to yield descriptive prescriptive knowledge. For example, one may make many observations either about what people believe the world to be like or about what the world actually is like. The categories into which the observations are grouped is what gives meaning to the observations, and those categories are derived from some theoretical view of the world. Finding solutions to practical problems requires, argued Johnson and Zerby, using theoretical, nonprescriptive beliefs about what people believe to be real as well as about what actually is real.

After reemphasizing that practical problems cannot be solved without reference to theoretical questions, Johnson and Zerby (1973) continued by pointing out that the application of knowledge in solving problems is a creative enterprise requiring objectivity. "Objectivity" is used to describe both the investigator and the kind of knowledge that results from objective investigation. The investigator is considered objective when he or she refrains from identifying himself or herself and his or her prestige with a particular concept and will thus be willing to submit the concept to various tests of objectivity. Knowledge or concepts are objective when they pass tests based on rules of evidence and valid means of justification.

To say that a statement is objective because it is true, or even that the statement is objective because it is an accurate description of reality, is incorrect, asserted Johnson and Zerby (1973). Asserting objectivity because something is an accurate description of reality implies that our experience tells us that there is a correspondence with reality—the only check on which is more experience, which may be as flawed as the first.

A concept is objective, Johnson and Zerby (1973) suggested, if it passes all of the following tests:

- it is consistent with other previously accepted concepts and with new concepts based on current experience,
- it has a clear and specifiable meaning, and
- it is useful in solving the problems with which one is confronted. (P. 224)

The first test of objectivity—the test of consistency—includes both internal consistency and external consistency. Internal consistency is an analytical test and requires that concepts bear a logical relationship to each other. The advantage of mathematical models as representations of theoretical knowledge is that they are, by definition, internally consistent. However, sometimes such models fail to pass the test of external consistency. The test of external consistency is a test of experience based both on synthetic knowledge (derived from experience) and analytic knowledge (deduced by logic from propositions). New or independent experiences can be derived through observation such as statistically designed experiments, survey research, or other approaches to observation. Observations or experience provide a basis for forming new concepts. To apply the test of external consistency, the newly synthesized concept is compared with existing concepts.

The test of clarity is simply the meaning of clarity. If a concept can be easily articulated and communicated, then it will pass the test of clarity. If the concept is not clear, then it does not pass the test.

The test of workability comes from pragmatism. The test of workability, argued Johnson and Zerby (1973), is primarily interested in the usefulness of knowledge. They illustrated the workability test by suggesting that the assumption that light moves in a straight line passes the workability test of objectivity if the problem being solved is the sighting of a rifle. Presumably, if either interstellar travel or molecular behavior is being contemplated, then quantum insights to the behavior of light must be considered to pass the test of workability. Similarly, the assumption that the earth is flat is workable when contemplating the construction of a building or a bridge, but not when plotting intercontinental air routes. To site a house for the best passive solar heating in the Northern Hemisphere, pure empirical observation will lead one to choose a southern exposure. To explain the empirical results, one will likely have to abandon the flat-earth assumption.

Two points are made from this formal discussion of the way that science is practiced and scientists behave. First, and contrary to Popper, the daily practice of science in less than falsification of basic theories but rather in applications or practical problem solving is not hack science, but a different brand of scholarship valued for the problems it solves. The second point is that this type of scientific practice has as much likelihood of contributing to Popper's falsification and ultimately to scientific revolutions, by virtue of the fact that in the solving of practical problems or puzzles, the scientist has some external discipline impelling a decision. If someone acts on the scientist's suggested solution to the practical problem, the additional test of workability will be passed.

By engaging in such problem-solving activity, the skill of the scientist is increased and he or she may, in Kuhn's (1970) terms, be more likely to be able to set up the experiment that actually tests the theoretical hypothesis. The test of objectivity that permits the scientist to work from his or her discipline on the practical problem is the test of consistency. The test that permits that an actual solution be found to the practical problem at hand is the pragmatic test of workability—light moves in a straight line or is influenced by gravity depending on the application. To restate the point, the exposure of the scientist and his or her theories to the rigors of application in a practical problem ("puzzle" in Kuhn's terms) not of his or her choosing provides a clear test of the capacity and knowledge of the scholar, and perhaps also of the theory.

Research and extension scholars within the Land-Grant-based agricultural science establishment compelled to provide workable answers to farmers' practical problems served to force the workability test of scientific objectivity on the whole enterprise. Part of the way that the test of workability was imposed was through the debates and tension between scholars with research appointments and those with extension responsibilities. The institutionalized and funded engagement via the extension function ensured the continuing exposure of the science to the rigors of that test of workability. The fact of its solving practical problems of real people elicited political support to continue and grow the appropriated funding.

In 2002, the state legal obligation to match federal contributions of appropriated funds for agricultural research (Hatch and MacIntire/Stennis monies) is dollar for dollar. The actual contribution from the states exceeds six dollars for each federal dollar provided (Hatzios 2002). The agricultural audience knows what a research university is and supports it.

Engagement and the relevance of the science practiced

Yet one more aspect of the power of engagement can be seen in the Land-Grant and extension experience. The issue is scholarly relevance. The quality of science practiced is different from the relevance of the science practiced. Relevance has more to do with the scientific agenda and the usefulness of the products of that scholarship in the society.

In the Twelfth Congress of the Universities of the Commonwealth, August 1978, the theme of relevance was a prominent one. Sir Charles Wilson, principal emeritus of the University of Glasgow, was somewhat hostile to the notion of a need for greater relevance in teaching and research as evidenced by greater responsiveness to local, national, and international problems. His objection was that "those who would make a whole philosophy out of 'relevance' would . . . like the universities to come closer to the world of action and practice and to sacrifice some of their detachment in favor of social involvement" (Wilson 1979, 22-23). For Wilson, the risks associated with involvement in daily events are a loss of scholarly detachment and neutrality. Wilson's (1978) concerns sound remarkably like Bok's (1990) concerns twelve years later, when he argued that engaging the world may be a distraction to the "more profound obligation that every institution of learning owes to civilization to renew its culture, interpret its past, and expand our understanding of the human condition" (p. 104).

John F. A. Taylor (1981), in his book *The Public Commission of the University*, poses an answer to Wilson and Bok.

> Of this only are we perfectly assured, that in the new relation of science and society there can be no such thing as a university beyond politics. A mere silence on public questions will not prove its innocence; quarantine will not prove its loyalty. The path of a university is unavoidably a political path for the reason that neutrality is unavoidably a political role. The problem of a neutral is not how to be out of the world but how to be in it—how to be in it without being of it. (P. 29)

According to this notion of the public commission of the university, part of scholarship is to be aware of societal issues related to the particular area of scholarship—to be relevant. The implication of relevance or irrelevance is usefulness or uselessness. The test of relevance affects both the agenda of the scholar and the conduct of the scholarship. Ensuring that this relevance in scholarship occurs is important to the administration of the university. As with academic freedom, relevance is important not just for the sake of the scholars but also for the sake of the university and the society.

For many academics, the exposure to real-world problems comes through consulting activities rather than through public service. Indeed, consulting, like public service, makes a positive contribution to scholarship through both the test of workability and the test of relevance. However, understanding the direction in which the flow of benefits is moving and not to confuse this benefit from consulting with public service is important. Similar observations can be made about the corporatization of the university. While the corporate owner provides real-world input (and funding) to the scholarly agenda, it is a far cry from an institutionalized test of scholarly relevance, where relevance is measured in societal terms. In the current scramble for funding support for higher education from corporate business, the danger is that university administrators will confuse usefulness to corporate America with usefulness to the society. The notion has long been rejected that what is good for General Motors is good for America.

This discussion of relevance also provides some basis for comment on the difference of perspective between Bok (1990) and the Kellogg Commission (1998) on the Future of State and Land-Grant Universities about greater engagement of universities in the society. Bok is concerned that without the engagement with the society, the society is in peril. The Kellogg Commission is concerned that without engagement with the society, the public universities are in peril. An implicit concern by the Kellogg Commission is that without engagement, the universities will have nothing to say to the society, which will be a social loss. Ensuring the involvement of university scholars in public service becomes an institutionalized test of their relevance.

The Bok (1990) view clearly comes out of the private, elite university culture and its remnant aristocratic view of the university and society. The public university/Land-Grant university leaders more closely reflect the public support/public obligation perspective that was part of the social contract between the American people and the Land-Grant universities.

Taylor (1966) provided a balance between Bok (1990) and the Kellogg Commission (1998) and the possibility that the university would become only an instrumental agency of the society:

> He who regards the university as an island, who lets it become one, is treasonable to it. He provincializes its community, and diminishes himself. He gains a province and loses the world. He may even gain the world, but he shall have denied its soul. (P. 225)

> In its relation to society, the university's function is, in the first instance, to provide the means to ends that society has chosen for itself. But it is a lame architect who houses an activity without civilizing it. You do not sensitively house the life of a man by providing only for the movement of his bowels, and if in seeking to serve his needs you search out only the known needs that he declares and will think to define, that he needs a kitchen and a place

to lay his head, you will serve him very ill indeed. He buys the services of an architect; you give him the services of a privy-carpenter. (P. 228)

Disaggregating the very high returns to investment in agricultural research and extension to identify the magnitude of the respective impacts of engagement through extension on science quality and on relevance is exceedingly difficult. Even measuring the contribution of extension in disseminating the results of scholarship is highly elusive and seldom done. Arguably the institutionalized and funded obligation for engagement of researchers with final users via extension is part of the explanation of the high success of the agricultural knowledge information system.

The Land-Grant principle

The principle of scholarly behavior that evolved from the growth and development of the Land-Grant colleges of agriculture into the Land-Grant universities as they struggled to address the problems of American society at the later part of the nineteenth century and throughout the twentieth century can now be discerned. Partly because of the character of the society and partly because agrarian interests acted politically to establish the Land-Grant colleges, the early agenda was directed to agriculture. The principle that emerged is general to all scholarship.

The principle revealed is that synergistic power derives from scholarship practiced where tests of workability and relevance are institutionalized—the power of engagement. Further synergy is generated when access to the knowledge is ensured for users who will find it useful in their lives. Some of the power from engagement and access to knowledge is intellectual by virtue of the contribution to both the quality and relevance of the science practiced. Other power is political, resulting from the engagement with users of the knowledge, the access they have to the scholarly product, and the usefulness of the new knowledge to them.

In the agricultural science experience, the power of the Land-Grant principle translated itself into high productivity of the AKIS and into substantial funding support for that system from federal, state, and local levels of government. Classroom instruction can also be enhanced by engagement through the greater relevance of both the instruction and instructor. The method of instruction may also become a part of the engagement.

The success of the Land-Grant principle as applied to the agricultural problems of the society can be used as a guide to the development of the larger university. The engagement that would emerge would ensure that universities, particularly research universities, play a larger, more useful role in the society. Furthermore, notwithstanding the fickleness of the political process, practice of the Land-Grant principle across the entire university should provide for greater support from the people and their representatives. This positive supportive relationship between the society and its universities would seem particularly likely in this period of our history when we call ourselves an information society.

Academic Agriculture Captured—
From Architects to Privy Carpenters?

Another, more cautionary lesson emerges from the Land-Grant universities and extension experience of more recent years. Part of the success of the Land-Grant principle at work on the agricultural agenda has been the continuing support by agricultural audiences for agricultural research and extension—the AKIS. However, as the success of the AKIS has grown and as a result of its success, the numbers of farmers producing the nation's food and fiber have significantly declined. The economic forces changing agricultural technology, global markets, and rising income expectations have resulted in ever fewer, ever larger farms. At the time of the 1862 Morrill Act, fully 60 percent of the people of the nation were engaged in farming. Today that number is less than 2 percent.

As Land-Grant colleges of agriculture grew into Land-Grant universities, so also did the range of scholarship practiced. At the beginning of the twenty-first century, there are 151 Doctoral/Research University–Extensive, out of a total of 3,941 institutions of higher education classified by the Carnegie Foundation. The 151 are the jewels in the crown of American higher education. Of these 151 universities, 44 are Land-Grant universities. The remaining Land-Grant universities established in 1862 are in the next category, Doctoral/Research University–Intensive category. All Land-Grant universities created in 1862 are classified as Doctoral/Research Universities (Carnegie Foundation 2001).

As the character of the Land-Grant institutions changed in response to the changes in the society, the agenda of the Cooperative Extension Services in the respective states did not follow suit. In most states, the portfolio of the extension service from the Land-Grant universities is still predominantly agricultural. In 1992, the last year for which complete statistics are available, extension to agricultural audiences on agricultural subjects still constituted 47 percent of the extension resources on a national basis (McDowell 1992). In most states, the extension service is still under the control of the college of agriculture and its leadership. Indeed, the Cooperative Extension Service associated with Texas A&M University, a Doctoral/Research University–Extensive, only changed its name from the Texas Agricultural Extension Service to Texas Cooperative Extension on 27 July 2001 (Texas A&M University 2001).

Within the Land-Grant universities, some of the most vicious internecine struggles of recent years have been over the leadership, control, and portfolio of the Cooperative Extension Service. Numerous university, college, or extension administrators within Land-Grant universities have lost their jobs in part because they attempted to move the extension organization toward a broader program portfolio and away from domination by the agricultural part of the program. Carcasses of such people in the 1990s are in Minnesota, Michigan, West Virginia, Virginia, South Carolina, Georgia, Iowa, Alabama, Illinois, and Missouri among others

(McDowell 2001). In 2002, legislators in the Minnesota House of Representatives filed legislation to direct the University of Minnesota Extension Service to refocus its extension programs back toward agricultural programs. The action was in response to a proposed reorganization of field staff made necessary by serious budget cuts in state, university, and extension budgets (Dick Hemmingsen, personal communication, 29 March 2002).

The Minnesota case illustrates the forces at work on behalf of the agricultural portion of the extension agenda in most of the states and their Land-Grant universities. In the face of some threat to agricultural extension programs, the agricultural community seeks to protect their programs, even if it means forcing the university to abandon other long-established programs. When the threat to agricultural programs is perceived to be the result of efforts by university or extension administrators to realign program resources, agricultural interest groups often participate in promoting the removal of the offending Land-Grant administrator.

These circumstances are so prevalent across the Land-Grant extension system that describing the system as being held hostage by agricultural interest groups is considered a fair characterization of the relationship between Land-Grant extension and the agricultural client groups at the beginning of the twenty-first century (McDowell 2001). The irony of the hostage relationship is that it grows out of the declining political power and inability of the agricultural community to maintain budgetary support for the university and extension. They use the power that farm groups continue to wield to win battles over internal university and extension allocations. The result is an ever narrowing of the extension portfolio and a downward spiral of support for the extension system.

Table 1 illustrates this narrowing of the extension portfolio in favor of the agricultural program at the national level from 1973 to 1992 (McDowell 1992).

This hostage taking of the Land-Grant extension system is insufficient to complete the argument that the AKIS has moved from architects to privy carpenters. The difference between the two, Taylor would say, is in the character of the housing envisioned and designed.

The character of the knowledge provided to agricultural producers at the end of the twentieth and beginning of the twenty-first century suggests that the AKIS has achieved the status of privy carpenters. Farmers are getting what they want, but not what they need. In the face of global economic forces, the factors affecting farm profitability are multitudinous. More and more farm profitability is dependent on successful strategic business behavior rather than simply the successful production of undifferentiated agricultural commodities. Notwithstanding this contemporary economic environment for farming in which at least one writer argues that we are seeing the end of commodity agriculture in the American economic portfolio (Blank 1998), the vast majority of the knowledge produced and distributed to farmers through the AKIS is precisely about on-the-farm production technology of commodities.

In 1992 at Virginia Tech, Virginia's Land-Grant university, the number of agricultural extension specialists time-committed to on-the-farm technology was fifty-five full-time equivalents as compared to six full-time equivalents directed to

TABLE 1

NATIONAL, STATE, AND LOCAL EXTENSION PROFESSIONAL FULL-TIME
EQUIVALENTS, BY PROGRAM AREAS, 1973, 1982, 1987, AND 1992
(IN PERCENTAGES)

	1973	1982	1987	1992
Agriculture and natural resources	38	44	46	47
Home economics	21	22	23	24
4-H and youth development	32	27	25	22
Community and rural development	9	7	6	7

SOURCE: Bottom 1992.
NOTE: More recent data were sought from the Cooperative State Research, Education and
Extension Service of the United States Department of Agriculture to bring this table up to the
late 1990s. The U.S. Department of Agriculture was unable to provide the data by these or any
other categories that would permit an estimation of these categories and still sum to 100 percent
of the full-time equivalents.

before and after the farm-gate issues in marketing, management, food technology,
and food processing. Similarly, the National Research Initiative of the U.S. Department of Agriculture, the major competitive grant source of funding for agricultural
research in the United States, had in that year approximately $85 million commit-
ted to on-the-farm production technology and its management and only $8 million
for trade, markets, policy, and food technology (McDowell, 1992). No appreciable
difference is seen in the emphasis of the National Research Initiative or agricultural extension programs across the country in 2001 from what was true in 1992.

Farmers ask for on-the-farm technology and its management because it can
more often be done from their tractor seats: the domain of actions and activity with
which they are most familiar and most comfortable. New knowledge in that arena,
even if its payoff is lower, is what they want. Other, more strategic behavior such as
forward contracting, other price risk-management activities, or collective action on
marketing or policy changes at the federal, state, and local levels are more difficult
to accomplish and require more exacting behavior of them as business people. As
hostage takers, farmers are used to getting what they want and in many cases are
not getting what they need.

Conclusions

The Land-Grant principle that emerged from the creation of institutions of
higher education to address the problems of a majority population engaged in agriculture in the nineteenth and early twentieth centuries represents one of America's
finest contributions to civilization and to scholarly practice. The principle applies
to all scholarship. When scholarship is practiced in an environment that institution-
alizes the engagement required by the principle, the scholarship is better and more
relevant.

The scholars who practiced under the Land-Grant principle throughout much of the twentieth century were the architects of America's agricultural success and also of the world's Green Revolution that emerged from the same scholarly practice in the latter half of the twentieth century. The capturing of that AKIS by being taken and held hostage by agricultural interest groups in more recent years appears to have turned the architects into privy carpenters. The trends toward greater corporatization of academic agricultural research will not likely offer any improvement.

Is it possible that Bok (1990) was correct? Is it possible that the part of the academy most engaged with society in the twentieth century—Land-Grant agricultural science—has succumbed to the blandishments, distractions, and corrupting entanglements that are Bok's concerns of the academy too closely engaging the society? The difference between Bok and the Kellogg Commission (1998) is the difference between relevance and irrelevance. In Taylor's (1966) terms, the difference between architects and privy carpenters is the difference between being objective, relevant scholars and subjective, relevant scholars.

The experience of the Land-Grant universities and extension in engagement suggests that great intellectual and political power can be garnered from creating environments where engaged scholarship is practiced. The experience suggests that institutionalizing and funding engagement in the whole university is important to achieving its benefits. Unfortunately, at the current point in the history of the academy, those in leadership roles who speak encouragingly of engagement have little more than exhortation to offer.

The exhortation of scholars to become architects of the use of particular kinds of knowledge in society is important in the absence of having anything else to offer. However, the Land-Grant experience in the agricultural sciences suggests that moving past exhortation to funding and formal expectations of engagement can achieve great things in the academy. That same experience also warns that being engaged is different from being held hostage.

America's universities, particularly its research universities, are struggling for support, including affirmation, from the society and the polity that house them. Former University of Michigan president James Duderstadt is reported to have joked that during his tenure at the University of Michigan, the university changed from being a state university, to a state-assisted university, to a state-related university, and finally to a state-located university (Kellogg Commission 1998). For universities, particularly public universities, to be related to society only by virtue of their location is to be truly disengaged. Those who have sought to capture the AKIS and hold it hostage have at least done so because they understood its importance to their part of the society and valued it. Helping the agricultural community to understand that the subjectivity they impose is costly to them is a second-order problem for agricultural science. That excess in engagement fades by comparison to those parts of the academy whose value is unknown, unappreciated, and at worst unused or completely owned by corporate interests and otherwise unavailable to the society.

References

Alston, Julian M., and Philip G. Pardey. 1996. *Making science pay: The economics of agricultural R&D policy*. Washington, DC: AEI Press.

American Association for Higher Education. 2002. Knowledge for what? The engaged scholar. 2001. Conference announcement for tenth American Association for Higher Education Conference on Faculty Roles and Rewards, 25-27 January, Phoenix, AZ.

Blank, Steven C. 1998. *The end of agriculture in the American portfolio*. Westport, CT: Quorum.

Blaug, Mark. 1980. *The methodology of economics*. Cambridge, UK: Cambridge University Press.

Bok, Derek. 1990. *Universities and the future of America*. Durham, NC: Duke University Press.

Bottom, John. Personal communication, 11 May 1992.

Boyer, Ernest L. 1990. *Scholarship reconsidered—Priorities of the professoriate*. Princeton, NJ: Carnegie Foundation for the Advancement of Teaching.

Busch, Lawrence, and William B. Lacy. 1983. *Science, agriculture, and the politics of research*. Boulder, CO: Westview.

Carnegie Foundation for the Advancement of Teaching. 2001. The carnegie classification of institutions of higher education, 2000 edition, with foreword by Lee S. Shulman. Available from http://www.carnegiefoundation.org/Classification/index.htm.

Eddy, Edward Danforth, Jr. 1957. *Colleges for our land and time: The land-grant idea in American education*. New York: Harper & Brothers.

Feldman, Kenneth A. 1987. Research productivity and scholarly accomplishment of college teachers as related to their instructional effectiveness: A review and exploration. *Research in Higher Education* 26 (3): 227.

Feller, Irwin, L. Kaltreider, P. Madden, D. Moore, and L. Sims. 1984. *Overall study report: Findings and recommendations*. Vol. 5, *The agricultural technology delivery system: A study of agricultural and food related technologies*. Prepared for Science and Education, U. S. Department of Agriculture. University Park, PA: Institute for Policy Research and Evaluation, Pennsylvania State University.

Graubard, Stephen R. 1997. The American academic profession. *Daedalus* fall: v, vi.

Hatzios, Kriton. 2002. *Virginia Agricultural Experiment Station annual report, 2000-2001*. Blacksburg, VA: College of Agriculture and Life Sciences, Virginia Tech.

Huffman, Wallace E., and Robert E. Evenson. 1993. *Science for agriculture*. Ames: Iowa State University Press.

Johnson, Glenn L., and Lewis K. Zerby. 1973. *What economists do about values*. East Lansing: Department of Agricultural Economics, Center for Rural Manpower and Public Affairs, Michigan State University.

Kellogg Commission on the Future of State and Land-Grant Universities. 1999. *Returning to our roots: The engaged institution*. Washington, DC: National Association of State Universities and Land-Grant Colleges.

Kellogg Presidents' Commission. 1996. *Joint statement, Kellogg Presidents' Commission on the 21st Century State and Land-Grant University*. Washington, DC: National Association of State Universities and Land-Grant Colleges. Retrieved 19 April 2000 from http://www.nasulgc.org/Kellog/STATEMENTS/comstate.html.

Kuhn, Thomas S. 1970. Logic of discovery or psychology of research? In *Criticism and the growth of knowledge*, edited by Imre Lakatos and Alan Musgrave. Cambridge, UK: Cambridge University Press.

McDowell, George R. 1992. The new political economy of extension education for agriculture and rural communities. *American Journal of Agricultural Economics* December: 1249-55.

———. 2001. *Land-grant universities and extension into the 21st century: Renegotiating or abandoning a social contract*. Ames: Iowa State Press.

Miller, Paul A. 2001. Foreword. In *Land-grant universities and extension into the 21st century*, edited by George R. McDowell. Ames: Iowa State Press.

Perie, Marianne, Zhongren Jing, Roy Pearson, Joel D. Sherman, and Thomas D. Snyder. 1997. *International education indicators: A time series perspective*. Washington, DC: National Center for Educational Statistics, U.S. Department of Education.

Peters, Scott Joseph. 1998. Extension work as public work: Reconsidering extension's civic mission. Ph.D. diss., University of Minnesota, Minneapolis.

Rainsford, George N. 1972. *Congress and higher education in the nineteenth century*. Knoxville: University of Tennessee Press.

Taylor, John F. A. 1966. *The masks of society*. New York: Appleton-Century-Crofts.

———. 1981. *The public commission of the university*. New York: New York University Press.

Texas A&M University. 2001. News Release: July 27, Texas agricultural extension service changing name, keeping commitments. College Station, Texas: Texas A&M University.

Wilson, Charles. 1979. Reconciling national, international and local roles of universities with the essential character of a university. In *Pressures and priorities—Report of the proceedings of the Twelfth Congress of the Universities of the Commonwealth*. London: Association of Commonwealth Universities.

Urban Universities: Meeting the Needs of Students

By
GERRY RIPOSA

Urban universities play an increasingly significant role in post-secondary education; however, little attention has been directed at these institutions. While not attempting to provide a comprehensive set of generalizations predicting the behavior of these educational institutions, this article seeks to be a gateway to focus our attention upon and examine the distinctive character, mission, and activities of urban universities. To that end, we build the context of education by discussing the rise of public education, in general, and urban universities, in particular. Next, using the California State University system, we set out the environment, philosophy, and challenges that distinguish urban universities from their traditional counterparts. From this research, we are able to better define urban universities and their environments, to begin mapping policy responses to the challenges these institutions face, and to suggest future areas of research of these important learning centers.

M ore than ever before, societies now look to higher education to promote social coherence, political stability, and economic prosperity. Global restructuring escalates competition for economic and political power; the emergence of information societies requires trained managers and workforce; and marginalized groups, as well as the general public, voice demands for a better quality of life in spite of conspicuous social problems (Castells 1989; Drucker 1993; Newman 1985; Reich 1991). Granted that societies have valued organized education for centuries, although predominantly as the purview of economic elites, and often as some bourgeois rite of passage to adult

Gerry Riposa is a professor of political science at California State University, Long Beach. His research interests are primarily in urban policy and, most recently, on the relationships among economic development, empowerment, and sustainable communities. His work has been published in scholarly book chapters and such journals as Policy Studies Review, Policy Studies Journal, Urban Resources, International Journal of Public Administration, American Review of Public Administration, Cities, *and* American Behavioral Scientist. *He is coeditor of* Texas Public Policy *(1987) and* City of Angels *(1992) and coauthor of* Doing Urban Research *(1993).*

DOI: 10.1177/0002716202238566

life. Today, access to postsecondary education is more democratized. For example, Dye (2002) observed that approximately 15 million students in the United States alone attend some type of institution of higher education. However, expansion of educational opportunities across class lines has demanded changes in institutional delivery systems; foremost in this shift has been the rise of the urban university.

With the ascendance of the urban university, questions of location where education will occur, who will have access, and how such knowledge and training will be disseminated assume a new urgency. By the 1960s, not only did every major city in the United States have at least one degree-granting institution, but even those medium cities with populations between 200,000 and 500,000 had one or more universities offering a range of programs and degrees to both traditional and non-traditional students (Elliot 1994). In the past, stereotypical university students were residents, typically attending school at some distance from home. They tended to be younger, be single, live on campus, work few outside jobs, and make steady progression toward a four-year degree, primarily attending daytime courses.

Urban universities tapped a different market of older first-time or returning students, many supporting families, and most working part-time or full-time jobs, yet still dependent on some form of financial aid. Race, class, and gender diversity expanded as inner-city, low-income residents, including minorities and women, gained access to advanced education. Most of these students are place bound and desire education as an economic necessity, but rank college as one of many competing priorities, thus needing in excess of four years to finish. To offer quality education to this new type of college student, urban universities have experimented with different philosophies and learning settings to find a balance between academics and off-campus obligations to their student constituencies.

Internalizing this obligation, urban universities contribute to an educated workforce, an informed citizenry, and increased national productivity; yet they face numerous and dynamic challenges inherent in providing education to diverse student populations. For example, how will universities prepare underequipped students to successfully engage rigorous study? What types of partnerships should these universities forge (Miller 1990)? And because they embrace a more diverse student body, how will these universities meld together multiple missions into a cohesive strategy (Aronowitz 2000)?

Given that the majority of our national population resides either within or at close proximity to urban centers, and that most of the working poor and minorities reside in cities, urban universities are poised to make even greater contributions today than in the past to national and individual development. Yet relatively few scholars have specifically addressed this phenomenon (Berube 1978; Elliot 1994; Giles 1972; Grobman 1988; Klotsche 1966; Weinstock, 1961). This article explores today's urban universities by setting out the rise, definition, and characteristics that distinguish this type of educational institution. To address that task, I will also set out the challenges and opportunities in this institutional environment. Next, moving the examination from general to applied levels, I will look at the California State University (CSU) system and, in particular, at two universities located within Los

Angeles County that service the metropolitan area and include low-income communities such as South Central Los Angeles, East Los Angeles, and Compton.

This article does not generalize about mission and best practices of urban universities; however, it does seek to broaden our understanding concerning these important educational centers and to suggest areas for future examination to meet the needs of urban university students.

Beginning of Education: From Groves Academus to Urban Universities

Efforts at formal education commenced shortly after the development of writing (3000 B.C.), when both Sumerians (developers of cuneiform system pictographics) and Egyptians (developers of hieroglyphics) established schools teaching students to read and write these systems. Semitic people in Syria, who developed the first alphabet between 1800 and 1000 B.C., established religious schools. Priests taught privileged students to read sacred Hebrew writings (Torah).

Confucius (551-479 B.C.) established the first open primary schools where students were taught music, literature, conduct, and ethics. He believed education should be available to all, regardless of class distinctions. As a scholar, he never refused a student even when "he came to me on foot, with nothing more to offer as tuition than a package of dried meat" (Ferguson 2000, 458). For him, any man, including a peasant boy, possessed the potential to be a man of principle.

The Western model of education is an extension of the ancient Grecian model emerging in the fifth century B.C., in which boys were trained in reading and writing, music, poetry, and military arts. Later in the same century, Sophists, teachers of philosophy and rhetoric, schooled young men in argumentation and political affairs. Subsequent centuries witnessed educational expansion but retained, for the most part, the notion that schooling existed to benefit elite males, a perception that ultimately retarded the growth of public education.

Not until the Age of Enlightenment did public schools begin to proliferate. Frederick the Great, a Prussian emperor, who was considered an enlightened ruler, established a public education system in the early 1800s. After Prussia united with Germany to form a more powerful state, other European countries began establishing public education systems. In the United States, public schooling began during colonial times. For example, a 1647 Massachusetts law required the establishment of public schools. By the early twentieth century, public education at the elementary level was free and compulsory throughout Europe and the United States.

Higher education made a similar climb through history. In the sixth century B.C., schools of medicine were started on the Greek island of Cos where philosophers theorized and taught students about the nature of man and of the universe. Pythagoreans (followers of Pythagoras the Greek philosopher and mathematician) began schools in southern Italy. Socrates, Plato, and Aristotle continued the

Pythagorean tradition, as did Epicurus and Zeon in the fourth century B.C. Universities also have traditions in the Arab world, such as Al-Azhar University, founded in 970 A.D. in Cairo, and considered one of the oldest universities in the world (Ferguson 2000).

In the Western world, universities took a major step forward with Pope Frederic I (1123-1190 A.D.), the Holy Roman Emperor, who asserted his authority and granted the first university charter to the University of Bologna (1158 A.D.). From this point on, universities began appearing in Europe throughout the Middle Ages; however, they were unlike those in today's educational settings. Often, groups of scholars and students gathered together for the free exchange of less doctrinaire ideas. The Sorbonne Liberal Arts and Science Division of the University of Paris became a beacon of new ideas at the largest and most famous university in all of Europe. By the 1500s, universities had been established throughout Europe. Some still survive today: Cambridge, Paris, Montpellier, Toulouse, Heidelberg, Bologna, Florence, Naples, Padua, Rome, Sienna, and Salamanca. The pedagogy of positing problems in lectures for students to ponder and research set standards for academic inquiry that today remain part of higher education traditions.

The first university in the Western hemisphere was the University of Santo Domingo, founded in the Dominican Republic (1538). Harvard University was chartered by legislative act on 28 October 1636 by the Massachusetts General Court. Approximately one year later, the General Court ordered that the college be constructed in New Towne, Massachusetts, renamed Cambridge after its English predecessor. The college was named after John Harvard (1607-1638), a philanthropist and colonial clergyman who bequeathed 800 pounds sterling and 400 volumes to the library (Ferguson 2000).

Some 150 years later, state governments began chartering public universities, notably the University of Georgia (1785), University of North Carolina (1789), University of Vermont (1791), University of Tennessee (1794), University of South Carolina (1801), University of Ohio (1804), University of Michigan (1817), University of Virginia (1819), and Indiana University (1801) (Grobman 1988). Yet it was the University of North Carolina, in 1795, that became the first public institution of higher education in the United States to enroll students. Other states soon followed.

The Civil War and the beginning of the U.S. Industrial Age heightened the need for a skilled workforce, especially in agriculture and engineering. Congressional passage of the Morril Act (Land-Grant Act) of 1862 helped to remedy deficits in these areas. Under this law, the national government made available income from federal lands to states for support of agricultural and engineering programs. Some states, such as California, channeled such funds into existing programs at previously established universities. Other states chose to use the resources to build separate institutions, such as Texas A&M, Purdue, Iowa State University, and Michigan State University (Grobman 1988). Still, university life catered to traditional students, but that would change.

The Rise of the Urban University

Societal forces converged to usher in the growing prominence of urban universities into the U.S. higher education landscape (Klotsche 1966). Because technological advances in agriculture and engineering reduced the need for farm labor, and because of rapidly expanded industrialization, located mostly in or around cities, demanding continually enlarging workforces, urbanization became the defining trend in twentieth-century social and spatial arrangements (Abu-Lughod 1991; Gottdiener 1994). People were also attracted to city living for its culture (Zukin 1995). Prior to the Civil War, 85 percent of the national population lived in rural areas; by the 1980s, 85 percent resided in urban areas (Grobman 1985). Technology generated a food surplus to support the cities, provided innovations for industrialization, and created systems to allow humans to live in concentrated spatial relations: industry provided the jobs; urbanization concentrated people in cities. Combined, they fostered the need for universities located within the city to educate a new class of students.

On the eve of World War II, 1.5 million students, or about 3 percent of a national workforce of 50 million, attended postsecondary education (Aronowitz 2000). However, the end of both World War II and the Korean War brought great numbers of veterans to the cities in search of jobs and also opportunities for education funded by the GI Bill. Along with the international and domestic civilian migration to the cities, vets joined this surge into the urban milieu needing continuing education. Adding weight to this demand was society's reaction to a knowledge explosion that demanded trained professionals. As a result, from 1941 to 1965, postsecondary attendance by young men increased 300 percent. To meet the needs of the burgeoning population, a new set of universities emerged (Berube 1978). By 1962, 150 branch campuses, operated by 43 universities in 31 states, had opened their doors (Elliot 1994).

By 1998, half of all Americans ages eighteen to twenty-two years attended university; by 1997, 15 million of a workforce totaling 114 million enrolled in higher education—four times the number in 1941. Demographics project that by 2010, 40 percent of all jobs will require a university degree; yet 30 percent of all jobs will be held by the working class. These working-class members, often older, often women, and often minorities, will push higher education to meet their needs, which happen to be located in urban areas. They are the sustaining catalysts in a globally competitive world that demands trained professionals.

The Urban University: Challenges and Opportunities

It is a mistake to assume that today's urban university is defined exclusively by its location or even by its particular student body. These factors are necessary but not sufficient conditions for a richer perspective of the urban university. Such a university must be located in an urban environ and should target and attract students who, for a myriad of reasons, are place bound and who wish to better themselves. However, it is the urban university's philosophy that distinguishes it from its counterparts (Berube 1978; Elliot 1994). That is to say, urban universities do not see themselves as "of the world, but not in it," to paraphrase Jesuit thought. On the contrary, the urban university must see itself inexorably connected to its urbanized milieu and thus seek to develop programs for a broad-based population on a wider range of issues faced by local communities and cities (Berube 1978). By looking outward, the urban university connects its educational mission to the needs of its immediate surroundings, creating a communication linkage between school and city (Elliot 1994). Indeed, the city becomes a learning center. Consequently, urban universities focus programs on ameliorating deep-seated urban problems. They foster student experience—jobs, internships, service learning—as an essential part of their program but focus impacts on the cultural, political, and economic development in local areas.

As important as these universities are for national productivity and individual opportunity, they continue to encounter considerable challenges (Kogan 1984). Like all of today's universities, urban institutions must overcome academic disengagement (The American freshman 2002). For urban students, external obligations and conditions—such as family, work, recreation, and economic strain—aggravate the disconnection between the ivory tower and the practical world. Although creating a richer educational environment, student diversity also generates its own set of unique problems. By the beginning of the twenty-first century, the increasing numbers of nontraditional, minority, and female students headed the list of most significant changes in higher education (Astin 2000). These students have a wide and uneven background in college preparation. Many are older and have both jobs and families; many are low income and disadvantaged (Grobman 1988). Embodying many of these characteristics, women compose a majority of the twenty-first century student body, a number of whom have taken long periods of time out during their college experience to birth and rear children or to become financially stable (Elliot 1994). It is not an uncommon occurrence for students to take six to eight years to complete a four-year degree. For all these students, education may be a goal, especially to gain economic and social mobility, but it is not their sole identity.

Faced with this type of student body, urban universities must first assess their environments and their constituencies to define student needs and then develop programs to meet those needs. Programs must accommodate the lives of the students, reaching through their cynicism and disengagement to help them achieve their goals (Aronowitz 2000). The goal must be not only to teach how to earn a living but, also in the process, how to live. To accomplish this task, urban universities must rethink routine policies such as scheduling, parking, advising hours, and child care provision, as well as more unique programs that require external collaboration such as service learning and networking opportunities. And most important, urban universities must reorient faculty trained at traditional research campuses to think about creating an intellectual delivery system that is rigorous yet accessible, rather than to perpetuate presenting the university experience as some rite of passage (Elliot 1994).

The Case of California: Urban Education in a Highly Urbanized Region

California is one of the nation's most populous and urbanized states, attracting approximately 25 percent of the country's foreign-born immigrants annually. These facts alone present California as the precursor of change in urban education for other states when reevaluating their own institutions of higher learning. The state's community colleges serve 70 percent of the total students enrolled in California's public colleges; the CSU system serves slightly more than 20 percent; and the University of California serves approximately 9 percent (http://www.calstate.edu).

Today, the CSU system is one of the largest educational systems in the United States. However, its beginnings portended a much more modest approach. California's first step into higher education established state Normal Schools in 1851 to train elementary teachers. In 1871, San Jose's Normal School—known today as San Jose State University—became the first such institution to open its doors, thus launching the beginning of the college system (Douglas 2000). Slowly, Normal Schools were opened in San Diego (1897), San Francisco (1899), Fresno (1911), and Humboldt (1913). By 1921, the state changed the designation of independent Normal Schools to Teachers Schools, and then to California State Colleges in 1935 (Douglas 2000). Additional campuses were added: California State College, Los Angeles (1947); California State College, Long Beach (1949); California State College, Fullerton (1957); and California State College, San Bernardino (1960).

A critical turning point occurred in 1961 when the state assembly, under the Donahue Higher Education Act (1960), combined state colleges into the California State College system and broadened their responsibilities to include offerings in undergraduate and graduate education in liberal arts, natural sciences, and engineering. As the state legislature created additional campuses, it designated the state college system as the California State University system in 1972 with an expanded mission (Douglas 2000). To paraphrase, the CSU mission statement calls for the extension of knowledge, opportunities for personal and professional development, preparation to make contributions to the state's economy and future, public service to communities, and guaranteed access to all who are prepared for collegiate study.

Today, twenty-three campuses compose the CSU system, serving 388,700 students through 22,000 faculty. Together, this university system offers 1,600 undergraduate degrees and 240 master's degrees. In 2000-2001 alone, CSU conferred 56,983 bachelor's and 14,327 master's degrees, along with 36 joint doctorates.

FIGURE 1
CALIFORNIA STATE UNIVERSITY STUDENTS RECEIVING FINANCIAL AID

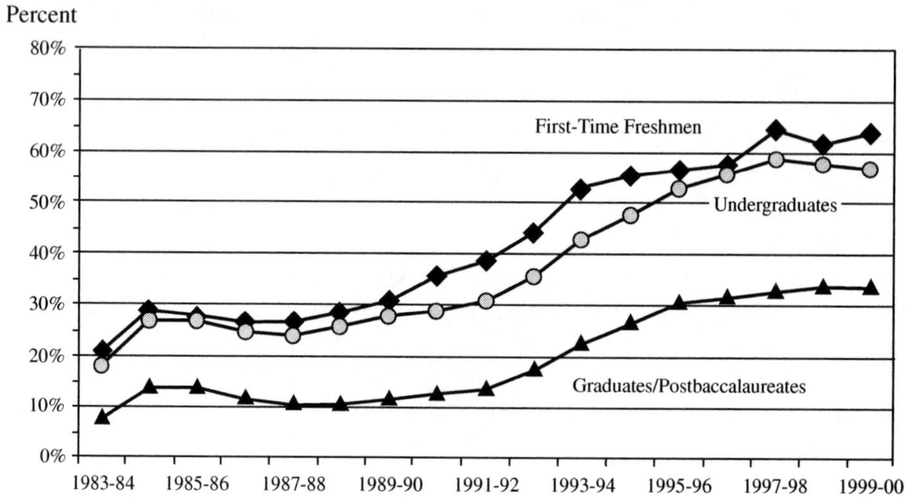

Percent

SOURCE: California State University Board of Trustees (http://www.calstate.edu).

Since 1961, it has granted approximately 2 million degrees (http://www.calstate.edu).

Students attending the CSU campuses reflect the state's rich diversity. By the late 1990s, no ethnic supermajority existed. The systemwide ethnic breakdown today stands as European Americans (47.2 percent), Mexican Americans (17.6 percent), Asian (15.3 percent), African American (7 percent), other Latino (6.2 percent), Filipino (5.1 percent), American Indian (1 percent), and Pacific Islander (0.5 percent). Women make up 58 percent of the student population. Across the board, CSU students tend to be older, with the average age of full-time undergrads at twenty-four years and at twenty-nine years for part-time undergrads. Seventy percent of the students are full-time; 30 percent are part-time.

To meet the needs of the state and of the current student population, Chancellor Charles Reed has translated CSU's mission into three objectives: (1) serve as an economic engine focusing on academic programs that produce a high-quality workforce, (2) provide access and opportunity to a high-quality academic program, and (3) take a larger responsibility for K-12 public school education. The state legislature has endorsed Reed's approach by authorizing funds to increase CSU enrollments by 12,000 students, while slashing funds for other state programs to offset deficits resulting from the recent energy scandal (Crane 2002).

To facilitate this mission, CSU institutions have set up extensive outreach and mentoring programs and have increased financial aid, recognizing that most of the system's students, particularly those in urban areas, work at least part-time and that many are disadvantaged. This increase in aid is especially evident with incoming freshmen (see Figure 1).

Because 60 percent of the state's teachers are products of CSU, Reed's administration works with various campuses to develop more effective programs to produce and train teachers. For example, one campus has established an institute to assist elementary and secondary educators communicate subject matter more effectively. CSU has established common admission standards for teaching programs, and Reed is lobbying for an extension of federal funding for teaching students in the fifth and final year of their program. Campuses have developed partnerships with K-12 school districts in which university faculty work with teachers to align math and English composition standards. Other faculty work with middle school teachers to enhance material presentation to reduce remedial needs. More than 80,000 workshops were offered to local teachers across the state in 2000-2001.

CSU also stresses the role of community relations and partnerships. For example, an agreement between the system and the state agriculture industry generates a 3:1 contribution of dollars, amounting to $5 million for applied research (Crane 2002). Between alumni and corporation donations, CSU raised $1.75 billion in external funding between 1999 and 2001, much of which will be spent on student programs. In the community, CSU and its campuses have established close working relations with numerous organizations such as California Association for Bilingual Education, National Association for the Advancement of Colored People, League of United Latin American Citizens, East Los Angeles Community Union, Greater African American Chamber of Commerce, and Mexican American Legal Defense Education Fund.

This mission is not without challenges. Because CSU is committed to an accessible and affordable education, problems of funding and unprepared students do arise (California Higher Education Policy Center 1995). The average cost of full-time tuition/fees is $1,876, so the system looks to other sources to generate funding to meet increasing student demands. Student proficiency is another challenge at CSU, where 7 percent of the recent freshman class failed to master basic math and English composition; 46 percent of incoming students require at least one remedial course in either math or English composition. The system has set a goal of reducing remedial education to 10 percent from the current base. To achieve this goal, CSU campuses offer course work and mentoring and dropped 2,200 students from enrollment last year for failure to master math and writing skills (Trounson 2002) (see Figure 2).

Nevertheless, Chancellor Reed maintains that "we're going to give students great opportunities to improve their lives and add value to everything they do. . . . That's what CSU does . . . it adds value to everything we do" (Crane 2002, 13). To gain a better view as to how two of the system's urban campuses work toward this mission, we now offer two vignettes.

California State University, Long Beach (CSULB)

CSULB first opened its doors as Los Angeles–Orange County State College in 1949. The first 169 students had choices from among twenty-five courses taught by thirteen faculty in support of five majors. The initial campus, consisting of two

FIGURE 2
CALIFORNIA STATE UNIVERSITY FRESHMEN SKILL LEVELS

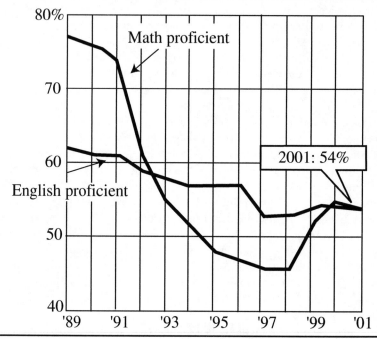

SOURCE: California State University Board of Trustees (http://www.calstate.edu).

apartment buildings in the central city, was soon eclipsed by the 320-acre site the city purchased two years later for the fledging university (http://www.csulb.edu). Legislators chose the city of Long Beach for the new university—later renamed Long Beach State College, then California State University, Long Beach—in response to rapid urban development. The city is now the second largest municipality in the Los Angeles metroplex.

Today, the university still serves the Los Angeles region and the northern part of Orange County. Having expanded from primarily teacher training—which is still a priority—to a large, comprehensive university with Colleges of Liberal Arts, Art, Education, Engineering, Business Administration, Natural Sciences and Mathematics, and Health and Human Services, the university now offers seventy-six undergraduate degrees, sixty-three minors, forty professional certificates, and sixty-four master's degrees. In accordance with the CSU mission, CSULB seeks to offer high-quality, accessible education, to promote equity, and to prepare students for lifelong learning and professional development in a culturally diverse society.

The 33,000-member student body ethnic breakdown is as follows: European American (42 percent), Mexican American (17.7 percent), African American (8 percent), other Latino (6.5 percent), Filipino (6.4 percent), Asian American (18 percent), American Indian (1 percent), and Pacific Islander (0.5 percent). Women maintain a 60 percent majority of the student population. The average age ranges from twenty-three years to twenty-eight years, depending on full-time or part-time classification. More than 80 percent of the students hold down at least one job, with many working in excess of thirty hours per week. Because of the city's proximity to low-income communities, many of the students are disadvantaged (http://www.csulb.edu). More than half of all students receive some type of aid; the same holds true for the minority cohort.

To increase accessibility for all students and to accommodate working students, the university schedules a majority of its classes in the afternoon and evening, so that students are able to earn degrees entirely through night courses, although that does extend time required to graduate. To assist students in selecting majors and career counseling, the university has established peer-advising centers, conducts career days, and subsidizes course reductions for departmental faculty advisors. Specialty advising is offered in the MESA Center for underrepresented groups majoring in engineering; Educational Equity Services advise educational opportunity programs; and Student Supportive Services Program assists students who are low income, first generation, or disabled. The university has established an acclaimed day care and child development center, servicing needs of students, faculty, and staff. In addition, the university, through federal and state government funding, offers a wide range of financial aid programs.

The university taps technology to expand accessibility as well. Professors are given incentives to bring online courses into the curriculum. These virtual offerings are found at undergraduate and graduate levels. For example, it is possible to earn master's degrees in occupational studies and social work at specified remote facilities through a combination of online course work and faculty visitations. Although it is not a realistic expectation that a majority of future courses will be offered online, the university does recognize that the adoption of such delivery strategies reduces the amount of time a student must be present on campus.

To give the university more visibility in the community, CSULB has established through internal funding a service learning center where students earn credit for doing jobs within their communities. Already, placements range from education to social intervention, from police work to policy work, from engineering to business. Not only do students gain experience but they also serve as university representatives interacting with community stakeholders to reassure all that the university is an organization of learners connected to their surroundings.

Through a multimillion-dollar external grant from the Knight Foundation in 1997, CSULB initiated a program to promote seamless education between the university and local schools. As part of the program, campus faculty have worked with secondary and middle school teachers on subject matter presentation. The goal is to bridge the gap between K-12 teaching and university standards. For the first time, the university has worked in an organized way to promote dialogue and identify best practices with local schools. From this effort, new standards and teaching practices have been adopted, and recent student admissions from the participating schools appear to have stronger educational backgrounds (http://www.csulb.edu).

Proficiency and persistence in the course work remain two real challenges for this urban university. Although it is encouraging that SAT scores have consistently increased during the past five years, still some 40 percent of students require some leveling work in math and reading/English composition. To address this deficiency, the university provides remedial courses to be taken during the freshman year and tutorial learning through the Learning Assistance Center and special mentoring programs for disadvantaged students. The Student Orientation, Advising, and Registration and the Learning Alliance are programs that advise and, through different mechanisms, mentor incoming freshmen. Both of these programs have shown success; for example, the Learning Alliance, which clusters and tracks students in classes to form learning communities, has a graduation rate of 70 percent compared to the university-wide rate of 30 percent. Unfortunately, all students do not benefit from this exposure, owing to limited program size or personal commitments or preferences.

Students who fall below a 2.0 GPA are placed on probation. Probation averages 5 percent across the university, with 14 percent for new regular admits and 20 percent for new special admits. First-year freshmen probationary rates can be as high as 16 percent but generally drop to 2.3 percent by the senior year. Following the lead of CSU, those who fail to master math and English skills after probation are dropped from university enrollment, although many of these students voluntarily withdraw. To help probationary students, the university has established the Strategies for Academic Success Program, which links students to appropriate campus resources. For participating students, the probationary program can be extended beyond one semester to allow time to acquire the necessary skills to mainstream.

CSULB exhibits the philosophy of an urban university, and it appears to be working. Student surveys indicate satisfaction with services; more than 88 percent of those graduating pass the writing proficiency test by their senior year; graduation rates are eking up (4,158 degrees were awarded in 1999-2000); and the community is perceived as part of the learning environment (http://www.csulb.edu).

California State University, Los Angeles (Cal State LA)

Cal State LA is located in one of the most characteristic areas for an urban university in the CSU system. Founded in 1947, this university sits on 200 acres of the old Rancho Rosa Castilla, originally inhabited by Franciscan missionaries in 1776. Only five miles from downtown Los Angeles, Cal State LA serves students across the city, especially from the Latino areas of East Los Angeles and the multiethnic areas of South Central Los Angeles. Although the institution began by sharing facilities with a nearby community college, today this university has six colleges, fifty academic departments, and 21,000 students, a quarter of whom are pursuing master's programs, particularly in applied fields such as public administration, teaching, and engineering. In line with the CSU system and CSULB, Cal State LA's mission statement emphasizes high-quality education, preparation for professional life and advanced study, respect for cultural diversity, and community partnerships (http://www.calstatela.edu).

The university student population is more ethnically diverse than that of some campuses in the system. Latinos make up 53.1 percent of the population, followed by Asian/Pacific Islanders at 21.6 percent, White/non-Latino at 16.4 percent, African American at 8.4 percent, and American Indian at 0.5 percent. Women make up slightly more than 60 percent of the student body. Seventy percent of undergraduates and 20 percent of graduate students are full-time.

Promoting accessibility, Cal State LA operates year round on a quarter system, scheduling classes daily from 8 A.M. to 10 P.M. and on Saturday mornings. The majority of classes are offered Monday through Thursday in late afternoons and evenings. Distance learning has been initiated in applied fields such as nursing and fire science and in general education courses.

Still, proficiency and persistence are challenges. Close to 70 percent of admitted freshmen need some remedial work in math and/or English composition. Many of these students come from the city's lowest-income areas, have few financial resources, and exhibit uneven preparedness. To increase academic performance, the university received a Title III Department of Education award specifically to increase retention. With these funds, Cal State LA created separate orientation courses for freshmen and transfer students. In addition, it created advising centers within each college that are open daily and staffed by the respective college's faculty through course-release time. Program administrators established a data system to track results for participating students. Math and English courses were mandated for the freshmen year.

This program has increased continuation rates; however, once federal dollars ran out, colleges were hesitant to adopt the costs of the centers, and the university did not name a director; hence, accountability and, with it, the program has collapsed. Advising is still carried out, but not with the coherence and tracking as before. In a student survey, respondents noted their frustration concerning advising (http://www.calstatela.edu).

To reach out into the community, the university's Pat Brown Center does research and outreach in a number of social areas such as gang prevention, economic development, nonprofit workshops, and political incorporation of underrepresented groups. The university has also used its connection with local schools to promote community linkages. For instance, the university has established on its campus a charter high school. Specializing in performing arts, this school has become popular, and admission is sought by artistic students from the surrounding area. Just as important, it has become a symbol of community pride and a program around which the university and community can find common ground for interaction. To increase the caliber of its freshmen, Cal State LA also works with high schools on early entrance and accelerated programs for local students. Using Department of Education Title V funding, Cal State LA cooperated with surrounding community colleges, which typically serve as feeder institutions to the university, to establish advising centers on their respective campuses to counsel students concerning course preparation prior to coming to Cal State LA.

Like CSULB, this campus has developed a philosophy of serving the surrounding communities and promoting student access to a quality education. The students at Cal State LA find the career center, financial aid, learning assistance, and tutoring to be strong elements of the university's overall program. Productivity can be seen in the matriculation rate. In school year 2000-2001, Cal State LA granted 2,490 undergraduate degrees and 860 master's degrees. Still, the attrition rate for freshmen is troubling and appears predominantly due to underfunding in student supportive services and advising (http://www.calstatela.edu).

Conclusion

This article does not provide a definitive set of generalizations concerning urban universities; rather, the purpose here is to draw our attention to the important role of urban universities in higher education. To that end, I have briefly laid out the contextual forces—social, economic, technological, demographic, and political—that drove the rise of public education and ultimately, urban universities. Given that these same forces are still strong influences in shaping society, one could hypothesize that the demand for urban university services will only increase.

More important, this research has underscored the philosophy that distinguishes urban universities from their traditional counterparts. Emphasizing access and outreach, these urban educational institutions have provided opportunities to nontraditional students and forged closer linkages with surrounding communities. This same philosophy generates a set of challenges such as how to meet the educational needs of the most diverse student body in the history of U.S. higher education and how to develop constructive partnerships with the community. To focus this examination, I have looked at the CSU system and two of its urban campuses that have mounted special programs to serve urban students. Some of these programs have been successful; some have not. Even though CSULB and Cal State LA were not offered as ideal types, their experiences are suggestive and allow for a sharper lens to determine which programs and policies are useful starting points to analyze future urban universities.

Understanding the character and actions of such universities is not a luxury but a necessity if one is to grasp the elements of higher education delivery in America today. A critical cultural and political change has occurred in society centering on who is entitled to a postsecondary education and who is not (Losco and Fife 2000). No longer, as was so in the past, is the postsecondary experience perceived as the personal domain for the privileged. In addition, society views the university process differently today. Most see education as one of many priorities rather than some exalted experience that takes precedence over all else. For example, taking five or six years to finish a B.A. degree no longer carries the stigma of lack of intellect or motivation but rather connotes that the person may have had other important responsibilities and interests. Urban universities have stepped forward to meet these new perceptions and expectations by building learning environments to accommodate the new university student constituency. Whether, and to what degree, they accomplish this task is grist for the mill of future research. Yet it is certain that future research on the effectiveness of U.S. higher education will demand a thorough analysis including urban universities.

References

Abu-lughod, Janet L. 1991. *Changing cities*. New York: HarperCollins.

The American freshman. 2000. *Advocate* 19 (4): 3.

Aronowitz, Stanley. 2000. *The knowledge factory: Dismantling the corporate university and creating true higher learning*. Boston: Beacon.

Astin, Alexander W. 2000. The college student: Three decades of change. In *Higher education in transition: The challenges of the new millenium*, edited by Joseph Losco and Brian L. Fife, 7-27. Westport, CT: Bergin & Garvey.

Berube, Maurice. 1978. *The urban university in America*. Westport, CT: Greenwood.

California Higher Education Policy Center. 1995. *Preserving the higher education legacy: A conversation with California leaders*. Report prepared by John Immerwahr and Jill Boese. Berkeley, CA: California Higher Education Policy Center.

Castells, Manuel. 1989. *The information city: Information technology, economic restructuring, and the urban-regional process*. Oxford, UK: Basil Blackwell.

Crane, Barbara. 2002. California state university system fuels state's economic engine. *Long Beach Business Journal*, 29 January, 1, 13.

Douglas, John A. 2000. *The California idea and American higher education: 1850 to the 1960 master plan*. Stanford, CA: Stanford University Press.

Drucker, Peter. 1993. *The post-capitalist society*. New York: Harper Business.

Dye, Thomas. 2002. *Understanding public policy*. 12th ed. New York: Prentice-Hall.

Elliot, Peggy E. 1994. *The urban campus: Educating the new majority for the new century*. Phoenix, AZ: Oryx.

Ferguson, Rebecca. 2000. *The history answer book*. Canton, MI: Visible Ink.

Giles, Frederic T. 1972. *Changing teacher education in a large urban university*. Washington, DC: American Association of Colleges for Teacher Education.

Gottdiener, Mark. 1994. *The new urban sociology*. New York: McGraw Hill.

Grobman, Arnold B. 1988. *Urban state universities: An unfinished agenda*. New York: Praeger.

Klotsche, J. Martin. 1966. *The urban university and the future of our cities*. New York: Harper & Row.

Kogan, Maurice. 1984. Problems of the urban university: Great Britain and U.S.A. In *The functions and problems of the urban university: A comparative perspective*, edited by Henry Wasser, 46-53. New York: City University of New York.

Losco, Joseph, and Brian L. Fife, eds. 2000. *Higher education in transition: The challenges of the new millennium*. Westport, CT: Bergin & Garvey.

Miller, Richard I. 1990. *Major American higher education issues and challenges in the 1990s*. London: Jessica-Kingsley.

Newman, Frank. 1985. *Higher education and the American resurgence*. Princeton, NJ: Carnegie Foundation for the Advancement of Education.

Reich, Robert B. 1991. *The work of nations: Preparing ourselves for 21st century capitalism*. New York: Knopf.

Trounson, Rebecca. 2002. Cal State ouster rate rises slightly. *Los Angeles Times*, 31 January, B1, B5.

Weinstock, Ruth. 1961. *Space and dollars: An urban university expands*. New York: City of New York Educational Facilities.

Zukin, Sharon. 1995. *The Culture of Cities*. Cambridge, MA: Blackwell.

Corporatization of the University: Seeking Conceptual Clarity

By
HENRY STECK

The notion of corporatization is the most ominous buzz-word in contemporary academic circles. A significant literature on the subject deals with the transformation of the American university. There has been substantial change—perhaps fundamental—in the direction of a university that displays the culture, practices, policies, and workforce strategies more appropriate to corporations. The article seeks to show what corporatization is and is not and to suggest some historical and contextual factors producing the change. The article seeks to deconstruct the term "corporatization" or "entepreneurial" to demonstrate the wide variety of meanings that the term covers. To the extent that a corporatized university is no university or corporate values are not academic values, the article concludes, it is the burden for faculty to address the issue of protecting traditional academic values.

The notion of the "corporatized" or "corporate" or "entrepreneurial" university is the most fashionable and ominous buzzword in contemporary academic circles. For those academics who stop to think about the institution in which they toil, corporatization is the specter haunting their lives, changing the reality, if not the appearance, of the university as an institution. From the Left, Stanley Aronowitz (2000), in *The Knowledge Factory*, argued that "by the mid-1990s, the corporate university had become the standard for nearly all private and public schools" (p. 83). For Lawrence Soley (1995), in *Leasing the Ivory Tower*, corporations, the military, and right-wing foundations had seized control of institutions of higher learning (see also Daniels 2000). So thoughtful and sober an observer as Robert Rosenzweig (2001) warned eloquently of the dangers inherent in the close relationship that has emerged between

Henry Steck is a political scientist at the State University of New York, College at Cortland. He is a Distinguished Service Professor and a professor of political science. He is the director of State University of New York Cortland's Project on Eastern and Central Europe. His current work deals with higher education.

DOI: 10.1177/0002716202238567

industry and the university. Whether as recipients of industry money for research or other purposes or as entrepreneurial institutions "selling their wares to a market outside their own student bodies" (Rosenzweig 2001, 203), universities have, such critics argue, gone down a path that threatens their deepest values and obligations. And the threat comes, as others warn, from more than big-time research activities or big-time athletics, although both are characterized by the same nonacademic elements of big money, big commercial pressure, and big-time celebrity super-stars.[1] It comes from a pervasive change in the university itself. The late Bill Readings (1996), in *The University in Ruins*, made the point that the university is not "like" a business corporation; it is a "corporation" (p. 22). The once slow to change, conservative institution—the university dating back to the thirteenth century—has undergone a "revolution" that has changed it from a community of scholars and students to an entrepreneurial university (Etkowitz, Webster, and Healey 1998, 1).

This is an issue that does not neatly divide Left from Right or even faculty from all administrators. Aronowitz wrote from the Left, but his ideas for curriculum reform are rooted in the traditional canon and could come from a National Association of Scholars playbook. Meanwhile, sensitive and thoughtful administrators who are on the front lines of change in a way most professors are not are equally troubled. Taking note of the pressures that play on the contemporary university, one humanist turned dean observed gloomily that "the university cannot *not* be a business" (Lewis 1998, 4). Within the American Council on Education (2002), the preeminent higher education administration organization, there is a sense that the key change has been in a direction it calls entrepreneurial and I call corporatization.

> In striking new ways, American colleges and universities no longer look or act much as they did 30, or even 20, years ago. Although they still teach students, confer degrees at all levels and in a range of disciplines, generate new knowledge, and serve their communities and states, today many colleges and universities are engaged in new and different activities, and they are developing new organizational structures in response to opportunities and challenges. Many, but not all, of these new ways of operating have an entrepreneurial focus; some new activities are responses to emerging social issues. In many instances, the academic programs offered have changed, as have their delivery mechanisms and pedagogies, and new and modified institutional structures have emerged. In sum, the enterprise of higher education is changing. (Ikenberry 2001)

Using the language of critics on the Left, the former president of the American Council on Education, Stanley Ikenberry (2001), warned in his farewell address to that very establishment body that higher education risks becoming a mere commodity, a change, he warned, that would undermine traditional academic values. In particular, he pointed to the impact of athletics, to conflicts of interest arising from corporate sponsorship of research, and to the commercial use of intellectual property. True, those who doubt that the university can survive this latest onslaught, this gale of destruction, may be too pessimistic, too radical, or even too conservative (in the best sense), but they are right to be gloomy.

But what exactly are they gloomy about? In this article, I want to disentangle the term "corporatization" and introduce a measure of definitional clarity to the discussion. As with any term that captures the Zeitgeist, "corporatization" is often used in a such an indiscriminate and shifting manner that it seems to say every-thing—or else very little. Examples and horror stories are piled on each other, and a variety of concerns tumble out on one another. Careful case studies[2] only fuel hot rhetoric and ardent indignation. It is time, then, to sort out the variety of meanings that are encompassed by the term "corporatization" to see what exactly is there.

And on this subject, neutrality cannot be avoided. On the basis of the available literature and the lived experience of a workaday academic, I fully believe there is a *there* there. My premise then is that the values of the market and the culture and organizational style of corporate life are changing the university. If I had to look for a metaphor, I guess I would turn to the classic film, *Invasion of the Body Snatchers*, a story of alien creatures who steal the soul and personality of individuals while retaining the identical and pleasant and amiable exterior. Where once college pres-idents meant what they said when they spoke of excellence or providing opportu-nity, today such sentiments come across as advertising slogans, carefully crafted with the latest market research findings in mind. Rosenzweig (2001) had it exactly right when he said, "The values of the market are not the values of the university" (p. 210), and the issue facing the academy is that the values of the market are steadily encroaching on and transforming the values of the university.

Looking at Context

Without delving too deeply into the causes for these changes, a few brief back-ground words might be appropriate. Quite aside from the long-term linkage of higher education to the business sector (discussed below in the What Is Not New section), higher education has been propelled along the path of corporatization by a series of developments. Clearly, the number and growing size of higher education institutions in the post-1945 era—including vast new state systems such as the State University of New York—confronted universities and colleges across the country with the task of dealing with vast numbers of students and complex new functions that changing times had thrust upon them. The changing environment called for managers trained in financial and bureaucratic management, and the labor market responded with a new breed of managers. Second, beginning in the mid-1970s, the long-running fiscal crisis of the state imposed harsh new realities on public and private universities and colleges alike. Such changes were concurrent with, as Slaughter and Leslie (1997) argued, the emergence of and intensified com-petition with the consequence that the university sector was mobilized into the rig-ors of global competition (see also Barrow 1996). Faced with recurrent budget cri-ses, distinct corporate language began to creep into the language of senior officials. "Downsizing," "restructuring," "realignment," "reengineering," and the like began to take precedence over concerns about the content and quality of education. Money troubles did not go away. George Keller (1983), in an influential work, warned that "a specter is haunting higher education: the specter of decline and bankruptcy," and his call for "strategic planning" heralded what he called the "management revolution in higher education" (p. 3). When the fiscal pressures did not let up, higher education managers were driven to cope with a Hobbesian environment by using the tools and techniques of corporate management, including increased pressure to replace public support with revenues raised by increasing student costs or by competing more aggressively in the market. When this tendency was accompanied by the evident distaste of conservative trustees—as in the case of the State University of New York—for public sector obligations, institutions had little choice but to undertake a host of "management" solutions taken from the corporate toolkit (Barrow 1993, 1996). *Rethinking SUNY* (State University of New York 1995), the neoliberal strategic plan for the State University of New York, was a major model of this approach to restructuring. And not to overlook the lure of the dollar, with higher education approaching something like $250 billion a year, the university had become too important to leave to academicians of the old school.

Finally, the radical impact of new information technologies has contributed significantly to and hastened the sense that the university is no longer what it used to be—or can no longer be what it once was. A number of analysts have argued persuasively that information technologies have undermined the role of faculty, increased the power of administrators, and failed to serve students well (Noble 2001). While most of us tend to think of the technological revolution as a 1990s development, the new technologies were making themselves felt by the late 1970s and early 1980s, and they brought with them increased pressures to and opportunities for cooperation with the corporate sector. Writing in 1983, Keller (1983) noted as clearly as anyone since the Faustian bargain that was struck,

> To enable students and faculty to have access to the latest electronic instruments and computer hardware in a time of growing financial hardships, colleges and universities have . . . (entered into) . . . a series of contracts with corporations, which seem increasingly ready to provide electronic equipment and research dollars in return for first options on the use of the research findings. (P. 21)

The presence of the new technologies and their potential has led observers inexorably to two conclusions. One is that the new technology will revolutionize—if it has not already done so—the university as nothing has since Gutenberg's invention of printing (Noam 1995), and the other is that only a corporate style strategy can realize the full potential and the opportunities of the new information technology. For those who argue that academia must adapt to new technologies or perish, the language of the corporate sector comes easily. Even some writers who appear sympathetic to traditional academic values endorse what seems to be the new orthodoxy, namely, that higher education is an industry that is being fundamentally transformed by the advent of information technologies. Arthur Levine (2000), president of Columbia Teachers College, disassociated the university from the idea of place when he noted that academia is not in the "campus business but the education business." William Wulf (1995) wrote that universities are in the "information business" and that technology is changing the university "industry" (p. 46). He argued that the exponential "improvement" in information technology will continue to revolutionize the university. Such developments as "Fathom on-line learn-ing" underscore the linkage of technology and entrepreneurial hustle on the part of universities. The time is not far off, it seems, when Wall Street will be talking about Educational Maintenance Organizations or Educational Service Providers.

There are those, of course, who have no problem with these trends, and they greet what *Business Week* (The new U 1997) called "the new reality" with positive if not gleeful enthusiasm. In 1997, the then president of the University of Florida had no second thoughts when he exclaimed, "We have taken the great leap forward and said: 'Let's pretend we're a corporation' " (p. 96). But for many universities, it is not "let's pretend" any more as they aggressively pursue a variety of corporate policies and strategies in areas including program design, licensing and franchising, dis-tance learning, and technology transfer. Jeanne C. Meister (2001) (president of Corporate University Xchange and advocate for corporate universities) advised universities to "think of themselves as business entities offering specific market-able services" (P. B10). For *Business Week* (The new U 1997), it is a deal that is signed, sealed, and delivered: "Higher education is changing profoundly, retreat-ing from the ideals of liberal arts and the leading-edge research it always has cher-ished. Instead, it is behaving more like the $250 billion business it has become." As one Stanford University official bluntly said about the idea that research is done for the sake of research and pure inquiry, "this is outdated. Research has to be useful, even if many years down the line, to be worthwhile" (Rosenzweig 2001, 210)

But those uneasy at this brave new world of higher education may be in the majority. They have watched with dismay as the humanities are downgraded; as presidents hustle their campuses and pressure their faculty to increase external funding; as campus offices of technology licensing sprout on campuses; as research is seen as a source of revenue, not knowledge; and as universities develop online, for-profit services. The idea that it is Campus, Inc. (White 2000) has become a per-vasive and critical way of looking at the university. Not since the campus turmoil of the 1960s have academics been forced to confront so directly so much uneasiness and uncertainty about the fundamental nature and role of the university.

Is this just another case of academics doing a chorus about a professor's lot not being a happy one? I do not think so. Certainly, professors have a lot to complain about. Since the 1960s, if not earlier, universities have been under fire for one thing or another. Admittedly, there is no end to large troublesome issues facing adminis-trators and faculties alike. A simple list will remind readers how stressed and con-flicted the university is: big-time athletics, college costs and student financial aid, shrinking budgets, an oversupply of Ph.D.s, new technologies, diversity and gen-der issues, student literacy (or lack thereof), student drinking, unionizing adjuncts, uncertain endowments, the so-called PC culture wars—the list seems endless. But many of these are, to some extent, manageable in one way or another. The conten-tion that the corporatization school of authors would make is that corporatization threatens the very institutional character and values of the university in fundamen-tal ways that other problems do not. And that is an argument that needs to be taken very, very seriously.

What Corporatization Is Not and What It Is

Let us be clear. The trend we call corporatization describes not one or another single element of the contemporary university, but a range of many features that link together in a systematic fashion. It embraces but goes beyond the observation that universities are becoming more bureaucratic in nature. It embraces but goes beyond the fact that universities are responsive to the priorities of corporate decision makers from corporations that are donors or contractors and that seek to influence overall university priorities. It goes beyond the unpleasant realities imposed on public colleges and universities by tightening state budgets and by the market strategies that university presidents are forced to employ to meet their payrolls.[3] It also goes beyond the important dynamic that many research universities are partnering with, raising money from, selling and leasing products to, and sharing important decision making with corporations. It goes beyond the notion that universities may be entangled in activities—such as big-time athletics—that are corrupting and not part of their core function and mission. It also goes beyond the notion that the modern university—Clark Kerr's multiversity—is so multifunctional and complex, so large and costly, that it must perforce adopt modern management methods to achieve efficiencies and hold costs down to students and their families. The corporatized university as a whole combines these and other elements into a comprehensive whole. But before we can say what corporatization is, let us try to see what it is not.

What it is not

To the extent that corporatization involves the entanglement of the business sector and the university, it is not a new development. It is misleading to assume the corporate university has emerged only in the past decade, and it is equally misleading to assume that there was a distant time when the university was pure, was in the world but not of it. It is tempting to look back to some golden age—to Newman's "idea of the university," to nineteenth-century Oxbridge, to the liberal education found in our best small colleges, or even to the Morrill Act—and to assume that these various moments have only recently been a paradise that is lost. Such models drawn from the history of the university can help define the deepest values of the university, but it is unlikely that they are a blueprint for reconstructing the university. On the plus side, they are the values that help define our critical awareness, our template, of what a university should be. They are, in Mannheim's terms, our utopia, our knife for critical incisions in the world around us. Undoubtedly, there are institutions that still embody these values to a significant degree. The so-called elite liberal arts colleges, for example, might be still regarded as "communities of learned discourse," devoted purely to teaching, learning, and scholarship (Graubard 1999, xi). But these are the exceptions. On the minus side, such models can become mere stereotypes or unexamined subtexts that mislead us about the real world.

The fact is, there is no golden age within historical reach. The modern American university has always been powerfully influenced by social forces. Beginning in the nineteenth and early twentieth centuries, there were business interests that influenced university governance, if in no other way than the presence of corporate managers as trustees and as substantial donors of buildings or chairs or programs named after themselves and their families. The precursor of the corporatized university is to be found early in the twentieth century.[4] As early as 1906, Veblen ([1906] 1957) pinpointed the role of corporate thinking in guiding America's universities:

> The intrusion of business principles in the universities goes to weaken and retard the pursuit of learning, and therefore to defeat the ends for which a university is maintained. This result follows . . . from the substitution of impersonal, mechanical relations, standards and tests, in the place of personal conference, guidance and association between teachers and students; as also from the imposition of a mechanically standardized routine upon the members of the staff. (P. 165)

Veblen's book, subtitled *A Memorandum on the Conduct of Universities by Business Men*, was written at a time when business interests exercised a powerful and controlling influence in higher education. Universities were obliged to meet the social and ideological needs as the captains of industry defined them (Barrow 1990).

No doubt, things have changed since then. The professorate is larger, more professional, more attuned to national disciplines rather than local campuses, and certainly more assertive than it was when Veblen ([1906] 1957) wrote and John Dewey struggled to form first American Association of University Professors and then American Federation of Teachers. The university is a more pluralized institution, and certainly professors have more clout and visibility than at the turn of the twentieth century. But despite the changes, there has never been a time in the modern era when the university has been free of the influence of capital or increasingly of the political domain. In the early 1980s, long before our current awareness of corporatizing trends, Barbara Ann Scott (1983) described the national university community as a complex network of overlapping administrative elites and organizations tied to major national corporate policy institutions. Rereading her work drives home the realization that the corporatizing world of academic managers—characterized as it is by networks of people, specialized associations, newsletters, position papers, and the like—is not a creature of the 1990s. Information technology may have made communications swifter and networks efficient. But organizations like the American Council on Education are long-standing trade associations of higher education administrators that promote and coordinate policy initiatives, lobbying of the government, and managerial models. Where they are probably different is that today, they more aggressively and coherently embrace the ideology of the new university, namely, that to make its way in a competitive market, the modern university must behave like a modern corporation. In short, the corporatizing trends have their precursors in the past.

There is another way in which current trends are not new, namely, the strong propensity—ideological, philosophical, cultural, pragmatic, call it what you will—of the American university to serve society in practical ways. At least since the mid-nineteenth century, if not before, the American university has demonstrated a strong utilitarian commitment: practical people doing practical things, whether the practicalities of the earlier colleges of agriculture and mechanical arts or the advanced research of a Massachusetts Institute of Technology or Cornell. Small or elite liberal arts colleges, perhaps, could and may still shun the practical, but serving society is very pronounced indeed. This is particularly true of public institutions that were created to meet concrete social needs. The Morrill Act defined the public university not only in democratic terms but in utilitarian terms, and that impulse has remained strong ever since (Nevins 1962).

Meeting societal needs took on direct and deadly seriousness during and after World War II, when the university was enlisted into the war effort. This was a period, as Rosenzweig (2001) put it, of "the most sweeping changes ever in American higher education" (p. 314). Americans are most likely to think of the postwar era in terms of the expansion of higher education—the GI Bill, new state institutions multiplying at a rapid rate, opportunities available to whole new segments of society. In the 1960s, of course, the campus was seen as the turmoil-ridden site of the counterculture, the civil rights movement, and the antiwar movement. But at the same time, and less visible to the public, the university became the primary locus for research and development, and the elite research university emerged almost as a new kind of institution and one that served as a model for less distinguished institutions. Sleepy little colleges and second-tier universities began to emulate, although on a lesser scale, the behavior of the research universities. Today, it is undoubtedly a rare president, no matter what the size or status of her or his college, who is not deeply concerned to pull in external funding from the federal government and foundations. The cause of this transformation, of course, was the decision by the federal government to center research activities in universities rather than in either industry or in free-standing research institutes.[5] In time, industry too turned to universities as the incubator of new products and as a willing partner in research, patent licensing, and marketing. As a sign of the change, the term "research" came to replace "scholarship," and star academics were now seen as researchers rather than scholars. The norms of academia were changing, not always necessarily for the worse (Jencks and Riesman 1969). As Hanna Holborn Gray (1997), former president of the University of Chicago, put it,

> The system . . . in which the faculty depend on grants for much of their research and which requires investment on a scale that only the federal government can manage, holds many dangers. . . . [The] funding system has spurred the vigorous progress in scientific knowledge. . . . At the same time (this change) continues to pose a critical challenge to the requisite autonomies of academia. (Pp. 149-150)

Business and political interests tapped into this utilitarian strain, as did the Left, with its 1960s demand for relevance and its 1990s concern for addressing issues of gender, race, and class. If we talk today about the pharmaceutical university or the information technology–university complex as if it were something new and sudden, we need only recall, as noted above, the role of the university in terms of the 1940-1945 war effort, the role of the university in terms of research and development for the military throughout the cold war, and the role of the university as a research arm of corporate and state interests, for example, agriculture (Chomsky et al. 1997). Senior faculty today will recall from their youth that the attack on the university's complicity in the Vietnam War was far more sharp, vocal, and violent than anything we hear today. The point is this: the linkage between business interests and the university as a social institution—particularly leading research universities and professional schools—is rooted deep in the modern history of the American university. There is no golden age, at least not one that provides anything more than an imagined utopia in an imagined time.[6]

What is new?

While contemporary developments reflect long-established trends, there is something unprecedented about the current period, perhaps to the point where it constitutes, as some have termed it, "a process of fundamental transformation" (Bronfenbrenner and Juravich 2001). Let us start with a rough definition and then proceed to examine the details.

For my purpose, the corporatized university is defined as an institution that is characterized by processes, decisional criteria, expectations, organizational culture, and operating practices that are taken from, and have their origins in, the modern business corporation. It is characterized by the entry of the university into marketplace relationships and by the use of market strategies in university decision making. Institutions will vary, of course, one from the other in the extent that they display corporatizing elements. It is important to emphasize, as I hope I do throughout, that the argument is not that universities have abandoned their primary functions of teaching, scholarship, and service. The academic culture is still present. There are strong continuities: the pursuit of teaching and learning, intellectual risk taking, critical discourse and sharp debate, commitment to liberal learning, and a defense of an institution whose central features date from the early middle ages. But the corporate culture has become commonplace if not yet pervasive, and corporate-style priorities, decisions, activities, and structures are very much in evidence. And it might be noted parenthetically that in many institutions, there is also an intrusion of political forces seeking to direct academic policy (Bowen 2001; Ryder 2001).

In what follows, I will set forth the variety of meanings encompassed by the notion of corporatization. I feel obliged, first, to provide a fair warning to the reader. What follows draws both on the very large literature on the subject and also on years of observations as an academic worker. It draws on the analyses of academic life to be found in the formal and the polemical literature and also on the pages of the *Chronicle of Higher Education* over the years. That said, my contention is that corporatization encompasses the following meanings.

First. The process of corporatization is more extensive than prior connections to the business community, in terms of both the depth and the scope of the penetration of the university by the corporate economy, culture, and practices. The change has roots in the past, but it represents a quantum leap forward.

Second. What is called "corporatization" is regarded by many academic administrators (who, of course, do not use this term) as a perfectly legitimate, necessary, desirable, and positive good thing. One would be hard-pressed to detect any strong sense of checks and balances by those responsible for opening the door to the corporate way of life. The corporate sector is seen as a credible partner, as an appropriate source of revenue, as a proper market to sell university goods, and as good people that one can do business with. Activities that might be seen by some as peripheral to the work of a university (licensing of commercial products such as baseball hats, logos, T-shirts; athletics; leasing of space) or even abhorrent (advertising) loom large on the fiscal side of things. It is no longer unusual to find administrators reflecting entrepreneurial zeal, eagerly seeking out venture capital, or making deals for start-up firms for technology transfer. Nor is it unusual to find faculty researchers moving, so to speak, from the liberal arts to the commercial arts or from looking on themselves less as disinterested scientists than as entrepreneurs with skills and products to sell. Nor is it any wonder that so much of the critique of the modern university flows from the pens of humanists, social scientists, and lit-crit types for whose work there are no patents, no technology transfer, no strategic plans, and but for a few superstars, no super incomes, and who constitute the pockets of resistance to the changes in the university.[7]

Third. Universities are administered by managerial and fiscal practices drawn from the corporate sector. University administrators look to the corporate sector for operational guidelines. These include some of the following:

1. The belief that market mechanisms are appropriate for the university and that the behavior of the market has a legitimate place in university affairs.
2. Acceptance of the culture and practices of corporate practices: mission statements and hierarchical organizational patterns, benchmarking, productivity measures and emphasis on institutional goals to be achieved, mission statements and strategic planning, best practices, and the like (Birnbaum 2000).
3. Conceptualization of departments or other units as "revenue centers" and the adoption of responsibility-centered management, a practice that obliges individual departments or colleges to be fiscally self-sufficient (Dubeck 1997).
4. Commercialization of the campus and campus culture.
5. The importation of managerial practices (e.g., total quality management) into the university environment.
6. Development of ancillary revenue activities, for example, athletics, conferences, facility rental, and so forth.
7. A customer service orientation.

8. The development of new entrepreneurial activities and the creation of new organizational structures and relationships.

Fourth. There is a change in the culture of the university. Today, many top university administrators look at their institutions as businesses retailing and wholesaling a product, whether research, information, or training. Indeed, with reference to technology transfer under the 1980 Bayh-Dole Act (more formally, the University and Small Business Patent Procedures Act), the argument has been made that "a profound alteration of culture in institutions of higher learning . . . was deliberately engineered by transnational corporations in a successful effort to get control of the federal investment in university research" (Minsky 2000, 95-105; Council on Governmental Relations 1999). Institutional claims to ownership of intellectual property used in distance learning or information technology–based learning modules are examples of the appropriation of intellectual labor for profit. What is involved is a shift of the university culture to a culture colored by values appropriate to the modern business corporation. Some of the elements include the following:

1. As noted above, a redefinition of the university as a corporate enterprise.
2. The definition of the student as a customer, a definition that if the notion that the customer is always right is obeyed, reverses the relationship between student learner, teacher, and curriculum. As this notion gains currency—whether by decisions on campus or by the impact of information technology in the larger culture—the university will come to be regarded (as Levine, 2000, suggested it already is) by students as simply a service provider, a convenience store for credentialing or self-enrichment. There will be more surveys to determine student satisfaction, and woe to the institution that scores low in the annual college ratings produced by weekly magazines. Service, quality, affordability, product, and customer satisfaction will become benchmarks of what *Business Week* (The new U 1997) calls the "New U."
3. The imposition of standards of efficiency, cost-effectiveness, and client appeal in decisions related to academic programs; for example, departments of philosophy or poetry with very few students will be eliminated or merged into a new humanities division to free up funds to pursue, say, studies in tourism or sports management.
4. Quality control—the intensified reliance on quantitative mechanisms of evaluation and measurement, for example, the current insistence on assessment measures to determine the value added to the product.
5. The broader belief, consistent with neoliberal thinking, that a college degree represents a private good not a public good and that it therefore rests on the student and her or his family to make the private investment. When the student is seen as customer, a host of corollary ideas follow: measures of customer satisfaction, marketing the product, adding product lines (e.g., food courts, athletic programs) that attract customers, engaging in forms of promotion (logos that reflect advertising design rather than traditional Latinate seals), advertising slogans ("students come first," "excellence," etc.) (Welcome to college 1999).
6. There is also the commodification of the university and the sale of its name. One recent writer urged universities to "brand the institution" (Meister 2001). Campus activities are now sponsored (e.g., cheerleaders at Syracuse University) in a way that extends beyond the naming of buildings or schools after wealthy donors.

7. Some have argued that colleges are not in the campus business but in the education business, thus disconnecting education from a sense of place. Compared to many universities elsewhere, one unique feature of American colleges and universities has been the grounding of academic life in a place, a campus, thus giving rise to a sense of community, of an enclosed space that is very special and that brings together scholars and students. Even the great urban universities have their place: the cafeteria, the lounges, and so forth. In the corporatized university, the once enclosed campus space becomes transformed into a commercial space and, indeed, into that most distinctive and contemporary of American commercial space, the mall. Whether Starbucks (for the faculty) or McDonalds or Taco Bell (for the students), through marketing agreements, sponsorship, sales, signs, and licensing deals, or whether a virtual electronic space, characterized by asynchronous contacts between students and teacher, the campus place is less a cloistered escape from the world outside—less a gathering place of a community of scholars and students. One need hardly mention here the overall impact of big-time college athletics. While we like to think that this is a phenomenon unique to division I schools, it is clearly making itself felt even at elite liberal arts colleges (Shulman and Bowen 2000; on athletics see also Menand 2001b; Sperber 2000; Hacker 2001; Sack 2001).

Fifth. Selection and evaluation of top administrators—perhaps even mid-level academic managers—by criteria and expectations more appropriate to a CEO of a corporation than of a dean or provost or president. This reflects not simply the changing expectations but the development of a cadre of professional administrators, a process that has most likely been under way for some thirty years or more.

Sixth. As the boundary between institutional sectors blurs, the university tends to lose its franchise: corporations that look at themselves as being in the information or education business reach into the academic marketplace while universities self-consciously restructure themselves as corporate enterprises. As Michael Carow (cited in Blumenstyk 2001), executive provost in charge of global-educational enterprises at Columbia University put it, "we are expanding what it means to be a knowledge enterprise. We use knowledge as a form of venture capital" (p. B10). Since the late 1980s, corporate universities—that is, universities established and operated by corporations—have increased in number by from 400 to 2,000, and of these, more than 300 have partnerships with traditional brick-and-mortar universities.[8] What is interesting is that a number of corporate universities are not only educating their employees, customers, and suppliers. They now offer courses to the general public, for example, distance education sponsored by Barnes and Noble University, which offers a course on film noir and Shakespeare.

Seventh. Perhaps most troubling for traditional academic culture is the host of commercial and corporate relations that breach the autonomy of research activity and crack, if not destroy, the wall between academics and commerce.

Press and Washburn (2000) detailed the agreement between the University of California, Berkeley, and the Swiss pharmaceutical firm Novartist, whereby Novartist funded basic research in the Department of Plant and Microbial Biology in exchange for the right to negotiate licenses based on the department's discoveries. In addition, Novartist was granted seats on the department's research committee. Nor is this unique: the literature describes a wide range of university-company arrangements including contracted research, patents and licensing, supplying services (distance learning, consulting), corporate role in defining research agenda, joint ventures and partnerships, creation of subsidiary corporations, confidentiality agreements that restrict publication of research findings, and corporate funding of programs, fellowships, faculty lines, and schools. Top—and not so top—research institutions see nothing but bold in start-up companies, patent rights, deals for licenses and options flowing from the patents, equity in commercial start-ups, and the like. Reviewing the extent of such commerce, one might well look on research institutions as technology transfer bazaars. (See detailed data on technology transfer in the *Chronicle of Higher Education* [How colleges get more bang 2002]). As one reads through the examples that authors like Press and Washburn related, one is driven to the cynical conclusion that the key motto for universities today is not "libertas" or "veritas" but "for sale" and "let's make a deal." The Haas School of Business at Berkeley is plastered with corporate logos, and Laura D'Andrea Tyson was the Bank of America Dean of the school.

Eighth. Not least of the aspects of corporatization is the impact on the academic profession itself. The point here is that academicians are being transformed from autonomous professionals to a salaried professorate. The very language of the profession is changing: research replaces scholarship and scholars become researchers; professors no longer profess but are teachers encouraged to adopt fresh new pedagogical methodologies, to undergo faculty development and to submit to assessment, preferably of the quantitative sort. The key trends are the following:

1. With the growing ranks of part-timers, contingent labor, and teaching assistants, the academy is following the corporate model of employing just-in-time labor as a flexible, fluid, and disposable low-cost labor force.
2. The treatment of professors as managed professionals rather than autonomous professionals (Rhoades 1998) and the strengthening of patterns of hierarchy within university organization.
3. The effort to eliminate or at least minimize a—if not, the—chief institutional pillar of the profession (i.e., tenure) with a host of new style employment arrangements and personnel philosophies drawn from the corporate sector.
4. Changing criteria of judgment, for example, the level of external research funding brought to the institution serves as a criteria for appointment, renewal, promotion, tenure, or access to laboratories.

5. Efforts of universities or corporate sponsors to gain control of intellectual property rights.
6. The unbundling of teaching as a result of distance learning: course design, material collection, and module preparation becomes the task of a team rather than the judgment and creativity of a single professor or of professor collaborators.
7. Although largely confined to public institutions, we see the role of faculty unions as self-defense mechanisms against "management" and the growing spread of unionization among teaching assistants and adjunct faculty (Smallwood 2002).

True, some of these developments might be straws in the wind, but the wind is blowing. There is, of course, a larger context to these trends. What is happening to the academic profession parallels the transformation of autonomous professionals elsewhere and also resembles the transformation of craft workers in the nineteenth century. During the past few years, to take one example, physicians have moved in the direction of unionization, signaling a profound backlash against changes in the medical profession. Significantly, this reaction to corporatization of medicine represented by HMOs comes from the professionals as much as from the patients. Sociologist Craig Little (personal communication 2000) noted that

> the issue that appears to be galvanizing physicians as no other is the loss of professional autonomy they experience daily when they are forced to defend their professional judgements about their patients' care to low-level, faraway medical bureaucrats working from insurance company manuals.

Faculty throughout the country are now faced with an analogous attack on their professional autonomy. Understandably, then, the most dramatic reaction to this trend, namely, the movement for unionization, has come from graduate students and adjuncts, for they are the least secure, most underpaid, and most exploited academic workers. They are, as it were, the canary in the mine for well-off faculty and staff.

Ninth. Corporatization also challenges, I believe, the public mission of the university, rightly understood. The Morrill Act defined a uniquely American and distinctly democratic role for higher education (Nevins 1962). This new mission broke with the notion of "knowledge—its own end" articulated by Newman, and it defined an articulated set of democratic purposes, among these, service to the broader society. But the social utility of the university has, in the age of corporatization, been turned not to serving society in general or to meeting some broad democratic mission but to working with if not bending to corporate interests. That, after all, is the deepest meaning of the technology transfer arrangement enacted by the Bayh-Dole Act. While many research advances that advantage private interests no doubt add to the sum total of social utility (e.g., in the area of medicine and pharmaceuticals), one is hard-pressed to see the same widespread devotion by universities to poverty, labor unions, the arts, addressing class divisions, and the like. The corporatized university is the university of neither Morrill nor Cardinal John Henry Newman, of neither Robert Lynd nor Max Weber.

Conclusion

I trust this brief deconstruction of a complex and emotionally charged concept demonstrates that corporatization covers a wide-ranging set of trends within the modern American university. To repeat an earlier caution against overgeneralization, not each and every element described above is found in each and every university; not each and every college president is a CEO *manque*; not each and every faculty member is an oppressed proletarian. The difficulty of pinning down the precise contours of the concept suggests the need for additional rigorous and empirically based analysis. One item on the research agenda would be, for example, how the academic culture adapts to the corporate culture—and vice versa. What are the tactics and strategies that permit both sides to continue to exist within an institutional structure that demonstrates such important continuities? What are the trade-offs that each side makes? What are the friction points? How effectively, if at all, do faculty senates and unions deal with a situation in which, say, a corporation seeks to influence a curriculum in exchange for endowing a center or graduate fellowships? How do faculty respond to the challenges?

And what are the challenges? At a macro level, the picture that emerges from the literature and from observation is that the American university today is increasingly seen to and expected to function in ways that are inconsistent with, alien to, and even hostile to more traditional academic values and culture. Loaded as it may be, the very concept of corporatization leads us to see that in both its internal and external relations, the modern American university has undergone a metamorphosis. Internally, it has changed in terms of how it is managed, how it regards its workforce, what its priorities are, what nonacademic purposes it services, what activities it encourages, and what its culture is. Much of this is subtle, hard to detect, and difficult to define, but academics know when, say, student pressures transform their campuses from a cloistered place to an extension of the mall culture that the students treasure. Internally, the academic culture—a traditional cultural of learning and scholarship and of the life of the mind—is eroded by a new culture. Externally, the university has changed in terms of its relation to the corporate and state sectors, what objectives it pursues in the marketplaces, how it sees itself vis-à-vis the wider society. The university sees itself as a corporation and sees its business sector as a legitimate part of the academy. That much traditional academic work takes place or that noisy radical or outspoken conservative academics still speak their piece does not gainsay this transforming change.

In sum, these trends together pose a strong challenge to[9]

- the integrity of academic research and of the priorities of research and scholarly agenda and the credibility of universities as the cradle of disinterested and objective scientific research;

- the integrity of the content of undergraduate, graduate, and professional curricula;
- the integrity of academic work itself, arising from unbundling, in which the preparation, presentation, and evaluation of courses are separated in a new division of labor that destroys the academic craft and subjects academic labor to central authority in the tradition of Frederick Taylor;
- the autonomy of academic workers;
- university employment from outsourcing and overreliance on part-time faculty and staff;
- tenure criteria, especially the weight given to raising money as a condition of tenure;
- peer and public access to research findings, instead of their proprietary control;
- the sanctity of campus space arising from commercialization and licensing deals for restricted access;
- priorities for decisions about allocation of public monies among university departments and programs at state universities; and
- the language used to characterize academic life, in which the search for knowledge and critical thinking are subordinated to a new language of students as customers or as investors out to get the maximum market return.

For pessimists who believe that a corporatized university is no university at all, the university has changed for the worse. For optimists, well, for optimists, the battle is still joined. What this article has sought to do is to lay out the main features of the battlefield and to leave it to academicians and students to define the strategies and objectives for reclaiming the university. This is an important and honorable task. Universities are one of the central pillars of civil society. The core values and mission of the university must be sustained if the university is to fulfill its traditional role of learning, scholarship, and service. A fully corporatized university is only a shell of a university, and the task facing the academic community is to ensure that the inner core as well as the outer shell are preserved. If academics do not attend to the governance of their own institutions, who will?

Notes

1. Recent headlines suggest that the movement of academics from one major league university to another is on a par with the move of athletes from one team to another or of movie stars from one studio to another (see Columbia gets star professor 2002; A Harvard black studies star 2002).

2. For the most detailed and revealing case study, see Press and Washburn (2000).

3. For the most recent horror story, see Morgan (2002).

4. That the idea of converting universities into corporations is not so recent is demonstrated by an interesting little 1905 essay by a Henry S. Pritchett, titled "Shall the University Become a Business Corporation?" (Barrow 1990).

5. The success of the Manhattan Project was a critical moment in demonstrating the potential of university-based research for the economy. Vannevar Bush's 1945 report titled "Science—The Endless Frontier" initiated the formal connection between research universities and the federal government. For an example of the issues involved with this connection and with the issue of technology transfer from universities to industries, see the Web site of the Council on Governmental Relations, an organization of leading research universities: http://www.cogr.edu/#cogr. See Rosenzweig (2001, chap. 1).

6. Louis Menand (2001a) did speak of a golden age, but in a quite different context. For Menand, the golden age refers to the period of expansion in American higher education, roughly 1945 to 1975 (pp. 44-47). In terms of the resources, the esteem, the growth, and the vigor of higher education, there is some truth to this characterization. Those looking at current trends, however, seem to me to imagine a golden age in a quite distant and unspecified past—a utopia, as I term it above.

7. It should be noted that external funding opportunities in the soft social sciences, the arts, and the humanities are small compared to the hard sciences, education, medical sciences, and similar fields. Moreover, external grants in those areas generally do not include overhead costs; that is, they do not create additional revenue streams for universities. There is, then, limited incentive for grants offices to extend themselves to help a poet, artist, or historian. If a National Science Foundation or National Institutes of Health grant can pull in, say, $3 million—not counting 50 percent or so in overhead costs—why should a grants office assist a poet looking for a summer National Endowment for the Humanities grant of a few thousand dollars or a museum director looking for $50,000 to mount a show of abstract art?

8. A corporate university provides training and education, usually for employees, customers, and suppliers. It may use its own faculty or outsource the job to traditional universities or other businesses. At the same time, the more common pattern is that corporations enter into partnerships with universities and the latter deliver the program. According to Jeanne C. Meister (2001), 92 percent of corporations outsource education and training while 60 percent outsource some aspect of the course design. This does not include firms that market programs for traditional university and college markets, for example, Kaplan.

9. What follows draws on Steck and Zweig (2000, 299).

References

American Council on Education. 2002. *The changing enterprise project "capitalizing" on the curriculum.* Working paper. Retrieved 27 March 2002 from http://www.acenet.edu/programs/change-enterprise/working-paper.cfm.

Aronowitz, Stanley. 2000. *The knowledge factory.* Boston: Beacon.

Barrow, Clyde W. 1990. *Universities and the capitalist state: Corporate liberalism and the reconstruction of American higher education, 1894-1928.* Madison: University of Wisconsin Press.

———. 1993. Will the fiscal crisis force higher ed to restructure? *Thought and Action: The NEA Higher Education Journal* fall: 17-24.

———. 1996. The new economy and restructuring higher education. *Thought and Action: The NEA Higher Education Journal* spring: 37-54.

Birnbaum, Robert. 2000. *Management fads in higher education.* San Francisco: Jossey-Bass.

Blumenstyk, Godie. 2001. Knowledge is "a form of venture capital" for a top Columbia administrator. *Chronicle of Higher Education,* 9 February, B10.

Bowen, Roger W. 2001. Conflicting cultures. Address to United University Professions, 11 May, Albany, NY.

Bronfenbrenner, Kate, and Tom Juravich. 2001. Universities should cease hostilities with unions. *Chronicle of Higher Education,* 19 January.

Chomsky, Noam, R. C. Lewontin, Ira Katznelson, Laura Nader, Richard Ohmann, David Montgomery, Immanuel Wallerstein, Ray Server, and Howard Zinn. 1997. *The cold war and the university: Toward an intellectual history of the postwar years.* New York: New Press.

Columbia gets star professor from Harvard. 2002. *New York Times,* 5 April.

Council on Governmental Relations. 1999. The Bayh-Dole Act: A guide to the law and implementing regulations. Available from http://www.cogr.edu/#cogr.

Daniels, Richard, with Lisa Blasch and Peter Caster. 2000. Resisting corporatization of the university. In *Campus, Inc.,* edited by Geoffrey White, 61-84. Amherst, NY: Prometheus Books.

Dubeck, Leroy W. 1997. Beware higher ed's newest budget twist. *Thought and Action* 12: 81-91.

Etkowitz, Henry, Andrew Webster, and Peter Healey. 1998. Introduction. In *Capitalizing knowledge: New intersections of industry and academia,* edited by Henry Etkowitz, Andrew Webster, and Peter Healey. Albany: State University of New York Press.

Graubard, Stephen R. 1999. Preface. In Distinctively American: The residential liberal arts college. *Dædalus* 128 (1): v-xii.

Gray, Hanna Holborn. 1997. Cold war universities—Tools of power or oases of freedom. *Foreign Affairs* 76 (2): 147-51.

Hacker, Andrew. 2001. The big college try. *New York Review,* 12 April, 50-52.

A Harvard black studies star heads to Princeton. 2002. *New York Times,* 13 April.

How colleges get more bang (or less) from technology transfer. 2002. *Chronicle of Higher Education,* 19 July.

Ikenberry, Stanley. 2001. Mission and market: A leadership struggle for presidents. Speech delivered at eighty-third annual American Council on Education meeting, 17-20 February.

Jencks, Christopher, and David Riesman. 1969. *The academic revolution*. New York: Anchor.

Keller, George. 1983. *Academic strategy: The management revolution in American higher revolution*. Baltimore: Johns Hopkins University Press.

Levine, Arthur. 2000. The soul of a new university. *New York Times*, 13 March.

Lewis, Philip E. 1998. The new university: Global and corporate perhaps; liberal and communal necessarily. *Arts & Sciences Newsletter* 19 (1).

Meister, Jeanne C. 2001. The brave new world of corporate education. *Chronicle of Higher Education*, 9 February, B10.

Menand, Louis. 2001a. College: The end of the golden age. *New York Review*, 18 October, 44-47.

————. 2001b. Sporting chances: The cost of college athletics. *New Yorker*, 22 January, 84-88.

Minsky, Leonard. 2000. Dead souls: The aftermath of Bayh-Dole. In *Campus, Inc.*, edited by Geoffrey D. White, 95-105. Amherst, NY: Prometheus Books.

Morgan, Richard. 2002. Ending class early in Tennessee public colleges become ghost towns amid a state-government shutdown. *Chronicle of Higher Education*, 12 July.

Nevins, Allan. 1962. *The state universities and democracy*. Urbana: University of Illinois Press.

The new U. 1997. *Business Week*, 22 December 22, 96.

Noam, Eli M. 1995. Electronics and the dim future of the university. *Science* 270:247-49.

Noble, David F. 2001. *Digital diploma mills*. New York: Monthly Review Press.

Press, Eyal, and Jennifer Washburn. 2000. The kept university. *Atlantic Monthly*, 39-54.

Readings, Bill. 1996. *The university in ruins*. Cambridge, MA: Harvard University Press.

Rhoades, Gary. 1998. *Managed professionals*. Albany: State University of New York Press.

Rosenzweig, Robert M. 2001. *The political university*. Baltimore: Johns Hopkins University Press.

Ryder, John. 2001. The American university today: A tale of three cities. Paper presented at the annual conference of Alliance of Universities for Democracy, 5 November, Belgrade, Yugoslavia.

Sack, Allen L. 2001. Big-time athletics vs. academic values: It's a Rout. *Chronicle of Higher Education*, 26 January.

Scott, Barbara Ann. 1983. *Crisis management in American higher education*. New York: Praeger.

Shulman, James L., and William G. Bowen. 2000. *The game of life: College sports and educational values*. Princeton, NJ: Princeton University Press.

Slaughter, Sheila, and Larry L. Leslie. 1997. *Academic capitalism: Politics, policies and the entrepreneurial university*. Baltimore: Johns Hopkins University Press.

Smallwood, Scott. 2002. UAW will represent part-time faculty members at New York U. *Chronicle of Higher Education*, 19 July.

Soley, Lawrence. 1995. *Leasing the ivory tower*. Boston: South End.

Sperber, Murray. 2000. *Beer and circus: How big-time college sports is crippling undergraduate education*. New York: Henry Holt.

State University of New York. 1995. *Rethinking SUNY*. Albany: State University of New York Press.

Steck, Henry, and Michael Zweig. 2000. Take back the university: Only unions can save academic life. In *Campus, Inc.*, edited by Geoffrey D. White, 297-319. Amherst, NY: Prometheus Books.

Veblen, Thorstein. [1906] 1957. *The higher learning in America*. New York: Hill & Wang.

Welcome to college. Now meet our sponsor. 1999. *New York Times*, 17 August.

White, Geoffrey, ed. 2000. *Campus, Inc.* Amherst, NY: Prometheus Books.

Wulf, William. 1995. Warning: Information technology will transform the university. *Issues in Science and Technology* 11 (3): 46.

Issues in University Governance: More "Professional" and Less Academic

By
WILLIAM L. WAUGH JR.

The pressures for efficiency and the achievement of performance goals are encouraging college and university presidents to focus more on the management of their institutions and less on the more collegial processes of academic decision making. Presidents are being held more accountable to external constituencies, particularly the public officials and business leaders involved in hiring them and the foundations and businesses that supplement their salaries and benefits, and, therefore, feel less accountable to the faculty and other internal constituencies. To increase efficiency and meet goals, presidents are increasingly hiring professional administrators without academic experience, who feel more accountable to their administrative superiors and less accountable to faculty, students, and others within the institution. The focus on managerial values is also filtering down to academic departments and nonacademic offices. The net effect is that the faculty role in university governance is decreasing and may be extinguished if current trends continue.

College and university presidents in the United States are becoming more responsive to outside constituencies and less sensitive to faculty and other internal constituencies, academic administration is becoming more professional, and academic institutions are becoming more bureaucratic. These changes are not universal in American higher education, but they are increasingly common. The question is what

William L. Waugh Jr. is a professor of public administration, urban studies, and political science in the Andrew Young School of Policy Studies at Georgia State University. His areas of teaching and research include administrative theory, human resource management, disaster management, and local government capacity building. He is the author of Living with Hazards, Dealing with Disasters *(2000),* Terrorism and Emergency Management *(1990), and* International Terrorism *(1982); coauthor of* State and Local Tax Policies *(1995); and coeditor of* Disaster Management in the US and Canada *(1996),* Cities and Disaster *(1990), and* Handbook of Emergency Management *(1990), as well as author of more than 100 articles, chapters, and reports. He has served in Georgia State University's Senate for eighteen years and has participated in accreditation and other academic reviews on more than a dozen other campuses.*

DOI: 10.1177/0002716202238568

ANNALS, *AAPSS*, 585, January 2003

effect the changes are having on the structures and processes of university governance. The short answer is that college and university presidents are responding to
pressures for greater efficiency and productivity (likely in that order) and are relying more on professional staff to achieve those ends. The longer answer is less simple. As organizations mature, they typically undergo changes that lead to greater
bureaucratization and, when the external environment is unfriendly, they adapt if
they want to survive. Professionalization of staff and responsiveness to external
constituencies are adaptations to new demands. While the changes are understandable, they are having a profound impact on the traditional faculty role in university governance and thus on American higher education. In fact, that role may
already be dead, according to Joanna Vecchiarelli Scott (1996).

The changing roles of college and university presidents should come as no surprise. Executive-centered management has been the cornerstone of organizational
theory and practice for the past century. Indeed, the good government movement
of the Progressive Era focused on executive-centered professional management as
a cure for political corruption and administrative inefficiency (see, e.g., Stever
1993). Executive-centered management was to ensure accountability by providing
leaders with ultimate responsibility for their organizations. Held accountable,
executives presumably would find it to their advantage to root out the unscrupu-
lous and the incompetent and to adopt techniques that would improve decision
making and administration. Reform measures included the development of executive budgets and tighter financial controls. The Brownlow Commission and its suc-
cessors encouraged executive-centered management in the executive office of the
president. The city management movement encouraged similar reform in local
government (see, e.g., Schiesl 1977).

In some measure, academic administration seems to have escaped the scrutiny
of reformers—until recently. The constituencies of universities and colleges were
not motivated to seek political and administrative reform through mechanisms to
enhance executive control. Colleges and universities tended to choose their leaders from the ranks of the faculty, often with academic qualifications outweighing
administrative skills. To some extent, many academic institutions still follow that
model. Presidents, provosts, vice presidents, and deans are still drawn from classrooms and labs, and their values reflect the consensus-building approach of academic decision processes. To be sure, there have always been authoritarians and
those with less than collegial inclinations, but the general pattern of academic
administration has been a decentralized, faculty-driven process. Now, however,
there is increasing pressure to recruit executives from the private sector armed
with skills in business management but without work experience in academic
administration. As a result, academic planning, budgeting, and day-to-day administration is becoming more like the management processes developed for the private sector and increasingly reflects values that conflict with the traditional values
of university governance.

The pressures for change in how universities and colleges are governed should
not be surprising. Economic constraints are forcing a focus on efficiency and
accountability. Governing boards and presidents are under increasing pressure to

be more cost-effective, and that pressure is being passed on to vice presidents, deans, and department chairs. Demands to do more with less are forcing institutions to reexamine how they operate. Programmatic changes are also taking place. Indeed, an executive in residence at Washington University suggested that universities "reinvent" themselves by first determining their core functions and then disposing of their "unproductive programs" and contracting out or sharing administrative functions with other institutions (Mahoney 1997). Reducing bureaucracy by identifying unproductive programs is the explicit goal, although it is uncertain what "unproductive" might mean for academic departments and programs. Does "unproductive" mean having only a few majors, generating few credit hours, or bringing in little or no sponsored research or training projects?

In addition to financial pressures on institutions and their officials, there are also inexorable processes that all organizations experience as they mature and adapt to the external environment. The processes of institutionalization, bureaucratization, and professionalization change the character and the culture of the organizations. They become more institutionalized as their structures become more differentiated. Lines of authority become more clearly defined. Tasks become more specialized. Relationships become more formal. Hierarchy grows as spans of control shrink and the needs for supervision and coordination increase. The institutionalization process makes for a much more complex organization, which in turn requires more accountability. Organizations also tend to become much more bureaucratic as they mature. Formal relationships require formal communication, rules and regulations, clear lines of authority, accountability, and so on. Procedural requirements, that is, red tape, ensure consistency in decisions. Professionalization reflects the movement to greater task specialization. Persons formally trained in financial management, human resource management, and other needed skills replace those who learned their skills on the job or as they were needed. In effect, professional managers are replacing the academics that previously filled those administrative roles.

All three of these processes are occurring in American colleges and universities today, and they are having a profound effect on the role of faculty and staff in university governance. While the faculty role in university governance has been a contentious one in many cases, a primary, if not dominant, view has been that faculty have lead responsibility for the design and implementation of academic programs. In many institutions, that role has been jealously guarded by university senates and faculty committees and by individual professors in the name of academic freedom. While some institutions have experienced debates concerning the authority faculty should have over curricular matters, the faculty role in hiring, promoting, and tenure decisions has been less controversial, although some presidents, provosts, deans, and other administrators do wield considerable authority in those decisions and may disregard faculty preferences.

Certainly it may be argued that the role of faculty in university governance has long been limited. However, that has varied from institution to institution. Many community colleges have tended to treat faculty as employees rather than the central technology of the institutions because there has been no scarcity of prospective faculty to fill those roles and because teaching loads have left little time for faculty to fulfill administrative duties. For-profit colleges have tended to treat faculty as employees subject to management prerogatives because they were hired much like other employees. The market, that is, student demand, determines programmatic priorities. By contrast, institutions less dependent on the market have tended to define their product in terms of the prerequisites of liberal arts or fine arts or scientific education. In other words, the curriculum determines human resource priorities. Finding enough qualified faculty to cover the desired range of courses is the goal. Institutions adjust to the market demand for liberal arts, fine arts, science, business, and other degrees, but not necessarily to demands for specific courses that might compromise the quality of the product. Notwithstanding the widespread adoption of programs to ensure computer literacy; an appreciation for diversity; an understanding of international issues, analytical skills, communication skills; and other cross-cutting skills and competencies, the content of core curricula has been defended by faculty in most institutions. What has changed? Why is university administration in the United States becoming more professional?

Academic Leadership and Executive Accountability

Higher education in the United States is clearly undergoing profound change. Issues of access, program quality, cost to students and their families, and cost to taxpayers are challenging universities and colleges to reexamine their products (or services). Public institutions are experiencing decreasing state support, and as a result, they are increasing tuition to make up the difference or face serious deterioration of program quality. The costs of education are not rising so much as public subsidies are decreasing, with students and their families picking up the tab (see Winston 1998). In many cases, raising special fees only reduces the state subsidy. Moreover, tuition discount or scholarship programs are increasing the number of students—further straining college and university resources. For example, the much lauded lottery-funded HOPE scholarships in Georgia are increasing the numbers of students in colleges and universities at the same time that state support is being cut.

In this environment, university presidents are under increasing pressure to meet performance standards, usually measured by the number of students enrolled and the credit hours generated, but increasingly measured by evidence of reputation and endowment growth (or occasionally by the success of the sports teams). In great measure, the pressure comes from politicians who know little about leading or running academic institutions and see the institution only in terms of its statistical profile. The pressure also comes from business and government leaders who do not understand the unique nature of academic institutions. The complaints of faculty are not taken seriously until academic stars choose to leave for more hospitable environs.

There is also a cultural divide that encourages politicians and business leaders to intervene in academic affairs. Roger W. Bowen (2001), president of the State University of New York at New Paltz, has criticized the interference of political leaders and their lack of tolerance for faculty, including faculty-administrator, opposition. Bowen concluded that the academic world, which values free-thinking, intellectual risk taking and challenges to authority and the rules, conflicts with the political world, which prefers "certainty, order, and rules" (p. B14). Political leaders do not like their authority to be challenged, and that is precisely what leaders face in academic institutions. Bowen went on to compare the academy with the Church and suggest the need to separate politics, the state, from the academy to preserve the search for truth, rather than power (p. B15). In essence, political leaders do not understand the nature of academic leadership and often encourage the hiring of administrators whose work experience fits their own notions of how leaders should lead.

There is also a problem of accountability to boards of regents or other governing bodies when presidents may receive a substantial portion of their compensation from third parties, such as the university or college foundation or a separate endowment set up by alumni. For example, the total compensation for the president of the University of Louisville in 2001-2002 was $597,455. The state of Kentucky contributed $263,305 in base salary, $21,000 in deferred compensation, and $8,250 for an automobile lease. The University of Louisville Foundation provided an additional $98,361 as compensation as a consultant to the foundation, $85,389 in performance bonuses, $121,151 in deferred compensation and benefits, another automobile, a club membership, and a house. If the president completes his ten-year contract term at the university, which will end in 2008, he will receive a $1.5 million bonus (Basinger 2001, A24).

It is not unusual for presidents to receive supplements to their base compensation from their university foundations, endowed chairs, and other sources. A 2000 report published by the Association of Governing Boards of Universities and Colleges indicated that about one-third of public governing boards said that their presidents received supplementary compensation from outside sources. The question is whether the outside compensation affects their accountability to institutional and state boards of directors or regents (Basinger 2001, A24). The boards that oversee the colleges and universities have little control over foundations; consequently, conflicts of interest may well be present. Corporate-sponsored chairs may also create conflicts of interest (Basinger 2001, A26).

Even the hiring process for university and college presidents has become more formal and legalistic. Contracts outline performance expectations, including fundraising and programmatic changes. These are not new issues for many of the business people on the institution's governing board or for the corporate recruitment services hired to provide a pool of candidates and to assist in the selection. The negotiations may result in agreements quite inconsistent with the institution's mission and the traditional responsibilities of faculty and administrators (Basinger 2002, A29).

Being held accountable to outside constituencies, whether foundations, corporations, or boards, lessens the chances that presidents will feel accountable to an institution's faculty, staff, or students. While most would feel that embarrassing votes of no confidence and other demonstrations of nonsupport would not be in their best interest, their jobs depend on those external constituencies that do the hiring and provide the salary and benefits. Hiring staff to ensure that those external constituencies' expectations are met only makes sense. Professional staff are more likely to feel primarily responsible to the president rather than to the faculty.

The Professionalization of Academic Administration

Pressures for efficiency and productivity encourage academic administrators to focus on management processes. Consequently, it should come as no surprise that academic institutions would choose to hire administrators trained in techniques designed to achieve management goals. The issue, however, is whether management goals and academic goals are the same or, at least, not conflicting. Unfortunately, the evidence is that the professionalization of academic administration is resulting in more attention to management goals and less attention to academic goals.

Certainly, there are still scholars and scientists serving in administrative roles in most colleges and universities. While the hiring of professional financial and human resource managers may be increasingly common and the hiring of executives, including chief executives, who do not have academic experience beyond their own undergraduate and graduate educations is growing, the administrative reins of most institutions are still largely in the hands of people who understand traditional academic values and have some appreciation for the central roles that faculty have had in university governance.

For those institutions in which professional staff has become the norm, the faculty may well find themselves left out of decision processes because staff feel primarily responsible to the president and vice presidents and do not share information that might cause disagreement with their decisions. In meetings, the staffers are representatives of the administration rather than resource persons for the faculty. While faculty may be involved in some decisions directly or in advisory roles, the participation is becoming more peripheral, and in some cases, it is disappearing altogether. The marginalization of faculty is all the more difficult to understand when faculty members have specific skills in planning, financial management, and other management techniques and often serve as consultants to private firms, nonprofit organizations, government agencies, and even other academic institutions.

The growing number of administrators lacking academic experience portends even more major changes in academic administration. Already, some institutions are making the argument that department chairs and division coordinators should be full-time administrators, rather than faculty members, because their duties may not permit time in the classroom and may require management skills not commonly found among faculty (see, e.g., Evelyn 2002). While that may be relatively uncommon in four-year and larger institutions, the numbers of professional managers are increasing rapidly. Staffs are expanding as business managers, assistant department chairs, and a proliferation of assistant and associate deans, provosts, and vice presidents are hired to manage nonacademic and academic offices. There are pressures on academic administrators to acquire management training to facilitate their work, as well. Harvard University, Bryn Mawr College, and other institutions have nationally recognized programs for university administrators. Their students range from presidents to department chairs to registrars. The courses cover strategic management issues from enrollment management to fund-raising and basic management techniques, from outcome assessment to strategic management to quality management. Administrators can also be trained in state-of-the-art course management systems in which many institutions are investing (see, e.g., Olson 2001).

As more and more senior administrators come from outside the institution and even academia itself, the concern about administrator interference in faculty governance is growing. Conflict between university presidents and faculty senates is only the tip of the proverbial iceberg. There is increasing conflict at all levels. A case in point is the recent conflict between members of Harvard University's Afro-American studies department and the university's president. One of the issues has been whether a university president should question a tenured faculty member's productivity. Interestingly, the initial report concerning the conflict cited the bureaucratic treatment received by a prominent member of the faculty and later by his colleagues. The tone of the interaction was confrontational rather than collegial (Wilson and Smallwood 2002, A-8). Rather than simply having a conversation concerning the faculty member's activities, the president challenged the value of the activities to the institution. While the president had some academic experience, most of his recent experience had been in government, where executive control is more accepted. Similar conflicts have arisen with public intellectuals who have the credibility to comment on the issues of the day and, thereby, may create political problems for administrators who wish to avoid controversies that might jeopardize the support of officials, alumni, and other constituencies.

Administrative values may also conflict with academic values. Because budgets so often are driven by credit-hour generation, encouraging the enrollment of more students in more classes makes perfect administrative sense. However, the weakening of standards to boost enrollments makes little academic sense unless the institutional leadership is consciously choosing to reduce the quality of its programs. Allocating resources with a strong preference for those programs with many students may well spell doom for degree programs and departments that are less popular, even though their courses are central to the educational mission. A better example that is becoming more common in American research universities is to favor those programs that generate indirect or overhead monies. To be sure, the pursuit of grants and contracts and the overhead that they bring may be affecting the allocation of university resources. But many departments and faculties may fail the market test if that is a principal criterion for allocating resources. In short, the policy choices that might be considered very desirable in management terms are often very undesirable in academic terms. Faculty participation in decision making can reduce the likelihood that academic interests will be ignored.

The Bureaucratization
of Academic Administration

The bureaucratization of academic institutions is a normal process, and the professionalization of staff is a major contributor to the process. Most institutions become more bureaucratic as they mature. Colleges and universities are taking on the characteristics of classic Weberian bureaucracies with increasing levels of hierarchy, divisions of labor, task specialization, formal communication, and impersonality. Standard operating procedures, plans, decision rules, and other administrative conventions reduce flexibility. The distance from the top of the organization, the offices of chief executive officer or president and chief administrative officer or provost, to the level of the organization at which services are delivered (including the level at which classes are taught) is increasing. There are more people, from vice presidents to deans to division and department chairs, between the chief academic officers and those laboring in classroom and lab. The growing numbers of non-tenure-track and other part-time faculty further lengthens the distance from the president's office to the classroom. As a result, seemingly simple decisions may involve layers of staff and officials over relatively long periods of time.

The bureaucracy is increasingly made up of people who have little or no academic experience and do not understand the academic enterprise. Their work experience has been in traditional private or nonprofit sector organizations that have regular business hours, well-defined products and/or services, a distinct market, and so on. Conflicts between faculty and bureaucrats over administrative and academic issues are understandable. While conflict may be frequent and acrimonious in some institutions, it is no different from conflicts between line and staff in many organizations. In academic institutions, the conflicts may be as mundane as the scheduling of early morning meetings when faculty teach late into the evening and scheduling classes in rooms which are inappropriate for instruction. Increasingly, however, the conflicts may involve extending registration periods to ensure higher enrollments, with the result that students join classes several weeks into the term, and reducing book orders to minimize costs to bookstores, with the result that there are not enough books for all students and instructors have to spend more time dealing with the issue. The first set of examples reflects differences in organizational culture, and the latter set reflects differences in the goals of faculty and administrators. As academic administration becomes more bureaucratized, the cultural and administrative conflicts between faculty and staff will increase. Indeed, the conflicts between staff and students will also increase, and faculty and students may find themselves with common complaints. The levels of conflict also tend to escalate as both sides become more frustrated in their interactions.

The development of a professional bureaucracy is creating a new culture. The language of higher education is increasingly punctuated with references to cost and revenue centers, customer-driven programs, and other terminology more common to the business world. While the profit motive is certainly appropriate in private for-profit institutions, profit or value is defined quite differently in academic institutions. The implications of business language, however, should not be dismissed lightly. The change in language reflects the change in values. Institutions are being "reinvented." Presidents, provosts, deans, and department chairs are becoming more "entrepreneurial," and their programs are becoming more "customer friendly." While some of the terms are simply buzzwords of the day and mean very little, the impact may be substantial (Waugh 2001). Allocating resources on the basis of economic measures affects more than the business functions of the institution. Administrators become more accountable and responsive to the chief executive or chief administrative officer. Faculty become a peripheral concern and may, in fact, be considered an obstacle to be overcome or avoided rather than participants in university governance (Waugh 1998). Moreover, the business techniques on which decisions are made may be ill suited to the kinds of decision processes that are associated with academic institutions.

It should be remembered that colleges and universities are not the same as businesses, and the same economic assumptions do not apply (Winston 1998). For example, strategic planning involves (or should involve) broad involvement of internal and external constituencies. However, the planning process is essentially top down in that senior executives guide the development of the mission and vision statements, the identification of strategic issues, and most important, the choice of participants. Many people may participate and there may be relatively open communication. But faculty become just another stakeholder group, along with students, staff, alumni, and local dignitaries. They may find themselves fighting for a niche in a new mission because that niche will determine their resource allocations for the coming years. Organizational change has become an administrative responsibility rather than a faculty responsibility (Waugh 2001).

Administrators may not understand the values inherent in their management techniques. The techniques are not value-free tools. They require a structuring of decision making and a selection of information that affect the range of alternatives considered and the choice. The selection of participants and the nature of their participation affect decisions. In academic institutions, the faculty are becoming stakeholders rather than the central technology of the institution (Waugh 1998). In strategic planning processes, as well as in the hiring processes for presidents and other high-level officials, faculty are one of many stakeholder groups and are often outnumbered by staff representatives and external constituents. The management processes effectively marginalize faculty in the institution. Decision makers tend to give numerical information, especially dollar amounts, more weight than qualitative information. Increased focus is on sponsored research, with indirect cost rates, faculty buyouts, and support for graduate research assistants, postdoctoral faculty, and equipment purchases. Some departments rely on indirect cost revenue generated by external research for their basic operating expenses and certainly for the amenities such as faculty travel. The revenue-generating departments and colleges often subsidize the units that do not or cannot generate their own revenue. Engineering, business, public policy, education, and other professional programs are often the cash cows of the university, while the humanities and others have far less opportunity for external funding. The allocation of indirect or overhead revenues is a controversial issue, with some universities absorbing all such revenue, some allocating a portion to the college and/or department that generated the revenue, and some ensuring that faculty who generate such revenue receive a portion large enough to encourage the pursuit of additional sponsored projects. In a large research university, successful grant writers can support legions of graduate students and finance state-of-the-art laboratories.

A more legalistic approach to academic activities may also be reflected in bureaucratic interpretations of academic parameters. For example, course length is generally expressed in terms of classroom or contact hours and specified by accrediting agencies. A regular semester system typically has two fifteen- or sixteen-week terms. However, the contact hours in a semester may be fit into a few days rather than three or four months. Forty-five contact hours in a typical semester, for example, could be satisfied in a long week or two or three three-day weekends, depending on the length of the class days. The literal or legalistic interpretation of standards may not be a problem in some courses, but it can be a serious problem in courses that require reflection and research. Creative curriculum design is an important marketing tool because students may appreciate the convenience and not the pedagogical problems.

Faculty, too, are often pressured to behave more like employees in a business. Requirements to wear business attire and work business hours are common. Many faculty experience serious problems fitting their activities into a typical, forty-hour, nine-to-five workday when research, professional travel, and even teaching may be done at night or on weekends and many faculty work fifty or more hours per week on average (particularly if they are seeking tenure or simply enjoy their work). Many faculty find it difficult to relate their work to a typical work schedule when projects frequently require long days and weekend work and professional conferences often span weekends. Smaller institutions often require that faculty have frequent contact with students and alumni outside of the classroom. Religious institutions may require attendance at services, as well.

Increasingly, the job of the department chairperson is to play the managerial game—to manipulate or, at least, to live with the performance measures. Success is getting courses inserted into core curricula to justify more faculty, increasing cost effectiveness as measured by cost per student or credit hour, creating graduate programs because the weighed credit hours may justify more faculty, eliminating outside electives to keep credit hours in house, lengthening programs to generate more credit hours, and increasing course offerings at the last minute to capture unanticipated demand. The point is that the management decisions are driving academic decisions, often at the price of academic quality.

Conclusions

Given the economic and political environment of higher education, it is understandable that college and university presidents, as well as other academic administrators, will focus on external constituencies. Given recruitment and selection processes, it is also understandable that presidents are more accountable to external constituencies, whether they be the boards that oversee the institution and hire presidents or the foundations that supplement salaries and provide amenities. Presidents, nonetheless, have a responsibility to their institutions, and academic quality should be a standard to which they are held.

It is also understandable that presidents will hire administrators who can help them reach economic performance goals. The pursuit of rationality and efficiency, without regard for the impact on faculty and students and others, may well be a form of what Adams and Balfour (1998) called "administrative evil." The application of business management techniques in universities may be saving money or more rationally allocating resources, but it may also be having a detrimental effect on students, faculty, staff, and other constituents. As long as efficiency is the sole criteria against which the techniques are measured, their effects on university governance will not be accurately assessed. Leaving faculty out of the decision-making processes that affect academic programs and other faculty concerns increases the likelihood that academic values will not be served and may well result in actions that are "evil" in their effects (Waugh 2001).

Cary Nelson (1999), a professor of English at the University of Illinois at Urbana-Champaign, has characterized the conflict between faculty and administrators as a "war" and called for a resistance movement to fight back against "evil" administrative actions (p. B4). The ethical choice may be to resist threats to academic freedom and to protect the faculty role in university governance. To do less would amount to complicity. Although budget cuts, resource reallocations, and mission redefinition may be necessary to the health of the institution, the choices should be made with full understanding of their academic, as well as their financial, implications.

Bureaucratization may be a problem for all—faculty, administrators, students, and external constituencies. It is common for bureaucracies to grow and to clog decision processes with standard operating procedures, regulations, and other impediments to innovation and flexibility. It is common for bureaucratic reward systems to encourage perverse behaviors. It is common for rational decision-making techniques to be utilized without a full understanding of the assumptions that underlie their method. In those regards, universities are suffering the same problems that other large organizations have suffered after long periods of growth. It is also common, however, for large organizations to reinvent themselves, reducing bureaucracy to provide greater procedural flexibility and to encourage programmatic innovation.

Traditional university governance processes, as aggravating as they may be for all involved, may be far more appropriate to the university role in society than centralized, bureaucratic processes. Collegial processes, in the long term, will be more effective in maintaining the health of academic programs. Admittedly, change is difficult in traditional academic institutions where programs are run by faculty with interests rooted in narrow disciplines and where departments are heavily dependent on internal resources. Changing a few courses in a core curriculum, for example, might radically alter the fortunes of a department faculty. It is no wonder that academic turf battles erupt over changes in core curricula when so many credit hours are generated through service courses, like those English, history, and political science courses that are required of all students. The loss of a course in the core curriculum can mean a loss of thousands of credit hours and result in the loss of one or more faculty members. Service courses also draw majors and minors and provide institutional visibility. Losing a faculty member or two might mean that there will be no one to cover Asian politics, contemporary European history, environmental chemistry, or other important academic areas.

To be sure, the articles and letters to the editor of the *Chronicle* indicate that while some faculty are experiencing a loss of power or control over curricula, courses, and instructional delivery, not all are. Moreover, not all faculty regret the loss of administrative responsibility. For some, expectations are different. They have little or no interest in academic policy making or politics. If the work environment becomes unpleasant, they will simply move on. The reduced administrative load means more time for consulting, research, student contact, and other activities. A question that should be asked is whether disconnecting faculty from those responsibilities contributes to a sense of disconnection with the institution itself.

The distinction between administration and governance is important, and it is a distinction that is increasingly overlooked as university presidents and governing board members extol the virtues of business management techniques in higher education and leaders seek to effect fundamental change in mission and method. Administration is those processes that are related to the allocation of resources, including planning, human resource management, and particularly financial management. Governance is those processes related to the technology of the university, including the academic programs, faculty, and scholarship. Preserving the distinction, so that the dog wags the tail, rather than the reverse, is essential for maintaining healthy academic institutions.

An answer may be to separate academic and nonacademic units. Ironically, businesses long ago learned that their more creative units may have to be located away from their production or factory units because of differences in organizational culture and operational imperatives. Research and development units also are often located in different buildings or in wooded industrial parks, away from the headquarters, so that creativity will be nurtured rather than managed. The cultures of some of the most technologically creative firms in our society have become the stuff of legend. As a result, creative organizations may now be more closely associated with nonhierarchical structures, informal relationships, casual attire, and minimal attention to the clock. In short, business campuses have come to look very much like traditional university campuses, and they have taken on the ivory tower role. Given that university faculty are generally considered the creative technology of the university, the logical answer might be to relocate the more factory-like business operations to the fringe of campus or to another site altogether to prevent contamination.

References

Adams, Guy B., and Danny L. Balfour. 1998. *Unmasking administrative evil*. Thousand Oaks, CA: Sage.

Basinger, Julianne. 2001. Private sources play more of a role in paying public university chiefs. *Chronicle of Higher Education*, 30 November, A24-A26.

———. 2002. For presidents and boards, a handshake is no longer enough. *Chronicle of Higher Education*, 24 May, A29-A31.

Bowen, Roger W. 2001. The new battle between political and academic cultures. *Chronicle of Higher Education*, 22 June, B14-B15.

Evelyn, Jamilah. 2002. Professors protest plan to replace faculty division heads with administrators. *Chronicle of Higher Education*, 18 January, A11.

Mahoney, Richard J. 1997. "Reinventing" the university: Object lessons from big business. *Chronicle of Higher Education*, 17 October, B4-B5.

Nelson, Cary. 1999. The war against the faculty. *Chronicle of Higher Education*, 16 April, B4-B5.

Olson, Florence. 2001. Getting ready for a new generation of course-management systems. *Chronicle of Higher Education*, 21 December, A25-A27.

Schiesl, Martin J. 1977. *The politics of efficiency: Municipal administration and reform in America: 1880-1920*. Berkeley: University of California Press.

Scott, Joanna Vecchiarelli. 1996. The strange death of faculty governance. *PS: Political Science and Politics* December: 724-26.

Stever, James A. 1993. The growth and decline of executive-centered intergovernmental management. *Publius: The Journal of Federalism* 23 (Winter): 71-84.

Waugh, William L., Jr. 1998. Conflicting values and cultures: The managerial threat to university governance. *Policy Studies Review* 15 (Winter): 61-73.

———. 2001. Entrepreneurialism and managerialism perceived as evil in university governance. In *Entrepreneurial management and public policy*, edited by Van Johnston. Commack, NY: Nova Science.

Wilson, Robin, and Scott Smallwood. 2002. Battle of wills at Harvard. *Chronicle of Higher Education*, 18 January, A8-A10.

Winston, Gordon. 1998. Economic research now shows that higher education is not just another business. *Chronicle of Higher Education*, 17 March, B6.

The Future of College Access: The Declining Role of Public Higher Education in Promoting Equal Opportunity

By
MICHAEL MUMPER

Beginning in the 1980s, a series of forces conspired to make access to public higher education more difficult for low-income and disadvantaged students. Rising tuition, changes in the federal student aid programs, and the decline of affirmative admissions all played a role. This article shows how, in the decades ahead, these troubling trends are poised to accelerate. The fiscal conditions driving up tuition will continue. The emergence of a new generation of student aid programs will further shift benefits away from the low-income and toward the middle- and upper-income students. Similarly, increased competition will make admission to public colleges even more difficult. The cumulative result will be diminished access for the most needy students. This development is likely to reverse the traditional role of these institutions in promoting equal opportunity. Indeed, public higher education may come to play the reverse role of reinforcing and widening the nation's income distinctions.

Americas public colleges and universities have long played a central role in the efforts of low-income and disadvantaged Americans to achieve economic success. The view that going to college was the surest path to the middle class was not only widely held, it was largely correct. It is no coincidence that improving access to higher education was a centerpiece of government efforts to promote equal opportunity since the 1960s. There is clear evidence that those efforts produced significant increases in the number of students from disadvantaged backgrounds who attended college and helped to close the wage gap between black and white Americans during the 1970s.

Michael Mumper is a professor and the chair of the political science department at Ohio University. He is a specialist in the politics of higher education finance and is the author of Removing College Price Barriers: What Government Has Done and Why It Hasn't Worked *(1996, State University of New York Press). His articles have appeared in the* Journal of Higher Education, *the* Review of Higher Education, *the* Journal of Education Finance, *and* Education Policy. *He served as member of the Task Force on Institutional Leadership for the National Association of Student Financial Aid Administrators.*

DOI: 10.1177/0002716202238569

But beginning in the 1980s and accelerating in the 1990s, college opportunities for low-income and disadvantaged people have declined. A combination of rising tuition, changes in the federal student aid programs, and new institutional admissions procedures have conspired to tighten access to public colleges. Looking to the future, these trends are poised to accelerate. As state budgets tighten, tuition inflation will continue. Federal student aid will increasingly emphasize loans at the expense of grants. Worse still, during the 1990s, federal and state policy makers developed a new generation of student aid programs that are both very expensive and much more effective at assisting middle- and upper-income students to cover college costs than they are at increasing access for low-income students.

What makes these developments so troubling is that the financial returns for earning a B.A. degree are increasing rapidly relative to those of high school graduates, and even to A.A. degrees. Today, however, just as access to higher education is becoming an even more central element in achieving financial success, the opportunities for low-income students to participate in public higher education are being sharply constricted.

In this analysis, I review the changing role that public higher education has played in promoting equal opportunity since 1965. I begin by looking backward at the design and development of the major government efforts to increase participation in higher education and to promote equal opportunity. Then I describe the factors that led to the unplanned collapse of those efforts since the mid-1980s. The analysis then looks forward to anticipate how government policies being put into place today are likely to exacerbate these trends in the decade ahead. The evidence presented shows that a combination of misdirected government subsidies in the existing programs, the creation of inappropriately designed new programs, and the changing demographics of college students are on the verge of undermining the role of public higher education in advancing equal opportunity. As a result, in the decades ahead, higher education is likely to serve to reinforce the existing patterns of stratification and exacerbate the nation's widening income gap. This role is precisely the opposite of the one it played a generation ago.

Higher Education and Economic Success

Going to college has never been a more important part of achieving economic success in America than it is today. Since the mid-1970s, the gap between the top and the bottom of the nation's distribution of income has been steadily widening. Table 1 shows the changes in household income by quintiles. In 1980, there was already a substantial gap between the highest and lowest income quintile. Since that time, however, the earnings of the highest two quintiles have grown much more rapidly that the lowest two. During that twenty-year period, the income of the lowest quintile increased by only $1,180, or less than 1 percent per year. At the same time, the household income of the highest fifth increased nearly $50,000[1] (see the U.S. Census Bureau at http://www.census.gov/hhes/income/histinc/h03.html).

TABLE 1

MEAN INCOME RECEIVED BY
EACH FIFTH OF HOUSEHOLDS: 1980 TO 2000

Year	Lowest Fifth	Second Fifth	Third Fifth	Fourth Fifth	Highest Fifth
1980	9,122	22,014	36,232	53,349	93,705
1985	9,096	22,485	37,242	56,007	103,310
1990	9,449	23,679	39,111	58,968	114,437
1995	9,631	23,527	39,340	60,475	126,202
2000	10,440	26,069	43,412	67,485	146,260
Percentage change in twenty years	14.4	18.4	19.8	26.4	56.1

SOURCE: Adapted from U.S. Census, Historical Income Tables, Households, Table H-3, http://www.census.gov/hhes/income/histinc/h03.html.

For purposes of this analysis, these income patterns are troubling for two reasons. First, it has made college more expensive to lower-income students. In 1981, for example, a student from a household earning the mean income of the lowest quintile needed to pay about 15 percent of his or her previous year's income to cover tuition at an average priced public college. By 2001, such students needed to pay 37 percent of their previous year's income. For a two-year college, the increase was from 9 percent to 17 percent. For upper-income families, the picture was quite different. The percentage of income required for a year at a four-year college still increased, but from about 1.5 percent to 2.5 percent.

The second reason for concern is that in America today, annual income is very closely linked to earnings. Table 2 shows the median household income by educational attainment. Household income increases steadily as education increases. Moreover, the rewards for higher earnings are heavily concentrated in the higher educational levels. Those leaving college with either an A.A. or a B.A. earn in the upper half of the income distribution. Those who do not earn a college degree are likely to be in the lower half. This has important consequences for the nation as a whole. A recent study estimated that

> if African Americans and Hispanics had the same distribution of college education as Whites, the nation could now fill college level jobs that now go begging or go to foreign students. Moreover, the upsurge in national wealth that would result from the infusion of human capital would be startling. African Americans would add $113 billion annually in new wealth and Hispanics another $118. Assuming an average federal, state, and local tax rate of 35 percent, the new wealth created by this new human capital would result in more than $80 billion in new public revenues. (Carnevale and Fry 2000, 44)

When this combination is viewed together, it presents an important challenge. Moving disadvantaged families up the income ladder generally means moving them up the educational ladder. Yet, during the past two decades, rising college

TABLE 2

MEDIAN HOUSEHOLD INCOME BY
EDUCATIONAL ATTAINMENT OF HOUSEHOLDER IN 2000

Educational Attainment	Median Income ($)
Less than ninth grade	17,994
Ninth to twelfth grade (no diploma)	23,305
High school graduate	37,545
Associate's degree	51,911
Bachelor's degree	68,475
Master's degree	80,516
Professional degree	102,791

SOURCE: Adapted from U.S. Census, Historical Income Tables, H 13, http://www.census.gov/hhes/income/histinc/h13.html.

prices and flat family income have increased the portion of the income lower earning families must pay to take advantage of the benefits of college. Policy makers have long recognized the problem posed by college price barriers. In fact, the federal and state governments spend billions of dollars each year toward that end. Unfortunately, as we will examine next, those programs are doing less and less each year to compensate for the rising price barriers facing college students from low-income families.

Higher Education and Equal Opportunity: The Collapse of the Traditional Framework

Beginning in the 1960s, states, the federal government, and public colleges and universities developed a loosely coordinated partnership to promote equal opportunity in which each level assumed a complementary role. State governments provided public campuses with sufficient funds to ensure that tuitions remained low. The federal government developed an extensive system of need-based grants to college students to ensure that all students who could be admitted to college could afford at attend. And individual institutions implemented admissions policies that gave advantages to students from racial minorities or disadvantaged backgrounds. While it was never explicitly planned, this combination of low tuition, grant assistance, and preferential admissions policies helped to increase access to college for the target populations (Heller 1999).

The traditional state role in maintaining equal educational opportunity was to maintain low public college tuition. This was done by providing generous subsidies to campus leaders who, in turn, used those funds to keep prices low. In a 1971 analysis of the relationship between prices and college admissions, Christopher Jencks found that the situation of the disadvantaged student improved between 1900 and the 1950s.

During the first half of the twentieth century the combined cost of room, board, and tuition rose considerably more slowly than family incomes. This meant that a substantially larger proportion of the population could afford to attend college in 1950 than at any previous time. (P. 88)

These long periods of low tuition at public colleges in many states did not happen by accident. It was the result of a sustained effort by state policy makers to provide public higher education at the lowest feasible cost. Indeed, a number of states have constitutional provisions that mandate such practices. This low-tuition approach was possible because the cost of providing higher education was relatively low, at least by today's standards, and the portion of the population attending public colleges was relatively small (Young 1974).

These conditions changed in the second half of the century, and public college tuition began to increase in the 1960s and 1970s. Those price increases accelerated in the early 1980s. Table 3 shows the average tuition and fees charged at two- and four-year public colleges and universities. Between the 1981-1982 and 2001-2002 academic years, constant dollar tuition increased by 166 percent at a public four-year college and by 112 percent at a public two-year college. The reasons for these increases have been the source of much controversy. In 1998, Congress was so concerned that it established the National Commission on the Costs of Higher Education to conduct a comprehensive review of college costs and prices. After months of hearings and staff investigation, the commission reached no consensus (National Commission on the Costs of Higher Education 1999). Some observers place the blame for rising tuition on declining levels of state support for higher education. To be fair, total state support to public colleges has increased steadily since 1980, but that increase has lagged behind the growth of personal income and declined as a percentage of state budgets. The result has been that state appropriations have declined as a portion of the revenue received by public colleges. Campus leaders have compensated for the declining state support by increasing the portion of their revenue from tuition (Heller 2001a). During the twenty-year period, tuition has increased from 16 to 24 percent of revenue at four-year public colleges. During that same period, the revenue they derived from state government declined from more than 60 percent to about 50 percent.

There are, however, other reasons for tuition inflation. Public college campuses now regularly provide students with services, programs, and amenities that were unknown a generation ago (Hauptman 1990). Technology costs have increased steadily, and employee health and benefit costs have experienced significant price increases (Mumper 2001).

Regardless of which of these causes are really driving the recent tuition inflation, there is every reason to expect that the trend will continue to increase in the next decade. State budgets have deteriorated rapidly since 2000, forcing further cuts to public higher education. Increased demand for new spending on Medicaid, law enforcement, and elementary and secondary education compete each year to draw revenues away from higher education. Barring any unexpected changes in the revenue structure of state governments, or the discovery of a reliable new reve-

TABLE 3

AVERAGE TUITION AND FEES AT PUBLIC COLLEGES AND UNIVERSITIES
(IN CONSTANT DOLLARS) FOR SELECTED YEARS
1971-1972 THROUGH 2001-2002

	Public Four-Year	Public Two-Year
1981-1982	1,414	819
1986-1987	2,051	1,048
1991-1992	2,706	1,504
1996-1997	3,323	1,636
2001-2002	3,754	1,738
Twenty year percentage change	166	112

SOURCE: Adapted from College Board (2001a).

nue source by campus leaders, tuition inflation will only accelerate. Similarly, campuses are spending more, not less, on new programs and services, and technology and health costs continue to rise at rapid rates. This will force disadvantaged and low-income students to find ways to cover these ever rising prices if they do not want to be closed out of the economic rewards that college brings.

These patterns are more troubling since tuition increases have a disproportionate impact on low-income students (Heller 1999). Thomas Kane has made a series of studies examining the link between rising prices and college participation. This research suggests that as the net price of higher education increases, the participation rates for low-income students declines (Kane 1995). Kane showed that this is true even in periods of time when both tuition and overall enrollments are rising. Looking at Massachusetts, which had especially dramatic increases in tuition in the 1980s and 1990s, he found that the gap between upper- and lower-income enrollment increased as tuition increased. Kane concluded that a $1,000 increase in tuition at four-year public colleges reduces enrollment in that sector by 13.7 percent by whites and 21.4 percent for blacks (Kane 1998).

Because state policy makers have been unable to keep tuition low, the role of the federal government has become even more important. The traditional federal role in maintaining equal educational opportunity was to provide a safety net ensuring that no qualified student was shut out of higher education. The centerpiece of this effort was the Pell Grant program, created in the Higher Education Act of 1965. Originally called the Basic Educational Opportunity Grant, Pell was established in the Higher Education Act of 1965. In its original form, the Basic Educational Opportunity Grant was allocated directly to institutions, which were left free to determine who would be eligible for aid and how much each student would receive. But with the 1972 amendments to the Higher Education Act, Congress created a national system of needs analysis in which each student applying for federal financial aid is subjected to a means test (Gladieux and Wolanin 1976). The estimated price of tuition and living expenses at an institution and the student's family income are used to determine eligibility for a federal grant or loan or for work study assistance.

TABLE 4
PELL GRANT FUNDING HISTORY

	Maximum Grant Awarded	Maximum as Percentage of Public Four-Year Price
1980-1981	1,550	69
1985-1986	2,100	54
1990-1991	2,300	44
1995-1996	2,340	33
2000-2001	3,300	39

SOURCE: Adapted from King (2000).

The Pell Grant was to provide the foundation funding that would ensure that the most needy would have substantial college support. In 1974, the first year it was awarded, the maximum Pell Grant (the one awarded to the most needy students) purchased 78 percent of the annual cost of one year at an average-priced public college or university. This went a long way toward removing price barriers for low-income students. By almost all accounts, the newly targeted Pell Grant produced some dramatic results in the years after the first awards were given out. A meta-analysis of six econometric studies of the Pell Grant and college enrollment found that as the program existed in the late 1970s, it raised lower-income enrollment by between 20 and 40 percent (Leslie and Brinkman 1987). However, almost since its creation, Pell funding has badly lagged behind the pace of tuition inflation. Table 4 shows the problem. While the size of the maximum award has increased slowly, its purchasing power has steadily eroded. Today, the Pell Grant covers less than 40 percent of the cost of a public four-year college. This has left disadvantaged students with fewer and fewer grant resources to pay the rising college costs.

Beginning only a few years later, the direction of federal student aid policy began a steady change that would eventually transform it from a grant-based system into a loan-based system (Hearn 1998). Congress also created the guaranteed student loan program, now called the Stafford Loan, in the Higher Education Act of 1965. While eligibility for these loans was also means tested, they were available to students from higher-income groups than were Pell Grants. Federal loan guarantees were originally intended to be a supplement to the centerpiece grant program, but almost immediately, the demand for loans exceeded expectations (Mumper 1996). As early as 1975, the federal government was awarding more student aid dollars in loans than it was in grants. However, the real explosion in student loans began with the enactment of the Middle Income Student Assistance Act in 1978. This removed the income eligibility requirements from the guaranteed student loan program and allowed virtually all full-time students to take out a government-guaranteed and -subsidized loan. The result was an explosion of student borrowing and a parallel growth in the loan components of the student aid programs. Between 1977 and 1981, the amount of student loans awarded increased from $4.2 billion to more than $13 billion (as measured in 2001 dollars), and the number of borrowers increased from 1 million to 3.2 million (Gillespie and Carlson 1983).

In 1981, the Reagan administration entered office determined to sharply reduce the size of the federal government's social spending. Large cuts were proposed for both the Pell Grant and the guaranteed loan programs. While those efforts were not successful at reducing overall student aid spending, they did slow the growth of the loan programs and restore an income cap for student loan eligibility, albeit at a higher level than it had been in 1978. But after the expansion, cutting back the student loan program proved virtually impossible. Middle-income students and their families were beginning to feel the effects of the tuition inflation discussed previously. They saw student loans as a simple, and subsidized, way to cover their rising costs. This set off an unprecedented expansion in student borrowing. The $13 billion dollars awarded in student loan aid in 1980 tripled to $40 billion in 1999 (College Board 2001b). During that same time period, total federal grant spending went from about $18 million to $27 million, an increase of only 33 percent.

The twenty years of growth in federal student loans and their growing cost to the federal treasury are undoubtedly a part of the reason for the decline in the Pell Grant program during the same period. While Congress was spending more each year on students, it was shifting subsidies away from the most needy to often considerably less needy middle-income students. The increase in student borrowing, and subsequent loan debt, among low-income students presented another important concern. Low-income students do not benefit from loans in the same way as middle-income students. Richard Fossey (1998) described the problem this way:

> Not all students who take out student loans are benefited. Many—low income students, single parents, and minority individuals, in particular—are defaulting. And many more who do not default are heavily burdened by their student loan commitments. Without any question, a certain portion of students see the quality of their lives decline rather than improve because the borrowed money to finance their education. (P. 4)

Finally, public college admissions procedures played a central role by advancing the cause of equal opportunity. The Civil Rights Act of 1964 established a national policy of nondiscrimination that was broadly understood to involve the elimination of overt discrimination and the adoption of color-blind practices (Sindler 1978, 12). However, within a short time of its enactment, this early view of nondiscrimination was judged by many to be too limited to achieve the desired results. In their view, additional and special efforts were needed to promote equal opportunity for minority groups. As a result, a number of varied, "something more" procedures were put into place by campus leaders. These came to be known as affirmative admissions policies. Such procedures became common in college admission through the 1970s.

These admission practices were challenged many times in court on the grounds that something more amounted to an unfair advantage and that college admissions should be race neutral. In 1978, the U.S. Supreme Court addressed this contro-versy in the case of *Allan Bakke v. Regents of the University of California*. In its rul-ing, the Court held that colleges and universities can consider race as a factor in determining admission but that they cannot establish a fixed quota of student slots assigned on the basis of race. This ruling allowed public universities to continue to consider race as a "plus factor" in an effort to ensure the campus maintained cam-pus diversity.

This all changed in 1996, when the U.S. Fifth Circuit Court issued its decision in *Hopwood v. Texas*. The court ruled that colleges, in this case a law school, cannot "give any consideration to race or ethnicity . . . for the purposes of achieving a diverse student body." The U.S. Supreme Court refused to hear the case on appeal, and the ruling stood. The state of Texas interpreted the decision as applying to admission at all public colleges and universities and to the allocation of scholar-ships (Hurtado and Cade 2001). At about the same time, the voters of the state of California passed Proposition 209, which, among other things, prohibited the granting of preferential treatment to any individual on the basis of race, sex, color, ethnicity, or national origin in admission to the state's institutions of higher educa-tion. A wave of race-blind admissions policies quickly replaced the long-standing affirmative admissions policies.

This change in admissions practices has resulted in a precipitous drop in the number of minority students admitted to the most selective institutions in those states. For example, resident freshman enrollment at the University of California dropped from 7.8 percent in fall 1997 to 3.7 percent only one year later (Pusser 2001, 138). In other cases, campuses responded to these trends by resorting to greater reliance on standardized tests in admissions decisions. Gary Orfield (1998) noted that "once affirmative action was stripped away . . . the consequences of rank-ing applicants by standardized tests became much more obvious." He went on:

> Under the new rules, there have been devastating declines in the admission of underrepresented minority students. A recent study suggests that even without the use of standardized tests, differences in grades alone would produce major drops in the enroll-ment of black and Latino students. (P. 7)

These actions compound the impact of the income and price trends discussed ear-lier. Minority students may now find it more difficult to gain admission to their institution of choice, even if they are able to overcome the financial barriers.

Looking Backward

From the perspective of 1980, the traditional framework for advancing equal opportunity in higher education was working well. States were keeping public col-lege tuition low. The federal government was providing need-based Pell Grants to help the most disadvantaged students cover their college costs. While an increase in the volume of federal student lending was well under way, the combination of

TABLE 5

AVERAGE ANNUAL UNMET NEED FACING HIGH SCHOOL GRADUATES,
BY FAMILY INCOME AND TYPE OF COLLEGE (IN DOLLARS)

Family Income	Annual Unmet Need
Public two-year college	
Less than 25,000/year	3,200
25,000-50,000/year	2,700
50,000-75,000/year	600
More than 75,000/year	100
Public four-year college	
Less than 25,000/year	3,800
25,000-50,000/year	3,000
50,000-75,000/year	1,500
More than 75,000/year	400

SOURCE: Adapted from Advisory Committee on Student Financial Assistance (2002, p. 6).

low tuition and Pell Grants was helping to close the college participation gap
between low- and middle-income students. Finally, public colleges were effectively implementing affirmative admissions policies that opened the door to college for many disadvantaged students to take advantage of higher education. Most
important, the gap in the college participation rates between lower- and middle-
income students had closed significantly.

But in the early 1980s, the traditional framework began to collapse. Public college tuition started a relentless climb. Simultaneously, the purchasing power of
Pell Grants sharply declined. Low-income students were left with no choice but to
take out student loans or give up on their dreams of a higher education. But there
are good reasons that some low-income students may be hesitant to borrow and
that those who do will have a more difficult time repaying the loans later. Finally,
the growing financial problems faced by potential college students from disadvantaged backgrounds were often made moot by their increasing difficulty in securing
admission to the college of their choice. The end of affirmative admission programs
forced many such students to attend less selective colleges and others to attend
none at all.

As policy makers shift subsidies away from the lowest-income students, the real
price of public higher education increases for the most needy. As shown in Table 5,
a recent study by the Advisory Committee on Student Financial Assistance (2002)
concluded that today, low-income, college-qualified high school graduates now
face an annual unmet need of $3,800 in college expenses not covered by student
aid. The result is a financial barrier that prevents 48 percent of college-qualified,
low-income high school graduates from attending a four-year college within two
years of graduation. That translates into a national total of more than 400,000
college-qualified students who are unable to attend a four-year college this year.
The committee described the consequences of these trends this way:

TABLE 6

COLLEGE PARTICIPATION RATES FOR DEPENDENT
EIGHTEEN- TO TWENTY-FOUR-YEAR-OLDS, BY
FAMILY INCOME (AVERAGE OF 1996-2000)

Family Income	College Participation Rate (%)
Less than $25,000/year	34.7
$25,000-$50,000/year	53.3
$50,000-$75,000/year	66.3
More than $75,000/year	79.9

SOURCE: Adapted from Mortenson (2001).

> While the considerable investment in need-based student aid over the last three decades has modestly improved postsecondary participation, persistence, and completion rates of low income youth, the shift in policy priorities at all levels away from access has caused a steep rise in unmet need. Thus, low-income participation and persistence rates continue to lag well behind those of middle- and upper-income youth. Each year, yet another cohort of low-income youth—academically prepared to attend postsecondary education full time—confront significant financial barriers making that aspiration nearly impossible. The root cause is a daunting level of unmet need, which has pervasive effects on educational decision-making. (Advisory Committee on Student Financial Assistance 2001, 10)

It should be no surprise, then, that these changes in the nation's pattern of higher education finance have translated into wide differences in the access to college for students from different income levels. As shown in Table 6, college-age students from families with income of more than $50,000 are now more than twice as likely to attend college than students with family incomes less than $25,000. This gap is greater than it was three decades ago and leaves little question that the traditional framework for removing college price barriers is no longer accomplishing its objective.

Looking Forward

The past need not always be a good predictor of the future. Yet, from the perspective of 2003, it is clear that the gap between the earnings of college graduates and nongraduates seems certain to widen. Public college tuition will accelerate as the real value of federal grants continues to decline. These trends alone are a significant cause for concern. But there are two ominous developments on the horizon that threaten to make a very bad situation worse. The creation of a new set of politically popular college finance initiatives in the 1990s and the changing demographics of the college-age population during the next two decades are likely to further constrain access to higher education for low-income and disadvantaged families.

The new generation of student assistance programs

During the 1990s, in the face of rising tuition and the limited availability of direct grants, state and federal policy makers undertook a major effort to overhaul the way the government finances higher education. They did not eliminate the existing programs or even reduce their subsidy levels. Rather, they constructed a new, parallel system of student support based on very different principles. These new programs represent the most fundamental change in the nation's higher education policy since the Great Society. During the next decades, this new generation of programs is poised to replace the traditional framework as the foundation of higher education finance. This will not happen through a direct replacement, but a slower process in which all new funds are directed to the new generation programs and the value of the traditional programs continues to erode.

These new programs are designed to make college more affordable to middle- and upper-income students. This is a noble goal, but in this case, realizing it seems likely to come at the cost of access for the low income. The programs that best exemplify this new approach to college finance are the federal HOPE Scholarship and Lifelong Learning tax credit and the various state-level merit scholarship programs modeled after Georgia's HOPE Scholarship.[2]

The Taxpayer Relief Act of 1997 created a number of new programs designed to help families pay for college. These included the federal HOPE Scholarship, the Lifetime Learning Credit, a student loan interest deduction, and an expansion of education IRAs (Wolanin 2001). The HOPE Scholarship and Lifelong Learning Credit, by far the largest of the initiatives, allow students to obtain credits that reduce their federal tax liability. They are designed to provide relief for those students who are already going to college rather than providing an incentive for others to attend. Also, unlike the need-based federal programs, the HOPE Scholarship and Lifelong Learning Credit were not designed to target benefits to the most needy. Instead,

> these two new programs are targeted toward students and families who generally are not eligible for need based grants but still need financial assistance to meet all of their expenses. The tax credit programs include income caps to prevent upper income students from qualifying for benefits while providing relief to middle income students. But they do relatively little to aid low income students, most of whom have no tax liability, and, therefore will not be eligible for the credit. (Hoblitzell and Smith 2001, 1-2)

These new tax credits involve no direct payment to students. Deductions are made from a family's tax liability, and it is assumed that those dollars saved will be used for educational expenses. Moreover, tax credits do not occur until taxes are filed, up to eighteen months later. Students must pay college costs from other sources and await reimbursement.

These programs carry a substantial cost, but it must be measured in forgone revenues rather than direct expenditures. The estimated cost of these new higher education tax credit programs is $41 billion over their first five years (Kane 1999, 43).

TABLE 7

ESTIMATED VALUE OF HOPE TAX CREDITS
BY TAXABLE INCOME (IN DOLLARS)

Taxable Income	HOPE Tax Credit at Public Four-Year	HOPE Tax Credit at Public Two-Year
10,000	0	0
20,000	0	0
30,000	550	550
40,000	1,500	1,250
50,000	1,500	1,250
60,000	1,500	1,250
70,000	1,500	1,250
80,000	1,500	1,250
90,000	750	625
100,000	0	0

SOURCE: Adapted from Wolanin (2001).

This is already roughly the same size as the Pell Grant program, and it is almost certain to grow during the next decade as more eligible students use the tax credit and institutions begin to set prices so that students can take full advantage of the program benefits.

The vast majority of these tax credits go to middle- and upper-middle-income students. Disadvantaged families who pay little or no tax are less likely to be aware of the tax credit and are more likely to attend lower-priced community colleges. Table 7 shows that the benefits of the tax credit are directed toward families with annual incomes between $40,000 and $80,000. This is far higher than the eligibility for the Pell Grant that usually is awarded to only those with taxable incomes less than $40,000. Thus, the HOPE credit represents a new type of targeting in which the most needy are left out entirely and awards are carefully targeted to the politically powerful middle-income families (Wolanin 2001). The result is a not so subtle redistribution of benefits to families higher up the income ladder. In annual appropriations battles, the funds for Pell Grants must come out of federal revenues that have already been reduced by revenues lost to the HOPE credits. Given these patterns, it seems certain that the federal government will continue to spend more on these tax expenditure programs (as well as the various student loan programs) and that it will have little positive impact on the college access available to disadvantaged students and their families.

State governments also made policy changes in the 1990s to address the problem of rising college costs. The fastest growing state initiatives in this regard are merit scholarships modeled on the popular HOPE Scholarship program in Georgia. These merit programs offer full or partial scholarships to all graduates of a state high school who earn a specified GPA and attend an in-state public college or university. On its face, such programs seem like an ideal way for states to encourage and reward academic achievement without regard for the student's racial or economic status. In practice, however, the early evidence is that like the federal tax credits, these merit aid programs direct a large portion of their funds to middle- and upper-income students. Lower-income students are less likely to meet the minimum GPA, less likely to maintain it through college, and more likely to attend less expensive institutions.

Since 1990, thirteen states have established new merit scholarship programs, and eight more operate programs that have a merit component (National Association of State Scholarship and Grant Programs 2001). While these programs vary in their structure, funding source, and eligibility criteria, all ignore the student's family income. The dollar growth of these merit programs is especially noteworthy.

> At the state level, new grant aid has shifted steadily in favor of merit based aid and against need based aid. Since 1993, funding of merit programs has increased by 336 percent in real dollars. During the same time period, funding for need-based financial aid programs had increased only 88 percent, which reflects the broad political appeal and support for these programs. (Advisory Committee on Student Financial Assistance 2001, 8)

Today, more than $900 million, or 23 percent of total state grants, are awarded as merit scholarships (National Association of State Scholarship and Grant Programs 2001), up from 10 percent in 1991 (National Association of State Scholarship and Grant Programs 1991). While these merit scholarship programs seem to be designed to appeal to all families, only those students who meet the requisite grade or test requirements earn the award. In most programs, the student must also maintain a predetermined GPA to keep the scholarship. In practice, this has meant that a far higher percentage of upper- and middle-income students receive the award. Lower-income and minority students, who often come from lower-performing high schools, receive these scholarships in much smaller percentages.

A study of Florida's Bright Futures merit scholarship program by Donald Heller and Christopher Rasmussen (2001) shows the desperate impact the award structure has by race. The Bright Futures program was created in 1997 and is now the second largest state run merit program. Initial awards cover 75 percent of tuition and fees at an in-state public college or a comparable amount at a private institution. To qualify, students must earn a 1280 on the SAT or 28 on the ACT. Eligible students who have completed seventy-five hours of public service can receive 100 percent of tuition and fees. Students must maintain a 3.0 GPA while in college to retain the award.

In analyzing participation in the program, Heller and Rasmussen (2001) found that whites were much more likely to win a Bright Futures scholarship. As shown in Table 8, in 1998, about 61 percent of Florida's high school graduates were white. But they received more than 76 percent of the scholarships. African Americans and Hispanics constitute 21 and 14 percent of the graduates, respectively. Yet African Americans receive only 7.5 percent of the scholarships while Hispanics receive 10 percent. There is no reason to believe that similar differences in the race and income levels of recipients would not be found in every state merit scholarship program.

TABLE 8

SCHOLARSHIP RATES FOR 1998 FLORIDA HIGH SCHOOL GRADUATES

Race	High School Graduates	Percentage of Total Graduates	Percentage of Award Recipients	Scholarship Rate	Percentage of All Recipients
Native American	196	0.2	55	28.1	0.2
Asian/Pacific Islander	2,695	2.8	1,145	42.5	4.5
African American	21,195	21.7	1,893	8.9	7.5
Hispanic	13,818	14.2	2,527	18.3	10.0
White	56,637	61.1	19,331	32.4	76.8
Multiracial	—	—	67	—	0.3
Other	—	—	157	—	0.6
Total	97,541	100.0	25,175	25.8	100.0

SOURCE: Heller and Rasmussen (2001).

NOTE: While the Florida Postsecondary Planning Commission allows students to indicate race as "other" or "multiracial," the state's Department of Education does not use these categories. Students with missing race data are excluded from the calculations, and the appropriate cells contain dashes.

In his testimony before the Advisory Committee on Student Financial Assistance, Heller (2001b) lamented this trend.

> There is no question that the focus of state scholarship programs is moving away from serving needy students. While the bulk of the state dollars spent for financial aid is still in need-based programs, virtually all of the new initiatives have been geared towards merit scholarship programs. And evidence is becoming available that merit scholarship programs do little to serve needy students, but rather, are addressed at the political interests of middle and upper income students and their families. (P. 3)

The emergence of this new generation of federal and state student aid programs has helped to undermine the goal of equal opportunity that characterized the earlier programs. These are explicitly not need-based programs. Instead, they are designed to make higher education more affordable to middle- and even upper-income families. There is substantial evidence that these programs are creating a future in which government spending on student aid is ever increasing and yet the access available to lower-income students is ever diminishing.

Despite these design problems, the politics of these new generation programs almost guarantees that they will expand. As college prices rise, there will be enormous pressure on policy makers to ensure that the value of the tax credits keeps pace with those increases. Similarly, state merit scholarship programs will cost states more each year as tuition increases, and this will bring enormous pressure to maintain the programs in their present structure. One commentator described it this way:

> The biggest problem with the scholarships may be simply that the public loves them too much. College officials and lawmakers alike complain that the merit programs have

become so popular that they are impossible to change. For some state policy makers, the scholarships are becoming to middle-class parents what Social Security is to an older generation. (Selingo 2001, A20)

Bruce Manlett (cited in Selingo 2001), executive director of the New Mexico Commission on Higher Education, echoed these concerns with New Mexico's merit program when he said, "If it isn't an entitlement yet, in folks' minds then it is getting pretty close" (p. A21). Georgia State Representative Charlie Barnes (cited in Selingo 2001) put it this way: "It's less painful to jump off a cliff than to change HOPE" (p. A20).

As the tax credit programs are more widely understood and institutionalized and the merit scholarship model migrates to other states, their cost will mushroom. It is almost inevitable that they will attract a larger and larger portion of the government spending on higher education which will, in turn, push tuition up and grant support down. Any attempt to restrain the growth of these new generation programs will mobilize their vast numbers of middle-income supporters. Breaking that spiral will prove even more difficult as a generation of middle- and upper-income families build their children's college funds on the assumption that these benefits will always be there.

A new generation of college students

In the 1960s and 1970s, the baby boom generation attended college in remarkably large numbers. The enrollment growth they produced fostered an expansion of our nation's public colleges and universities. New campuses were opened, and expansions took place at virtually all existing campuses. Today, a new tidal wave of college enrollment is on the way. In 1988, there were more than 4 million births in the United States. That was the highest number since 1964. This baby boom echo generation is crowding elementary and secondary schools across the country, and they are on the verge of going to college. Table 9 shows that between 2001 and 2011, projected college enrollment will increase by 15.6 percent to nearly 18 million.

Some of the reasons for this increase are obvious. The National Center for Education Statistics has projected that public high school graduates will increase by more than 10 percent between now and 2011. The college continuation rates of recent high school graduates is now 64 percent, up 59 percent from a decade ago. That means more students are graduating from high school and a higher percentage of them are going on to college. But this is by no means the only factor driving the pending enrollment surge. A recent report by the Educational Testing Service identifies three other factors that seem destined to crowd our colleges in the next decades. First is immigration. Since the 1980s, 800,000 immigrants have come to the United States every year. This has already changed the character of elementary and secondary education. As recently as 1990, about 15 percent of all school-age children were the children of immigrants. By 2010, it will have increased to a remarkable 22 percent. Second, the changing labor market will force many work-

TABLE 9

**PROJECTED ENROLLMENTS IN DEGREE-GRANTING INSTITUTIONS
OF HIGHER EDUCATION, BY ATTENDANCE STATUS
AND AGE, 2001-2011 (IN THOUSANDS)**

	2001	2011	Percentage Change
Full-time			
Younger than 24	9,271	10,979	18.4
24-35	3,086	3,760	21.8
Older than 35	2,943	2,948	0.1
Part-time			
Younger than 24	7,233	8,715	20.4
24-35	1,186	1,425	20.2
Older than 35	616	605	−1.8
Total	15,300	17,689	15.6

SOURCE: Adapted from Carnavale and Fry (2000).

ers to return to school or add to their skills. These new students might be looking for midcareer advancement, looking for education, preparing for a career change, or retooling after a layoff. The federal HOPE and Lifelong Learning tax credits will make returning to college even more affordable to many Americans. Finally, better academic preparation among high school graduates will mean that more of them are prepared for college than at any time in the past. Comparing academic readiness is always difficult. But most empirical evidence suggests that student achievement levels have been rising during the past thirty years. In explaining this trend, Carnevale and Fry (2000) were careful to point out that "rising scores do not necessarily imply that our schools are performing better, however. The apparent rise in cognitive skills could reflect improvements in other areas such as better preparation or higher family income" (p. 15). Regardless of the reason for the improvement, better prepared students will head to college in larger numbers and move toward graduation at higher rates.

These factors leave little doubt that the next decade will bring an influx of new students hoping to enroll in public colleges that are already operating close to capacity. This growth in demand for seats will force institutions to tighten admission requirements to manage enrollments. Selective schools will be forced to be more selective. Students who might have previously been admitted to public flagship universities may now find slots only in community colleges. And those new students with the lowest levels of academic preparation may find themselves shut out of even the open-door institutions.

It may be comforting to think that these new students can always attend low-priced community colleges. There are two limitations to this solution. First, tuition and fees at these institutions are rising as well and, in many states, have already reached the point where they are unaffordable to many needy residents.

TABLE 10
PROJECTED NATIONAL GROWTH IN THE TRADITIONAL
COLLEGE-AGE POPULATION: 2001-2015

	Increase	Percentage Increase
Asian/Pacific Islander	689,554	64
Black	679,496	18
Hispanic	2,076,667	56
Native American	35,233	15
White	776,161	4

SOURCE: Advisory Committee on Student Financial Assistance (2001, p. 6).

Second, many potential four-year graduates stop after they complete their two-year degree.

> Among traditional college age students, only 29 percent of Whites and 27 percent of Hispanics, and 20 percent of African Americans transfer to four year schools after completing two-year programs. This has an important impact on future earnings. While a worker with an associates degree earns 21 percent more than a high school graduate, a bachelors degree commands 31 percent more and a masters degree 35 percent more. (Carnevale and Fry 2000, 32)

Forcing low-income students into community colleges rather than allowing them to begin at a four-year campus dramatically lowers their chances of earning a four-year degree and unnecessarily limits their life chances.

Exacerbating these trends is the fact that states will not have, or will not be willing to spend, the funds to build or expand the physical capacity of their public colleges. The enrollment surges brought on by the GI Bill and the baby boom each produced an enormous expansion in the number of campuses in the country and the capacity of those campuses. In the decades ahead, however, states are simply not going to be able to add capacity in that way. With more students fighting for a fixed number of college seats, competition for admission will increase.

Not only will the next decade bring a growth in the number of students hoping to enter college; the new applicants will be of a much different racial and ethnic mix. Table 10 shows how the number of Asian/Pacific Islanders and Hispanics will increase by 64 and 56 percent, respectively, while the number of black and white students will increase by only 18 and 4 percent. Many of these potential students will be seeking to become the first members of their families to attend college. Those who come from low-income families will face higher tuition, fewer grants, more loans, no preferential admissions policies, and increased competition for admission. And if they look to federal and state policy makers for help, they will find that while there are growing budgets for higher education, more and more of the funds are going to tax credits and merit scholarships.

What Can Be Done?

In the past two decades, higher education's role in promoting equal opportunity has steadily declined. Turning to the future, the trends are even more troubling. Public higher education is rapidly becoming a barrier to equal opportunity in America rather than its promoter. Is there anything that can be done to reverse these trends and improve college opportunities for disadvantaged students? Fortunately, there is substantial evidence that shows what public policies are effective in getting low-income and disadvantaged students into, and through, college. Interestingly, the programs that work best look a great deal like the ones implemented in the 1970s. A larger number of low-income and disadvantaged students are drawn to college as price barriers are removed. Given this, an essential first step in any such public policy is to ensure that low-income and disadvantaged students can afford college. Both low tuition and need-based grants have been shown to be effective in doing this. The growing unmet need faced by these students must be reversed. The problem is not so much insufficient spending; it is that the funds are being spent on programs that help the middle- and upper-income families while ignoring the worsening situation of the most needy. To fix this, all sides must play a role.

State policy makers are not in a position to return to the days of low public college tuition. While this was effective, it is certainly not an efficient way to help those who need it most. Instead, states should continue to let tuitions rise and find ways to ensure that the additional revenue generated by those increases is used to support need-based student aid programs that target the funds to the most needy. This might be through a high tuition/high aid funding strategy. But that is not the only way. Private colleges have long used income-based price discounting to maintain access for low-income students in the face of very high prices. There is no reason that public colleges could not do the same thing. Moving away from ill-advised merit scholarship programs would be an important first step in securing the additional funds.

Federal policy makers have already designed a program that efficiently targets its funds to those who need it most—the Pell Grant. The problem is that Congress has allowed the purchasing power of the Pell Grant to erode and redistributed funds to the student loan and tax credit programs. This can be reversed, but it will take a sustained effort and substantial political will. It requires making access to college for everyone, regardless of income, a priority. It also means sharply reducing the subsidies now given to middle- and upper-income students who would be going to college without the subsidy. Phasing out the badly designed tax credits and reducing eligibility for federal loans would save millions of dollars to rebuild the crumbling Pell program.

Finally, institutions must look to control costs. At least a part of the current price spiral is caused by campus spending patterns. In their search to attract the highest achieving students, many public colleges have been willing to spend money on new facilities and programs that appeal to upper-income tastes. But as net prices rise, the low-income and disadvantaged are left behind. In addition, campuses must work harder to ensure that they are attracting and retaining economically and racially diverse student bodies.

These remedies may seem simplistic—a call for a return to a golden age of lower prices and more generous need-based aid. Certainly, such an approach presents enormous political obstacles. Returning public colleges to their traditional role as engines of equal opportunity requires challenging middle-income families. All levels of government need to redirect their attention and subsidy dollars to those who need them most. In the next century, higher education may well become the only door to the good life for most Americans. As the century begins, however, the trends discussed here are threatening to close that door to many low-income families. Achieving the goal of an equal opportunity society requires policies to be put in place to force it open again.

Notes

1. All dollar figures have been converted to constant 2000 dollars.
2. The Federal HOPE Scholarship was loosely based on the Georgia program. While the federal program operates differently, it retains the same name given to Georgia's program by then governor Zell Miller.

References

Advisory Committee on Student Financial Assistance. 2001. *Access denied: Restoring the nation's commitment to equal educational opportunity*. Washington, DC: Advisory Committee on Student Financial Assistance.

———. 2002. *Empty promises: The myth of college access in America*. Washington, DC: Advisory Committee on Student Financial Assistance.

Carnevale, Anthony, and Richard Fry. 2000. *Crossing the great divide: Can we achieve equity when generation Y goes to college?* Princeton, NJ: Educational Testing Service.

College Board. 2001a. *Trends in college pricing*. Washington, DC: College Board.

——— 2001b. *Trends in student aid*. Washington, DC: College Board.

Fossey, Richard. 1998. Introduction. In *Condemning students to debt: College loans and public policy*, edited by Richard Fossey and Mark Bateman. New York: Teachers College Press.

Gillespie, D., and Nancy Carlson. 1983. *Trends in student aid: 1963-1983*. Washington, DC: College Board.

Gladieux, Lawrence, and Thomas Wolanin. 1976. *Congress and the colleges*. Lexington, MA: Lexington Books.

Hauptman, Arthur. 1990. *The college tuition spiral*. Washington, DC: American Council on Education.

Hearn, J. 1998. The growing loan orientation of federal financial aid policy; A historical perspective. In *Condemning students to debt: College loans and public policy*, edited by Richard Fossey and Mark Bateman, 47-75. New York: Teachers College Press.

Heller, Donald. 1999. The effects of tuition and state financial aid on public college enrollment. *Review of Higher Education* 23 (1): 65-90.

———. 2001a. Trends in the affordability of public colleges and universities: The contradiction of increasing prices and increasing enrollment. In *The states and public higher education policy: Affordability, access, and accountability*, edited by Donald Heller, 11-38. Baltimore: Johns Hopkins University Press.

———. 2001b. Remarks before the Advisory Committee on Student Financial Assistance in response to *Access Denied*, 20 February, Washington, DC.

Heller, Donald, and Christopher Rasmussen. 2001. Merit scholarships: Evidence from two states. Unpublished manuscript.

Hoblitzell, B., and Tiffany Smith. 2001. *Hope works: Student use of education tax credits*. Indianapolis, IN: Lumina Foundation New Agenda Series.

Hurtado, C., and Heather Wathington Cade. 2001. Time for retreat or renewal? Perspectives on the effects of Hopwood on campus. In *The states and public higher education policy: Affordability, access, and accountability*, edited by Donald Heller, 100-20. Baltimore: Johns Hopkins University Press.

Jencks, Christopher. 1971. Social stratification in higher education. In *Financing higher education: Alternatives for the federal government*, edited by M. D. Orwig, 71-115. Iowa City, IA: American College Testing Program.

Kane, Thomas. 1995. Rising public college tuition and college entry: How well do public subsidies promote access to college? Working paper no. 5164, National Bureau of Economic Research.

———. 1998. Taking stock at the end of three decades of federal financial aid. Unpublished manuscript.

———. 1999. *The price of admission: Rethinking how Americans pay for college*. Washington, DC: Brookings Institution.

King, J. 2000. *Status report on the Pell Grant program*. Washington, DC: American Council on Education.

Leslie, L., and Paul Brinkman. 1987. Student price response in higher education. *Journal of Higher Education* 58 (2): 181-204.

Mortenson, T. 2001. College participation by family income, gender, and race/ethnicity for dependent 18-24 year olds: 1996-2000. *Postsecondary Education Opportunity* 144:1.

Mumper, Michael. 1996. *Removing college price barriers: What government has done and why it hasn't worked*. Albany: State University of New York Press.

———. 2001. The paradox of college prices: Five stories with no clear lesson. In *The states and public higher education policy: Affordability, access, and accountability*, edited by Donald Heller, 11-38. Baltimore: Johns Hopkins University Press.

National Association of State Scholarship and Grant Programs. 1991. 21st annual survey report conducted by the National Association of State Scholarship and Grant Programs. Harrisburg: Pennsylvania Higher Education Assistance Agency.

———. 2001. 31st annual survey report conducted by the National Association of State Student and Grant and Aid Programs. Available from http://www.nassgap.org/researchsurveys/31stAnnualSurveyReport.pdf.

National Commission on the Costs of Higher Education. 1999. *Straight talk about college costs and prices*. Washington, DC: American Council on Education.

Orfield, Gary. 1998. Campus restratification and its alternatives. In *Chilling admissions*, edited by Gary Orfield and Edward Miller. Cambridge, MA: Harvard Educational.

Pusser, B. 2001. The contemporary politics of access policy: California after Proposition 209. In *The states and public higher education policy: Affordability, access, and accountability*, edited by Donald Heller, 121-50. Baltimore: Johns Hopkins University Press.

Selingo, J. 2001. Questioning the merit of merit scholarships. *Chronicle of Higher Education*, 19 January, A20-A22.

Sindler, Allan. 1978. *Bakke, DeFunis, and minority admissions*. New York: Longman.

Wolanin, Thomas. 2001. *Rhetoric and reality: Effects and consequences of the HOPE scholarship*. Washington, DC: Institute for Higher Education Policy.

Young, Kenneth, ed. 1974. *Exploring the case for low tuition in public higher education*. Washington, DC: American Association of State Colleges and Universities.

Housing Students: Fraternities and Residential Colleges

By
GUILLERMO DE LOS REYES
and
PAUL RICH

Many American campuses are dominated by their fraternities and sororities. Administrators are caught on the horns of a dilemma because the housing that these Greek letter societies offer would require an enormous capital investment to replace. Moreover, old graduates are often more devoted to their "frat" than to their alma mater. But there seems no end to the difficulties, including hazing, poor study habits, de facto segregation, and alcoholism, attributable to the fraternity system. The historical background dating back to the eighteenth century, the arcane rituals, and the future prospects of one of the most controversial aspects of college and university life are surveyed, along with the arguments of both enemies and friends.

The election of George W. Bush briefly focused attention on his student life at Yale, which included the presidency of the fraternity Delta Kappa Epsilon and membership in the secretive Skull and Bones. College fraternities are the subject of much romantic misinformation, the target of film fun as well as of criticism for low intellectual standards. Bush's fraternities intrigued the press (Fraternity leaders 1996). The problem of college residential facilities is not so interesting to reporters. The membership of Al Gore, his opponent, in Dunster "college" at Harvard, actually Dunster House, or of President Bush in Davenport College, went unremarked.[1]

Guillermo De Los Reyes is completing his Ph.D. at the University of Pennsylvania. He received his bachelor's and master's degrees from the University of the Americas–Puebla, Mexico, where he received the university's highest academic honor, the silver medal for scholarship. He has written and published extensively on civil society and voluntarism.

Paul Rich is the president of the Policy Studies Organization and of Phi Beta Delta, the international honor society. He is the Titular Professor of International Relations and History at the University of the Americas–Puebla, and a visiting fellow at the Hoover Institution at Stanford University. A member of the Lasswell Award Committee of the American Political Science Association, he is the editor of the Lexington Press series on policy research.

DOI: 10.1177/0002716202238570

Although many fraternities and sororities at universities are residential, both Bush and Gore lived in universities where they are not residential[2] and where the majority of the students live in Oxford- and Cambridge-style residential colleges along with some faculty. The problems, such as drinking, associated with Greek fraternity houses are therefore under much closer supervision since professors in the Harvard and Yale residential colleges are literally neighbors:

> Yale is not MIT. MIT students are scattered in different types of housing; the vast majority of Yalies live in the University's residential colleges. MIT's fraternities are the backbone of the Institute's social life and drinking scene; much of Yale's alcohol activity takes place within 500 feet of a college Master. (Altschuler 1997)

Few American universities have the college residential system that Harvard and Yale maintain. Some, like the University of Pennsylvania, are developing it. The cost is high since residential colleges are not just deluxe dormitories. Typically, they have incorporated suites and even houses to attract senior faculty, dining halls, libraries, and sports facilities such as squash courts. Seminars and classes are conducted. The number of undergraduate and graduate students is usually around 300 or 400, and so the socializing is similar to that in a small liberal arts college. Educators find this to be an answer to many problems of university housing but are frustrated by the inability to find the resources to provide such buildings. It was the Edward Harkness gift to Harvard and Yale that made their colleges possible:

> The Harvard House system was established in the 1930s by the university's president, Abbott Lawrence Lowell, with a gift from Edward Harkness, an alumnus of Yale University, Harvard's traditional rival. The irony of a Yale graduate making a large contribution to Harvard was lost on no one at the time, and it has been the source of many an inside joke over the years. Soon after his gift to Harvard, Harkness did in fact make a major contribution to his own alma mater to establish a residential college system at Yale University as well. Although his name is little known outside those two institutions, it can be truly said that the entire residential college movement in the United States owes its existence to the generosity of Edward Harkness. (Samuel Eliot Morison 2002)

The Harvard and Yale colleges benefited from the Great Depression since skilled craftsmen were available at low wages. The result was a great deal of ornamental ironwork, wood carving, and other architectural details that would have been financially prohibitive just a couple of decades later:

> Each House has single, double, and quadruple suites for students; suites for residential and non-residential tutors; a dining hall, common-rooms for students and tutors, and a house library—a feature insisted upon by the masters, which has proved one of the most useful in the plan. Adams has a swimming pool, and several have their own squash courts. (Samuel Eliot Morison 2002)

The nearly 15 million students in higher education institutions in the United States all have to live somewhere. A good many live in facilities owned or sponsored by more than 5,500 fraternity chapters. The Greeks boost that

Seventy-six percent of all Congressmen and Senators belong to a fraternity. Forty of the forty-seven Supreme Court Justices, since 1910, were fraternity men. One hundred of the one hundred fifty-eight Cabinet members, since 1900, were fraternity men. All but two United States Presidents, since fraternities began in 1825, have been Greek. Of the Nation's fifty largest corporations, forty-three are headed by fraternity men. Eighty-five percent of the Fortune 500 Executives belong to a fraternity. (http://web.umr.edu/~betasig/rush/rush.html)

Fraternities and sororities have existed in the United States since the founding of Phi Beta Kappa in the eighteenth century. They can be considered in two major categories: the honor or recognition societies and the so-called Greeks or social fraternities such as the ones Bush joined. This separation into honorary and social and ritualistic societies did not at first exist; for the first part of the nineteenth century, social and academic purposes were common to all.

There is little to Phi Beta Kappa's activities today that suggests its ties with ritual or with purely social affairs. For many years, the honorary fraternities devoted to scholarship, which have done so much to foster intellectual activity on campuses, have contrasted sharply with the social fraternities. Arguably, some of the social fraternities have done as much damage to intellectual life with their *Lord of the Flies* initiations as the honorary fraternities have done in the way of encouragement of scholarship.

The honorary fraternities retain some ritualistic features, but ceremony is not their focus. It is the social fraternities that often have kept elaborate ceremonies, many of which are suggestive of Masonry. The conversion of some of the Greek societies into purely social organizations is sometimes blamed on their acquisition of property in the nineteenth century:

It is tempting to see the arrival of the fraternity chapter house as the closing of the fraternity's intellectual, moral, and cultural "golden age." When a fraternity got together only once a week or so for a chapter meeting, the occasion was extraordinary. Gathering in a rented hall or classroom, fraternity brothers could invest their time together with a sense of special purpose. That was what stimulated the establishment of the Yale societies. Whether they met to discuss a passage from Aristotle's Nicomachean Ethics or Erasmus's Agagia or the Missouri Compromise, they could engage each topic, serious, or not, with undistracted freedom. (Owen 1991, 1-2; cf. Shea 1995, A32)

The rituals also allegedly changed:

Spectacle and mystery, rather than humane learning and ancient wisdom, came to prevail. Primeval myths, powerful in austerity, were distorted into gorgeous but ludicrous pageants. What the Greeks of old may have inspired, latterday vulgarians did their damndest to obscure and confuse. Coffins and hooded robes, burning crosses and stakes, swords and armor, cauldrons and grails, lions and dragons, terrifying oaths and incantations, the regalia of crusaders, cavaliers, feudal knights, holy pilgrims and sainted martyrs, stage machinery and special effects—all these were elevated into the mythical means that transformed lowly pledges into bonded brothers. What light and truth may have failed to accomplish, sensation dared to attempt. (Owen 1991, 1-3)

The initiations as the years passed increasingly involved elaborate staging and were often conducted, and still are, in purpose-built temples.[3] Mock burials and resurrections, labyrinths, and secret sliding panels required purpose-built structures, and these lodge rooms for adolescents were incorporated into buildings that eventually provided not only social facilities but housing. American higher education expanded more rapidly than did its ability to provide accommodation to increasing number of students, and fraternities were glad to fill the gap. They offered a freedom that college-run dormitories did not have, along with a solidarity enforced by handshakes and passwords.

Although the fraternity houses helped solve the accommodation problem, they brought with them other problems. They were difficult to control, and universities found that even the best efforts at regulation did not end the difficulties with drinking and substance abuse, deaths and injuries because of hazing, and low academic performance because of a generally lax atmosphere. The students appreciated the relaxed atmosphere of the fraternities and sororities, with their bendable rules, and have not greeted a recent return to university-controlled housing:

> The new in loco parentis powers of universities, critics argue, are in the hands of political partisans who employ them to transform students according to their own ideological desire, with disastrous consequences for freedom of conscience and independent thought. According to recent polls, most students agree. (Menashi 2000)

A rebuttal has been that the presence of oath-bound secret societies on the campus, some racist or discriminating on religious grounds, is much more damaging than a housing shortage. University fund-raisers complain that donations that should have gone to them are diverted to chapter and national fraternity projects. In recent years, the difficulties have prompted many institutions to seek substitutes:

> These are difficult times for Greeks, whose traditions are being changed by societal forces, both at Cornell and around the country. The rise of lawsuits against the organizations has placed a high cost on the follies of youth. The campus has become much more of an ethnic and cultural mosaic than it was a generation ago, and only a third of students are interested in pledging. In addition, university faculty and administrators nationwide are becoming less sympathetic to the Greek system, and are questioning its relevance to campus life. . . . Dartmouth, that fraternity bastion where the Animal House legend was born, became the latest school to effectively dismantle its Greek system when it announced all houses would have to go co-ed. At Cornell, Greeks are preparing for the move of all freshmen to North Campus over the next few years. This may leave fraternities near West Campus—long considered prime recruiting ground, with its allegedly more social atmosphere—working harder to keep their numbers up to pay bills and to weather attrition. (Conroe 1999)

For the supporters of the Greek system, the efforts of universities to regulate or outlaw fraternities and sororities are the heavy hand of socialism, an invasion of constitutional rights, and a surrender to political correctness. To attract students, the Greeks have struck back with high-speed Internet access, gourmet meals cooked by chefs, and beach volleyball.

For harried administrators, the Greek houses are an ever-present danger to the university's prestige, a time bomb waiting to explode. Fraternities and sororities, however, are not going to cede their ground without a fight. The Center for the Study of the College Fraternity at Indiana University, Bloomington, has developed an impressive list of favorable research publications about campus fraternities. Its sponsors include the American College Personnel Association, Association of Fraternity Advisors, College Fraternity Editors Association, Fraternity Executives Association, National Association of Student Personnel Administrators, North American Interfraternity Conference, National Pan-Hellenic Council, National Panhellenic Conference, and Professional Fraternity Association. Its investigations have highlighted the centrality of the peer group to the educational experience. Its research claims that Greek members are more liable to be involved in university life than non-Greeks, and that Greek alumni are more likely to support their alma mater than non-Greek alumni (http://www.indiana.edu/~cscf/).

Proponents of the residential university have made much, over many years, of the pedagogical value of students and in some cases faculty living together. Certainly, the early history of the university is intertwined with the fortunes and frequently the misadventures of such solutions as nationality housing at Paris and the founding of the first colleges at Oxford and Cambridge. No one residential system has ever emerged as the predominant one. The three major solutions are still in contention—the largely American one of Greek fraternity and sorority houses, the provision of university-sponsored dormitories, and the tradition (strong, e.g., in the British Commonwealth), of residential colleges. There are also arguments for letting students seek out their own accommodations largely without university involvement.

Dr. Robert J. O'Hara, who was a tutor in a Harvard residential college and then started the residential college system at the University of North Carolina at Greensboro, has this to say about the current situation:

> The real crisis in higher education today does not have to do with the curriculum, it has to do with the **poverty of student life**. At many large universities in the last forty years the faculty have given up all responsibility for the lives of students outside the classroom, and the resulting vacuum has been filled by non-academic residence life departments. Out-of-control and endlessly rescrambled dormitories, alcohol abuse and vandalism, social isolation, institutionally-promoted segregation, and a complete lack of connection between the classroom and student life outside the classroom—all these troubles have for a generation plagued institutions that advertise themselves as "caring" and "student-centered."
>
> If universities are to have the **transformative effect** they ought to have on the lives of young people then the faculty must once again become the principal influences on student life throughout the institution, instead of being merely teachers in classrooms. On some campuses this is already beginning to happen through a revival of one of the oldest models of university structure in existence: the **decentralized residential colleges** of Oxford and Cambridge Universities in Great Britain. Within these small collegiate communities—communities that include young and old, rich and poor, student and professor, artist and scientist—a stable, challenging, and diverse social and intellectual environment can be restored. (The collegiate way 2002, emphasis in original)

Perhaps future residential systems will try to include something of the fellow-ship and ritual that has made the Greek system so formidable, along with the responsibility and civility that makes the residential college system seem attractive. The immense variety of residential solutions on campuses guarantees that the experimentation and innovation are not over. With their large financial endow-ments and devoted alumni, the fraternities and sororities are not down for the count, but they are on notice that *Animal House* is not the residential image that universities in the twenty-first century are anxious to project.

Notes

1. Harvard was reluctant when it inaugurated its residential colleges to usurp the traditional name of the university, Harvard College, so the residential colleges are known as houses. Interestingly, Bush's daughter also was a member of Davenport College.

2. There are fraternities at both, although they are outnumbered by unique clubs that have no counter-parts elsewhere. Bemused critics claim that is because Harvard and Yale students are snobbishly unwilling to offer hospitality to visitors from other institutions and hence will not belong to national fraternities. An instance of a secret university society that is neither honorary nor social in the normal sense is Scroll and Key at Yale. The Yale secret societies have a culture of their own, but Scroll and Key too owed something to Phi Beta Kappa (Mack 1978, 4-5). "Though endowed from the beginning with a winning doctrine, the society's real strength has flourished from its ritual, in which it has generally been happy" (Mack 1978, 42).

3. "Young Protestant middle-class men sought their rituals not only in the fraternal and beneficiary lodges, but also in scores of voluntary associations with primarily religious, reform, political, or economic objectives. College fraternities are an obvious example. . . . What is less appreciated is the extent to which founders and members regarded ritual as important in and of itself" (Carnes 1989, 6).

References

Altschuler, David. 1997. Mixing alcohol and Yale's colleges. Available from www.yaleherald.com/archive/ xxiv/ 11.7.97/news/front.html.

Carnes, Mark C. 1989. *Secret ritual and manhood in Victorian America*. New Haven, CT: Yale University Press.

The collegiate way residential colleges and higher education reform. 2002. Available from http:// www.collegiateway.org/.

Conroe, Scott. 1999. Fraternities forever. Available from http://cornell-magazine.cornell.édu/Archive/ May1999/MayFrats.html.

Fraternity leaders . . . 1996. *Chronicle of Higher Education*, 15 November.

Mack, Maynard. 1978. *A history of Scroll and Key, 1841-1942*. New Haven, CT: Scroll and Key.

Menashi, Steven. 2000. James Wright is watching you. Available from http://www.dartreview.com/issues/ 1.24.00/report.html.

Owen, Kent Christopher. 1991. Reflections on the college fraternity and its changing nature. In *Baird's man-ual of American college fraternities*, edited by Jack L. Anson and Robert F. Marchesani Jr. Indianapolis, IN: Baird's Manual Foundation.

Samuel Eliot Morison on the origin of the Harvard houses. 2002. Available from http://www.collegiateway. org/reading/morison-1936.html.

Shea, Christopher. 1995. Hamilton College to bar students from living in fraternities. *Chronicle of Higher Education*, 17 March.

Trends in Postsecondary Science in the United States

By
DAVID D. KUMAR

This article deals with trends in postsecondary science in the United States. Analysis of the literature indicates that science is undergoing a subtle but steady metamorphosis in higher education as follows: a shift in the research paradigm, the rising tide of commercialism, more stringent human subject research regulations, teaching for a scientific workforce, the instructional technology invasion, pressure to participate in teacher education, ethnic and gender inequalities, a proliferation of research disciplines, and fading public influence. It is time that the university science community comes to the realization that science in higher education, like any other human enterprise, is as good as the people who learn, teach, research, and work in it and, most important, that the future of science depends on how it is used for the welfare of all mankind.

Postsecondary science in the United States is the envy of the world. Known for generating countless patents, research contributions, and Nobel prizes, science in American universities enjoys the attention of the international community. It is the dream of many international science and engineering students to earn graduate degrees from U.S. universities. However, science is undergoing a subtle but steady change on the higher education scene. According to Hurd (2000), "the image of today's science is vastly different from that of the past decades. Science and technology as a whole have become integral part[s] of our economic, social, and political life" (p. 282). In this context, an important question is, what is the current trend in science in universities and colleges in the United States?

There are many important issues affecting postsecondary science in the United States. Globalization of the free market since the fall of

David D. Kumar is a professor of science education at Florida Atlantic University. His research involves evaluation and policy in science and technology education. He is a Fellow of the American Institute of Chemists.

NOTE: Thanks to Dr. Penelope Fritzer and Dr. Susanne Lapp at Florida Atlantic University for thoughtful critiques.

DOI: 10.1177/0002716202238571

the Soviet Union brought additional commercialism into university science. Increasing legislative intervention in research is putting public universities and colleges in a precarious position by forcing them to collaborate with for-profit industries. Recent developments in information technology place enormous amounts of scientific information at the click of a mouse. Distance education courses are on the rise. Scientific developments since World War II have paved the way for countless subspecialties. More and more American students are pursuing nonscience majors, creating a shortage of eligible candidates for science-related careers. Ethnic and gender equity issues continue to haunt postsecondary science. These and related issues will be addressed in this article.

Discussion

A search of the literature in science and higher education using the Educational Resource and Information Center (ERIC), the *Chronicle of Higher Education*, and the American Association for the Advancement of Science sites resulted in a sizable number of citations. However, a careful review of the abstracts showed a handful of them relevant to this article. Secondary and other more direct sources of information were also consulted. The analysis of the literature indicates the following trends in science in higher education: a shift in the research paradigm, the rising tide of commercialism, more stringent human subject research regulations, teaching for a scientific workforce, the instructional technology invasion, pressure to participate in science teacher preparation, ethnic and gender inequalities, a proliferation of research disciplines, and fading public influence.

A shift in the research paradigm

A shift in paradigm is evident in science research, and very few university science faculty get to stay exclusively in their ivory towers anymore. A shift from hypothesis-based research to more problem-based, interdisciplinary research addressing societal needs (e.g., sustaining natural resources, protecting the environment, improving human health) is obvious in the contemporary science literature (Hurd 2000; Gibbons et al. 1994). Also, in recent times, the science research orientation has shifted toward the generation of context-specific knowledge (Gibbons et al., 1994). Biological scientists work hand in hand with social scientists to solve pressing social problems of a scientific nature on university campuses. For example, since the 11 September 2001 incident, microbiologists, chemists, political scientists, social scientists, and medical personnel from many universities have been working together to develop response readiness to bioterrorism. Such collaborations help to break down the walls of separation between science and other disciplines.

Community-oriented, problem-based research approaches help to win large federal grants when intense intradisciplinary wars are involved, another example of the shifting paradigm in science research. Recent increases in funding for biomedical and health research make "many physicists and chemists worry that federal funding has boiled down to a popularity contest among disciplines" (Brainard 2001b, A19). Such a contest would effectively mean that research areas that capture public interest and support (e.g., genetic engineering, heart disease, cancer, alternate energy), often housed in nonacademic settings (e.g., national laboratories) and settings in partnerships with industries (e.g., research parks) get access to more tax dollars.

Increasingly, it is becoming difficult for university scientists to refrain from getting involved in pressing societal issues of scientific origin to find practical solutions. However, this paradigm shift seems to have a slowing effect on basic research. According to the U.S. Commission on National Security, "the U.S. in recent years has seriously underfunded basic scientific research" (Ember 2001, 11). The commission went on to state that "if the serious crisis in basic scientific research and education needs is not addressed quickly, the U.S.'s economic and security supremacy will be overtaken in the next 25 years by other countries now making the necessary investments" (Ember 2001, 11). There is also a need for basic research that can form a foundation for future discoveries to improve life on earth. In this regard, science in higher education is in a state of flux.

The rising tide of commercialism

So far, most science policies developed and implemented in the United States have emphasized university research. This emphasis is perhaps the major reason for the strength of U.S. science and technology. Even though universities house the largest number of research scientists, the general public seems reluctant to invest in isolated research at universities, which often ends up in obscure refereed journals gathering dust on library shelves. According to Schmidt (2002), "state lawmakers are no longer willing to support universities' research simply for the sake of expanding knowledge and improving the reputations of higher education institutions" (p. A26). Rather, university research is expected to create new jobs and businesses. With the emphasis on free market enterprises, there is a shift in emphasis from isolated university-based research to more research endeavors involving university-industry partnerships.

In the name of generating revenue for research and technology transfer, partnerships between university science programs and local industries are on the rise (Schmidt 2002; Gibbons et al. 1994). "State lawmakers are sending public universities a clear message. It's time to begin commercializing your discoveries to promote local economic development" (Schmidt 2002, A26). Research parks offer science and technology industries the opportunity for research and development as well as partnerships with universities.

Some of the advantages are that industry partners can interact with the university science and engineering departments and take advantage of their facilities and expertise, have applied research efforts directed at their specific needs, provide opportunities for faculty and students to work for the industry partner, and take advantage of the university's advanced degree programs. Nevertheless, often universities may be forced to compromise their independent scholarly research endeavors for industry-dependent for-profit enterprises. In an ever increasing age of commercialism, "corporate infiltration of science" (a term borrowed from Beder 1998) should make one wonder about the future of scholarship-based university science if married to dollar-motivated industrial science. In addition, as in Canada (Kondro 1997), disputes over intellectual property rights may hamper university-industry relations and interfere with the research productivity of university scientists.

More stringent human subject research regulations

More regulation of human-subject-based research has become the norm in university science. Increasingly, scientists at universities are under pressure to exercise a more humane treatment than in the past of human and animal subjects used in their research. In the words of the National Bioethics Advisory Commission (2001), "research involving human participants has become a vast academic and commercial activity, but this country's system for the protection of human participants has not kept pace with that growth" (p. 1). The need to protect human subjects in research arose from scandals concerning psychological and medical studies on Holocaust victims in World War II Europe, which came to light during the Nuremberg trials, and experiments involving sexually transmitted diseases among socioeconomically disadvantaged minorities in Tuskegee (from the 1930s to 1970s) in the United States.

The National Bioethics Advisory Commission (2001) has several strongly worded recommendations: all researchers who use human subjects should be educated and certified in research ethics (e.g., see the Education for Research Teams by the National Institute of Health at http://cme.nci.nih.gov), all university institutional review boards that review research protocols must be accredited, institutional review boards should closely monitor voluntary informed-consent procedures, and Congress should pass laws to federally regulate all research involving human subjects. Although these recommendations are made with purely good intentions, they add layers of bureaucratic paperwork to university science research. In addition, the commission also recommends that institutional review board membership include at least 50 percent nonscientists. (Current laws mandate that one member be from outside the university community.) This recommendation may not be pleasing to the university science community, as nonscientists serving on institutional review boards may not have the technical competence to evaluate scientific research (Brainard 2001a). These regulations, besides several other ongoing litigations in several universities, gradually will limit the freedom of research so far enjoyed by university science faculty and will affect their capacity to go after research grants since university research scientists have no choice but to comply with the additional bureaucratic regulations concerning human subject research.

Teaching for a scientific workforce

There is a critical need for preparing students for the modern work environment dominated by science and technology (National Research Council 1995; Mervis 1997; Chubin 2000; Steiner 2000; Kumar and Chubin 2000). Unfortunately, "students educated with a narrow disciplinary focus and with solitary learning styles can have difficulties in adjusting to such an environment" (National Research Council 1995, 4). The obvious solution is to move away from narrow subspecialty to more science, technology, and society (STS)–based approaches to graduate as well as undergraduate science education in the United States (Kumar and Chubin 2000).

> We are citizens of an increasingly global society influenced by an explosion of knowledge, advances in technology, and a progressive expansion of the free market. The hybrid character of science, technology, and society mirrors this changing scene. STS [science, technology, and society] draws on a range of intellectual sources: scientists and engineers seeking more than textbook treatments; educators focused on content that matches pedagogy; social scientists who insist that context imbues the science and technology with values, politics, and consequences. (Kumar and Chubin 2000, 2)

How to prepare students for the modern scientific workforce remains a major challenge to universities and colleges.

There are initiatives from federal agencies such as the National Science Foundation, universities, and colleges to broaden the scope of graduate and undergraduate training to address the science and technology needs of the community at large (Mervis 1997; Hackett 2000). STS programs are a part of the curricula in major universities such as Stanford, Harvard, Massachusetts Institute of Technology, Virginia Tech, and Pennsylvania State. In Canada, a public campaign has been launched to encourage students to prepare for the modern workforce. "Learn how to think critically, and you'll be prepared for almost anything—and land a good job besides" (Birchard 2001, A6). This is part of an advertisement by Canadian universities aimed at increasing the pool of available workforce in a science and technology–oriented society and encouraging college students to learn science for the sake of education and not just for preparation for professional careers in medicine and engineering. However, in Steiner's (2000) view, "the skills, attitudes, and values required for science work in industry have not been clearly articulated" (p. 123). More research is required in this area to help universities understand the needs of the science and technology workforce and to develop programs to meet those needs.

Instructional technology invasion

Information technology has opened up opportunities for developing technology-based instructional resources in science. Technology helps to bring attention to science and enables students to engage actively in science learning (Burdge 2001). Increasingly, faculty members in science use technology in their class presentations, post their lecture notes and assignments on the Internet, and develop and offer science courses via distance education technology (Video Conference, WebCT). As technology-based instructional delivery systems are being developed and implemented in higher education, what role faculty plays in instruction remains a critical question.

According to Bork (1999),

> teaching faculty, in the sense that we know them today, may cease to exist, except for in smaller, advanced courses. But their skills and experiences will be important in the design of learning modules. This raises many issues about the structure of universities, such as the need to maintain research. (P. 49)

This so-called attempted takeover of teaching by technology has not spared science, as an increasing number of sophisticated, interactive, online science courses are offered by colleges and universities across the United States. In this context, it seems that the "more intelligent and capable these [instructional technology] systems are, the less need there is for highly educated [science] content experts to serve as mentors" (Croy 2000, 108). To complicate this matter, recent trends in allowing for-profit companies to offer college courses and programs (e.g., teacher education in the state of Florida) challenge the role of the university faculty.

As Bork (cited in Croy 2000) pointed out, "universities will not survive competition with certificate- and degree-granting companies and corporate continuing education programs unless faculty construct high-quality interactive courses" (p. 108). This trend might force "faculty to reallocate their resources and redirect their efforts" (p. 108) to teaching by slowing down research. This is a dilemma facing faculty in all disciplines, especially science, where research is often valued over teaching. Since full-time equivalent (FTE) based on student enrollment plays a major part in the revenues of universities and colleges, it will be practically impossible for universities to "abandon their teaching tasks and support themselves as pure research entities. The only hope of salvation is through increasing the quality of learning by means of technology" (p. 108)

Pressure to participate in science teacher preparation

Recent school reform efforts, especially in science, have asked college of science faculty to work with college of education faculty in the area of teacher preparation (Mervis 2002; Gregorian 2001). Often, traditional undergraduate science courses taught by teaching assistants from non-English-speaking countries and professors dedicated to laboratory research over teaching fail to motivate students to learn science. As Roy (2000) said, "word has gotten around for generations about such science. Two words especially: hard and dry, and not connected to life" (p. 10). There is a trend to increase the required number of science credits required in elementary science teacher education programs. Weiss et al. (2001), in a national survey, found that "very few" elementary teachers have had a major in science and about 56 percent had less than six credit hours of college course work in science. As Tobias (1999) pointed out,

> to the extent that future elementary and middle school teachers are obliged to study science and mathematics in traditional courses, the science faculty is under pressure (1) to reform those courses to reflect "best practice" in pedagogy and (2) to fit them specifically to the needs of future teachers. (P. 27)

This means that a step toward improving the science competency of elementary teachers involves college of education professors working together with college of science professors who teach lower-division science courses, to develop undergraduate science content courses that would help prospective teachers learn meaningful science. An exemplary example of such a collaboration between education and science faculty is evident at Vanderbilt University (see Kumar and Altschuld 2002 for more details). In states like California and Florida, there are directives to require science faculty who teach undergraduate science content courses to prospective teachers to visit and work with local schools.

Ethnic and gender inequalities

Ethnic and gender inequalities are prevalent in science in higher education. According to the Commission on the Advancement of Women and Minorities in Science, Engineering and Technology Development, "the economic stability of the United States depends on the ability of government agencies and educational institutions to integrate women and members of minority groups into science and technology" (Read 2000, 1). Among the 1,637 tenured/tenure track chemistry faculty in the top fifty research universities in the United States, eighteen were black, twenty-two were Hispanic, and three were Native Americans (*AWIS Magazine* cited in Jacobson 2001). However, it is surprising to note there is inequality among minority groups. For example,

> Black scholars have kept pace with their Hispanic peers in the number of chemistry Ph.D.'s earned, yet since 1991, not a single Black scholar has been hired to a tenure-track post at one of the top 50 chemistry departments. In that same period, 12 Hispanic chemists have found jobs in the top departments. (Jacobson 2001, A12)

Similarly, only 6.6 percent of faculty members in physics at the top fifty research universities are women (*Tenure/tenure-track faculty at the "Top 50" physics departments*, n.d.), even though in the past ten years, the percentage of women working in undergraduate science departments has climbed to 40 percent (Research Corporation 2001). This disparity between women scientists in graduate and undergraduate institutions is a serious one. Considering the seriousness of this issue, leaders of nine major research universities have "pledged to smash the glass ceiling that hinders women from advancing at their institutions" and they discussed paying special attention to hiring practices, mentoring junior faculty, and providing possible child care at science meetings (Lawler 2001, 805). (A note must be made that the enrollment of ethnic minority and woman students in science courses and degree programs is not encouraging. See Astin and Astin 1993 for details.) Underrepresentation of ethnic minorities (especially African Americans), and gender inequalities (e.g., low percentage of women in graduate research institutions) are some of the most critical issues increasingly haunting postsecondary science in the twenty-first century.

Proliferation of research disciplines

There are too many subdisciplines in science (Hurd 2000). "As knowledge in a field increases, it is again fractionalized to make it more comprehensible for researchers" (Hurd 2000, 283). Also, almost every scientist in his or her quest to create a niche ends up creating a subdiscipline. For example, traditionally, chemistry has four major divisions—physical chemistry, analytical chemistry, organic chemistry, and inorganic chemistry. Now there are a number of research divisions in chemistry such as bioinorganic chemistry, organometallic chemistry, and biopolymer chemistry. Likewise, biology has now more than 400 research areas. Often, competition for research funds among these subdisciplines may be fierce. There are no real winners in such turf wars, more precisely ego wars, and the university scientific community in general ends up paying the price—poor public image.

Fading public influence

Brainard (2001b) pointed out

an acceleration of a long-term trend. For at least the last 30 years, academic scientists have largely stayed on the sidelines while the White House and Congress have ignored them or made controversial decisions that ran counter to their conclusions. (P. A19)

This "waning influence" in the public arena is due to several factors (Brainard 2001b): university science faculty have taken for granted their public respect over the years and kept themselves from interacting with the general populace, and recent increases in pork barrel funding has let special interest groups and legislatures determine science funding priorities, limiting the influence of academic scientists on funding decisions. The fading influence of university scientists is also felt in the decreasing number of them being appointed to serve on federal commissions and committees involving science and technology.

In dealing with chemists, McCarthy (2001) pointed out,

In the end, innovations derive not only from ideas but also from the interface among various technical subjects and a spectrum of individuals. Are you able to grasp subjects outside of your area of expertise? Can you work effectively with international coworkers . . .? Can you explain to nonscientists what you do for a living? The answer has to be yes. (P. 166)

These questions also apply to science faculty at universities.

Summary

Postsecondary science in the United States is in a state of flux. The national need for a science and technology–literate workforce is demanding undergraduate science teaching to address societal applications and implications of science and technology. An increase in funding opportunities in society-based science research endeavors is configuring science research to societal needs and to an extent causing a paradigm shift from hypothesis-based to problem-based research. Free market interventions entice academic science to seek for-profit ventures. Federal regulation of human subject research adds layers of bureaucracy to an already saturated university research administration. A slowly but steadily encroaching instructional technology is challenging the status quo of college science teaching. University science professors are encouraged and in some instances required to invest time in teacher education and work with local public schools. Ethnic and gender equity issues continue to torment the scientific community in higher education. The rising turf wars among scientific subspecialists for tax dollars along with the somewhat diminishing influence of academic scientists adds more damage to the public image of science.

Science is one of the most interesting areas of inquiry. Postsecondary science is privileged to be at the interface of the academic world and the real world, and the responsibilities of its members are critical. Being slowly evicted from their ivory towers, the university science community must come to grips with the fact that science in higher education, like any other human enterprise, is as good as the people who learn, teach, research, and work in it. Its survival depends on how it is used for the welfare of all mankind. The days of selfish research projects at the expense of taxpayers, boring science lectures, insensitivity to societal needs, and immunity to public scrutiny are numbered. Those who want to believe that postsecondary science is unshakable may be living in the past.

References

Astin, Alexander W., and Helen S. Astin. 1993. *Undergraduate science: The impact of different college environments on the educational pipeline in the sciences*. Los Angeles: Higher Education Research Institute, UCLA.

Beder, Sharon. 1998. The corporate infiltration of science education. *School Science Review* 80 (290): 37-42.

Birchard, K. 2001. Arts and sciences want you! *Chronicle of Higher Education* 47:A6.

Bork, Alfred. 1999. The future of learning: An interview with Alfred Bork. *EDUCAOM Review* 34 (4): 24-27, 48-50.

Brainard, J. 2001a. Panel proposes new guidelines for research with human subjects. *Chronicle of Higher Education* 47:A24.

———. 2001b. The waning influence of scientists on national policy. *Chronicle of Higher Education* 47:A19-A22.

Burdge, J. R. 2001. Using technology to teach chemistry. *Chemical & Engineering News* 79 (13): 192.

Chubin, Daryl E. 2000. Reculturing science: Politics, policy, and promises to keep. In *Science, technology, & society: A sourcebook on research and practice*, edited by D. D. Kumar and D. E. Chubin. New York: Kluwer Academic/Plenum.

Croy, M. J. 2000. Faculty as machine monitors in higher education. *Bulletin of Science, Technology & Society* 20 (2): 106-14.

Ember, L. 2001. Science key to national security. *Chemical & Engineering News* 79 (7): 11.

Gibbons, M., C. Limoges, H. Nowotny, S. Schwartzman, P. Scott, and M. Trow. 1994. *The new production of knowledge*. London: Sage.

Gregorian, Vartan. 2001. Teacher education must become colleges' central preoccupation. *Chronicle of Higher Education* 47 (49): B7-B8.

Hackett, Edward. J. 2000. Trends and opportunities in science and technology studies: A view from the National Science Foundation. In *Science, technology, & society: A sourcebook on research and practice*, edited by David D. Kumar and D. E. Chubin. New York: Kluwer Academic/Plenum.

Hurd, P. D. 2000. Science education for the 21st century. *School Science and Mathematics* 100 (6): 282-88.

Jacobson, J. 2001. Study documents lack of diversity in chemistry departments. *Chronicle of Higher Education* 47:A12.

Kondro, W. 1997. Spat over intellectual property threatens Canadian networks. *Science* 275:922-23.

Kumar, D. D., and James W. Altschuld. 2002. Complementary approaches to evaluating technology in science education. In *Evaluation of science and technology education at the dawn of a new millennium*, edited by J. W. Altschuld and D. D. Kumar. New York: Kluwer Academic/Plenum.

Kumar, D. D., and D. E. Chubin, eds. 2000. *Science, technology, & society: A sourcebook on research and practice*. New York: Kluwer Academic/Plenum.

Lawler, A. 2001. College heads pledge to remove barriers. *Science* 291:806.

McCarthy, T. J. 2001. A window on chemistry. *Chemical & Engineering News* 79 (13):166.

Mervis, J. 1997. NSF revamps graduate training grants. *Science* 275 (5302): 918.

———. 2002. U.S. programs ask faculty to help improve schools. *Science* 295 (5553): 221.

National Bioethics Advisory Commission. 2001. *Ethical and policy issues in research involving human participants*. Bethesda, MD: National Bioethics Advisory Commission.

National Research Council. 1995. *National Science Foundation convocation on undergraduate education*. Arlington, VA: National Research Council Center for Science, Mathematics and Engineering Education and Training.

Read, B. 2000. Colleges should recruit aggressively to diversify ranks of scientists, report says. *Chronicle of Higher Education*. Available from http://chronicle.com/daily/2000/07/2000071402n.htm.

Research Corporation. 2001. *Academic excellence: The sourcebook—A study of the role of research in the natural sciences at undergraduate institutions*. Tucson, AZ: Research Corporation.

Roy, R. 2000. Real science education: Replacing PCBS with s(cience) through STS throughout all levels of K-12 materials as one approach. In *Science, technology, & society: A sourcebook on research and practice*, edited by David D. Kumar and Daryl E. Chubin. New York: Kluwer Academic/Plenum.

Schmidt, P. 2002. States push public universities to commercialize research. *Chronicle of Higher Education* 48:A26.

Steiner, C. J. 2000. Teaching scientists to be incompetent: Educating for industry work. *Bulletin of Science, Technology & Society* 20 (2): 123-32.

Tenure/tenure-track faculty at the "top 50" physics departments by race/ethnicity and by rank (FY 2002). n.d. Available from http://www.awis.org/statistics/PhysicsTable.pdf.

Tobias, S. 1999. Some recent developments in teacher education in mathematics and science. A review and commentary. *Journal of Science Education and Technology* 8 (1): 21-31.

Weiss, I. R., E. R. Banilower, K. C. McMahon, and P. S. Smith. 2001. *A report of the 2000 national survey of science and mathematics education*. Chapel Hill, NC: Horizon Research, Inc.

Information Communication Technology and the New University: A View on eLearning

By
CHEOL H. OH

The purpose of this study is to explore aspects of learning that are perceived as helping foster successful eLearning for all participants separated by time and distance. The author argues that learner-centered practice is necessary to improve the quality of learning on the Internet. To this end, this study deals with the issues of potential or actual students as they relate to eLearning. In two different surveys, most respondents expected information communication technology to play a key role in shaping the form of future education. The surveys also revealed several real or potential problems facing students taking courses on the Internet. Most important, students' needs and demands are perceived as being given a lower priority than other aspects of designing courses on the Internet. In short, client orientation is the key mode of operation in the information age, and a user friendly environment is thus critical to ensuring the success of eLearning.

U ntil recently, information communication technology (ICT) was viewed primarily as a means of helping organizations function more efficiently. However, rapid advances in this area are changing the ways in which government governs, business operates, and individuals conduct their daily lives (see Oh in press). Increasingly, modern society is moving into an era when all practitioners of higher education will have an information technology component. Teachers

Cheol H. Oh is a professor in the Department of Public Administration at Soongsil University, Seoul, Korea. He was director of Government Research and Services at Arkansas State University. He has also served as director of the Information Brokerage Center of the Asia-Pacific Forum for Small Business. He has directed research and written on information utilization and policy making, information communication technology and public policy, and eGovernment. Currently, he is writing a book, Evaluating eGovernment: Logic and Reality, and is involved in projects on information technology, critical theory, and policy analysis as well as on human resource management in the digital era and transaction cost and information process.

NOTE: The author would like to thank Charles Hartwig for helpful and constructive suggestions about making revisions.

DOI: 10.1177/0002716202238572

and trainers are thus faced with a bewildering array of claims about the impact of ICT and the ways in which it can and should be deployed to our advantage or disadvantage (see Ryan et al. 2000).

The availability of ICT can provide opportunities and possibilities as well as threats and dangers to teachers and administrators. Understanding, directing, and managing information-related activities within educational institutions have become critical to the success of education programs and policies. Despite the importance of information-related activities, such activities have not been systematically examined. Students of higher education seem to neglect the meaning of ICT—especially the key questions of why and how ICT affects many activities in higher education.

Most important, ICT significantly changes the way learning is conducted. With the increase of information and communication technologies for instructional design and delivery, technology-supported learning models are eroding the dominance of traditional classroom learning (Barclay 2001). Although unlikely to completely replace face-to-face learning in the classroom, technology-supported learning—also referred to as distance education, distributed education, online learning, or eLearning—was expected to grow at a compound annual rate of more than 50 percent from 1996 through 2002. For example, colleges and universities are the most wired community on the Web, with more than 90 percent of college students accessing the Internet, 52 percent daily. Furthermore, 2.2 million students are expected to enroll in distributed learning courses in 2002, up from 710,000 in 1998. Likewise, approximately 84 percent of four-year colleges are expected to offer distance learning courses in 2002, up from 62 percent in 1998. U.S. colleges and universities offer more than 6,000 accredited courses on the Web (see Merrill Lynch 2000, 169). The expanding use of ICT thus challenges historical classroom and instructional models of how successfully training and learning take place.

Research has often focused on technological aspects of eLearning, with relatively few academic studies written on the human aspects of teaching and learning on the Internet. In general, three areas—program design, effectiveness of technology, and general distance learning research—constitute the majority of articles in mainstream distributed learning research (see Barclay 2001; Cardenas 1998; Johnston and Krauth 1996). For example, an analysis of student achievement relative to traditional classes is the starting point for most studies of educational technology (see Hiltz 1994). Likewise, many evaluation studies have been conducted on Web-based courses, resulting in mixed outcomes (see Bothun and Kevan 1996; Cox 1996). However, student learning experience, or effectiveness of instructional methods, has received relatively minimal attention (for a few examples, see Edelson, Pea, and Gomez 1996; Ruberg, Taylor, and Moore 1996). That is, the instructional design process has the biggest effect on final course/program quality—not the use of technology.

How content is prepared, how and to what extent person-to-person interactions are arranged, and how the whole learning environment matches learner needs should be the important issues for technology-supported learning. Past studies, however, tend to deal with instructors who have experience with synchronous online learning as the major focus of research but do not seriously consider another important player in eLearning, that is, students or potential users (for a similar view, see Biggs 1987; Norman and Spohrer 1996). Past studies thus pay little attention to real or potential users of distance education; rather, they focus on providers or managers (i.e., instructors or administrators). As a result, users' needs and demands have been often neglected in studying the designing and implementing of eLearning, while administrators' or instructors' demands or assumptions have been the major source of investigation.

One reason for this line of research may be that administrators of higher education tend to view eLearning not from students' perspectives, but from an internal organizational or technological perspective (see Rapp and Poertner 1992). For example, people say that investment in technology is the key to education quality as we enter the new millennium (see Fiske and Hammond 1997; Roth and Sanders 1996). Yet it is also said that students choosing online courses are not getting what they pay for (see Guernsey 1998; Mingle and Gold 1996). To make the best of technology-supported education, administrators, instructors, and students should be all considered as an integral part of the learning process. As a way of keeping our understanding of eLearning balanced, this study focuses on issues of potential or actual students as they relate to eLearning. Any university or college that does not provide the levels of service that students or potential learners expect will suffer from students' poor attitude toward that institution. This will gradually undermine the very foundation of the institution.

As a way of shifting our attention from providers' to learners' perspectives, we need many preliminary studies. Especially, we need to base our eLearning programs on reality by conducting periodic examination of students' (or users') needs and attitudes associated with eLearning. From this factual understanding, we are expected to propose suggestions, if any, for improving eLearning. That is, learner-centered practice is required to improve the quality of learning on the Internet (see Barclay 2001). This study will explore aspects of learning that are perceived to help foster successful eLearning for all participants (e.g., instructors and students) separated by time and distance. Simply put, the purpose of this study is to understand eLearning in the context of higher education as it relates to potential or actual learners' needs.

There are a lot of important questions related to technology-based learning. This study focuses on the following: What are the current human and social learning issues associated with the use of ICT for eLearning? What are the possible ways to resolve problems, if any? Since this study does not intend to make an in-depth analytical examination of a specific segment of eLearning, it is rather descriptive and general in its presentation and content. To this end, this study first briefly touches on the meaning of the digital ear for higher education by examining the potential of cyberspace. Second, some major issues associated with distance teaching and learning will be explored. This will be followed by a cursory review on the client (i.e., learner)-centered approach and its implications for distance learning.

Third, two surveys on both students' and adults' feeling and awareness of eLearning are presented and discussed. Finally, a set of suggestions for helping improve the quality of eLearning will be made.

One caveat is that the use of survey data about Korean cases may raise a question about the generalizability of the arguments made in this article. Readers are thus advised to be cautious in interpreting and applying the findings and discussions in other contexts.

A Changing Environment and Higher Education: The Emergence of eLearning

The digital era and its meaning for education

The world is changing. It is changing so fast that it is even almost impossible to predict what it will look like in the near future. Most important, this change is fundamental in its nature and scope and is driven by ICT. We may understand the meaning of such changes from a variety of perspectives. Especially from a social development perspective, such a change can be understood as a fundamental shift from the industrial society to a newly forming society, that is, the knowledge-based information society. Under the circumstances, the environment of higher education can be characterized as uncertainty, discontinuity, and turbulence (for more detail, see Oh 2001).

The use of ICT has the potential to radically alter our very social structure and mode of operation, and this social change will in turn force our educational institutions to react and change as well. So far, the central question a large number of academic universities and colleges seem to be, according to Postman (1992), asking themselves with regard to the impact of ICT is, "How do we integrate this new technology into the way we already do things?" This question is, however, misleading. Rather, the central question surrounding the adoption of new technology should be something more like, How does the very nature of new ICT force us to change? It is because any new technology carries along with it its own rules for operation and that these rules alter what has gone before (Kroeker 2000, 143). In this sense, any new technology is a double-edged sword, creating opportunities for growth in new directions (for a few examples of an optimistic view, see Denning 1997; van Dusen 1997), while at the same time destroying, or at least causing the abandonment or rethinking of, an old way of doing things (for a similar view, see Garson 2000).

With respect to the role of technology in higher education, Shields (2000, 162) broke down the sociotechnological movements into three stages (or acts). The first stage, the first personal computing movement of the early to mid-1980s, spawned the second, the networking movement of the late 1980s to mid-1990s; the latter, in turn, envisions the rise of virtual universities during the 2000s (also see Rosenberg 2001, 20-28; Kearsley 2000, 2-12). What is interesting about the third movement is that some of the advocates of virtual education believe that the traditional model of campus-based teaching, learning, and scholarship must adapt to new technological realities (e.g., the Internet, digital libraries, broadband multimedia capabilities, etc.) or die. Proponents of distance learning believe that an ICT-driven revolution can make higher education more affordable and more accessible. For example, the university will be, according to Wulf (1995, 50), no longer defined in terms of a place but rather with a set of functions distributed in space and possibly in time. Remote scholarship is the direct analog of telecommuting in the business world.

On the other hand, while we recognize the tremendous potential of ICT for education, it can be and sometimes is overstated. The investment in ICT is based on the assumption that it will change and improve teaching and learning. Holmberg (1998), however, raised a fundamental question about the real effect of ICT on education. He argued that the developments of the past couple of decades may not represent such a revolution of methods and media that we have reason to describe their result as a paradigm shift. It is true that we need to disentangle the hyperbole from reality. Despite pros and cons, we cannot deny that we are already seeing a strong commitment to the introduction and application of ICT into teaching and learning at all levels.

In the middle of perplexing and contested arguments, just what will become of universities and colleges is not clear yet, as it often takes many years for an influential technology to come into its full stride. Certainly, students and the general public are already expecting many different things from institutions of higher education, chief among them increased access to learning, not to mention information of all kinds.

What the rise of the Internet (or ICT in general) means for learning in higher education is that it is now presented with hardware and/or software tools that can allow institutions of higher education to solve some of the limitations associated with the lack of linkage between instructors and learners separated by time and place. As for the impact of ICT on education, Tony Blair (cited in Ryan et al. 2000), the U.K. prime minister, once said,

> Technology has revolutionized the way we work and is now set to transform education. Children cannot be effective in tomorrow's world if they are trained in yesterday's skills. Nor should teachers be denied the tools that other professionals take for granted. (P. 8)

More specifically, ICT represented by the Internet or the World Wide Web enables institutions of higher education to overcome traditional in-house (or face-to-face) learning's lack of features for networking or linkages as well as provide the ability to create a virtual site (or cyberspace) where they can create an electronic presence that participants in the learning process can easily interact with without actual face-to-face contacts.

Simply put, ICT offers the means to deliver courses to new and different audiences who may be dispersed geographically and who may not have had the opportunity to study in a conventional setting (see Ryan et al. 2000, chaps. 9-10). But ICT's influence is not limited to the teaching and learning process. It also significantly affects staff and institutions of higher education themselves. For example, some universities are seeking to compete directly in the global market, perhaps through strategic alliances with other like-minded institutions somewhere in Asia or Europe. This study only touches on the learning aspect of ICT's influence on higher education.

An understanding of eLearning

Universities have an increasing interest in making available their resources to a wider audience than the traditional one that comes to live on or near the campus. This interest is driven in part by the need for funding, but it also carries with it possibilities for the more effective education of a larger and more dispersed number of students (Taylor 2000). It is ICT, more specifically the Internet, that makes all these expectations and guesses possible.

Technological developments make the whole world online accessible on a PC or a notebook. This means that time and space are decreasingly limiting and are, thus, becoming irrelevant factors. Virtual reality and ICT offer numerous possibilities to create, construct, and simulate realities (see Slevin 2000, chaps. 1-5). Consequently, time as a relevant factor in the processes of organizations becomes compressed. Likewise, organizational boundaries lose their traditional meanings. Organizations including institutions of higher education become virtual within themselves, and thus, boundaries will be trespassed. The spatial location of activities becomes irrelevant (for an example of organizational transformation, see Keider 1995; Lucas 1998). Among the more specific implications of ICT for education, the following are worth noting:

- integration of technologies and media makes distance in space and time increasingly relative; long distance "on-line" connections are possible, so that simultaneity and nearness are less and less bound by limits;
- consequently, the experience of a limited territory in which one can act and communicate becomes less relevant;
- communication relations and actions can thus be organized on the basis of the desired level of scale and scope, the desired participation and the desired information provision. (Frissen 1996, 276)

Likewise, the mode of education consequently changes because it has always been based on limitations in time and space. The technological developments thus seem to lead to deterritorialization (Frissen 1998, 37) because neither time nor space poses significant constraints. Higher education cannot ignore this change.

In this volatile climate, institutions of higher education are dramatically increasing their reliance on ICT to support diverse learning environment, cost-effectiveness, and productivity goals for education and training. At the center of this changing environment lies distance teaching and learning. The term "distance education" became popular when technology was added to correspondence courses. It implies a geographical or temporal separation between teacher/instructor and student for most of the instruction.

According to the Center for Adult Learning and Education Credentials of the American Council on Education (American Council on Education 1996, cited in Barclay 2001, 12), distance learning is defined as a system and a process that connects learners with distributed learning resources, for example, the Internet, computer-based training, satellites, virtual reality, or teleconferencing. On the other hand, the National Council for Open and Distance Education (2002) of Australia defines distance learning as an integrated set of strategies to promote student-centered learning through a combination of specially designed learning resources and inter-active media and technology. To be more specific, distance learning (or learning on the Internet, eLearning, Web-based learning, distributed education) in this article is understood as a just-in-time learning process in which the right people and/or organization acquires the right amount of contents at the right time at the right place through the use of Internet technologies, thus helping people enhance knowledge and performance.

Despite a wide variety of definitions, all eLearning is characterized by (1) sepa-ration of time and/or place between instructor and learner, among learners, or between learners and learning resources; (2) interaction between instructor and learner, among learners or learners and learning resources conducted through one or more media, especially through the use of ICT; and (3) a teaching and learning process not limited by time and/or place (see Cardenas 1998; Holmberg 1998; Keegan 1986; Porter 1997). More specifically, in comparison with traditional class-room learning, eLearning focuses on the operation of homepages for different lev-els (or steps) of learning programs, paperless classrooms, emphasizing problem-solving strategies, building eLearning communities, and connecting before and after learning. Consequently, eLearning is the adaptation process of education institutions to the changing environment, resulting in the swift move from in-house learning to learning on the Web (for more detail about technical aspects of eLearning, see Rosenberg 2001, chap. 6).

Major Issues of eLearning and a Client-Centered Approach

A glimpse at major issues

Recent development in ICT (e.g., network technology, digital cable, the Internet, etc.) has provided multiple options for live and remote distance educa-tion. Like the analogy of eGovernment (for a brief review, see CNN.com 2000; G-7 government on-line project 1996; Kauver 1998; Oh 2001; Zittel 2000), the new technologies expect to offer the promise of anytime, anywhere, and anyway teach-ing and learning intended to produce greater learning effectiveness, improved cli-ent (or learner)-centered approaches, and better quality of interaction. But whether the promise has been achieved is the question.

Failures of eLearning to get any attention in a university are often related to the quality of their plans for eLearning. In the past, universities and colleges have tried several approaches to build enthusiasm and support for learning. This has been most notable when they seek to expand their influence. The impact or influence, however, has often not been up to their expectations. This led scholars and practitioners of higher education to wonder what might be the problems to tackle. For example, Cravener (1999) has found that while distributed education increases access to education, one can easily find decreases in instructional quality brought about by increased faculty workload, problems of adapting to technology, difficulties with online course management, and other related matter. These issues need further examination in future research studies.

More specifically, the quality of online education, for instance, has emerged as a major topic for distance learning conferences. Hillesheim (1998), for example, distinguished three dimensions to quality standards: (1) organizational criteria (e.g., leadership, record keeping, etc.), (2) technological criteria (e.g., student support through process teams), and (3) instructional criteria (e.g., relationship between students and faculty, faculty and student empowerment). Achievement of goals in the first and second dimensions is necessary but not sufficient for obtaining quality education in eLearning. Much more depends on the third dimension such as establishment of authentic relationships (for a detailed discussion on quality education and eLearning, see Garson 2000).

Likewise, one of the major concerns for most students is to understand computers and other technological systems well enough to use them effectively. This seems to be a more serious problem for older students than for young children. Clearly, the computer proficiency of real and prospective students affects their success in school. The question is, then, How much attention should be given to teaching computer skills and investments in building information infrastructure (see Kearsley 2000, 71-72; Rosenberg 2001, chap. 6)?

In addition, what is most distinctive about eLearning is that it provides the learner with a great deal of autonomy—the choice of when, where, and how to learn. This is part of the student-centered understanding of distributed education. However, this autonomy also brings with it responsibility. Students must possess initiative and self-discipline to study and complete assignments. Otherwise, online courses would experience high attrition and dropout rates. Similarly, online education is as much a social activity as an individual one. Thus, social skills are another important aspect of interacting via computer networks, especially when collaboration is involved (Kearsley 2000, 65). Students and instructors need to be sensitive to this matter and think about how to reduce the difficulties possibly brought about by the lack of social skills early in the course. Furthermore, extended interaction via computer networks can develop its own patterns of social behavior in cyberspace. This also deserves special attention (see Rosenberg 1997; Young 1998).

The issues briefly mentioned above are important for the successful operation of eLearning. But placing students at the center of designing eLearning is as important or, perhaps, more important. As organizations including educational institutions move to ICT-based operations, those operations should be user friendly. While the precise meaning of this concept is not well specified, institutions of higher education should certainly pursue strategies that aim to maximize the ease of use of ICT-based teaching and learning and to limit the negative impacts on participants in the learning process that are caused by ICT.

Universities and colleges need to see the student as the client. The client is the person who pays for the learning. Therefore, serving clients should be based on an understanding of what they need and want. This fact-based understanding can lead universities and colleges to build more effective strategies. It can, subsequently, help them articulate plans on eLearning in a way that is meaningful to all stakeholders, particularly real or prospective students. With any new revolution, the challenge is not to throw out "the baby with the bathwater" (Rosenberg 2001, 308). In a technological world, we must continue to preserve the people-centric nature of learning. If so, why and how can we see students as clients?

A view of the client-centered approach

One common characteristic of online education is that it is student centered. Although teachers and faculty still play a key role in creating and organizing classes, students largely determine its direction by virtue of their participation and activities. Moreover, we cannot deny that the popularity of online education at universities and colleges is in part due to the presence of mature, motivated students capable of the independent study required in many online courses (Kearsley 2000, 16). It is thus natural and, perhaps, a must to intentionally pay attention to what students expect from online education and to adjust, if necessary, the overall design of eLearning.

The client-centered approach is one prominent perspective in the field of social work (see Rapp and Poertner 1992), and it is also related to a key public administration theme—client-oriented service delivery (see Heeks 1999; Kearney and Berman 1999; Kettl 1994). According to this approach, eLearning is said to rest on the assumption that the principal justification for learning on the Internet is to improve the quality of education for students. Therefore, separation between students and instructors can cause the results of eLearning to be less than desired.

The centerpiece of eLearning is the benefits accrued by students as a result of taking courses on the Internet. This benefit may act as the bottom line of universities and colleges in much the same way profit serves business. As Farrington (1999) observed, the realities of the University of Phoenix model, its customer orientation, are central to the competitive strategy of purveyors of online education, although critics resist the passing of the academic community of scholars to the academic marketplace of customers. To paraphrase Etzioni (1964), the purpose of eLearning is to achieve the desired and intended ends. These ends should be in large measure to provide some form of benefits (e.g., affective changes, learning, behavioral changes, etc.) for the students taking courses on the Internet.

The current practice of eLearning, however, seems to be dominated by means, not ends. The most common form of eLearning begins with "to provide," "to teach," or "to establish" (Rapp and Poertner 1992, 8). Consequently, this can produce acute goal displacement, whereby the means of eLearning becomes its end. Simply put, technology can prevail over the quality of education or the benefit students may get from distributed education (also see Barclay 2001; Eddy et al. 1997). Likewise, instructors can engage in reactive teaching practice, premature embracing of new technology that consumes large amounts of resources before they are discarded.

Most important, we cannot ignore even the slightest possibility that students seeking help, direction, or relief can experience processes or protocols unresponsive to their problems. Even though the means for online interaction and participation are provided (e.g., e-mail, real-time conferencing, Multi-User Dungeon, etc.) (for more detail, see Kearsley 2000, chap. 3; Porter 1997, chaps. 6-8; Rosenberg 2001, chap. 7), students still need encouragement or motivation to get involved. Narrowing the spatial gap between students and instructors via the Internet can quickly create cyberdistance rather than building a virtual community, unless students are given more consideration in planning on eLearning (e.g., designing courses, content development, monitoring, assessment, etc.). The challenge of student (or client)-centered eLearning is therefore to make the student's benefit the centerpiece of education.

The vision of client-centered eLearning briefly described above may be only an ideal or in a sense premature. Yet what we need is to demonstrate that the ideal can be created out of current realities. In this regard, a set of guidelines or principles is helpful as the foundation required to create the ideal. Rapp and Poertner (1992, 16-26) proposed four principles of the client-centered approach in social administration: venerating clients, creating and maintaining focus, demonstrating a healthy disrespect for the impossible, and learning for a living. What is particularly interesting is the principle of venerating the people called clients.

According to Rapp and Poertner (1992, 17), managers whose programs are effective for those they serve are managers who create helping environments wherein consumers are seen and treated humanely—as people and less like patients. Likewise, instructors whose courses on the Internet show effective results for students are those who create helping environments wherein students are seen as a critical factor in the success of the courses. Central to student-centered eLearning is the view that students have strengths and change over time. This belief is the core of so-called lifelong education as it relates to eLearning. From such a perspective, individual students are valued for their ability to adapt and continue to learn.

How do instructors view students as having abilities? There are a few things worth considering. First, instructors need to know the students who take courses on the Internet—their motives, expectations, purposes, backgrounds, and so forth. Second, instructors need to promote the idea that students are major players. This point is particularly meaningful in the sense that eLearning courses often face multiple constituencies, that is, students with different histories and backgrounds. Third, instructors need to have a student advocacy perspective toward their own jobs. The provision of quality education is the central purpose of eLearning, but students are only one of many major participants making demands on the learning process. When facing this situation, instructors should listen to students' voices.

An Understanding of Learner as Client: A Look at the Reality

The technological possibilities offered by the rapid development of ICT should not compromise one of the fundamental aims of higher education institutions: to offer high-quality teaching and learning opportunities to students. Putting a course on the Web does not in itself guarantee the quality of teaching and learning. It may help students access learning opportunities, but it is unlikely to prove acceptable unless learning on the Web is carefully and appropriately designed. One critical factor for designing appropriate student-centered eLearning is to understand what students expect from it. This is what the client (or student)-oriented approach argues for. In this regard, two surveys on both students' and general adults' needs and awareness of eLearning in Korea are worth noting and will be briefly presented below.

A survey on students' attitude toward distance learning or eLearning

A survey was conducted to examine some critical aspects of eLearning (e.g., university management, teaching and learning, infrastructure, etc.). The survey was conducted on the Internet from 16 June through 30 June 2001. It was administered to samples of students who enrolled in nine distance learning universities in Korea. Of the samples, 166 students actually responded to the questions on the Web (for more detail, see http://www.freechal.com/cyberok).

The survey consists of fifty-seven questions of interest associated with the overall picture of eLearning. Among them, twenty questions are about teaching and learning, while ten questions are about students themselves. As mentioned earlier, this study touches on only how potential or actual customers of distance learning understand and perceive eLearning. The following is a brief summary of the result about teaching and learning as well as students' perceptions (for more detail, see the Korean Ministry of Education and Human Resources 2001, 104-13).

Table 1 shows respondents' satisfaction about teaching on the Internet. Overall, satisfaction about preparation for teaching according to the syllabus (4.0 on a 5-point scale) is larger than respondents' satisfaction about motivating students to learn, including appropriate teaching methods (3.4 on a 5-point scale). This indicates that distance learning in higher education institutions needs to improve ped-

TABLE 1
SATISFACTION WITH ELEARNING AND INTERACTIONS

	Course Preparation	Course Management
Satisfaction with eLearning		
Question	Is course syllabus provided before the beginning of course?	Are teaching methods effective?
	Is course syllabus well written and information rich?	Does the instructor motivate you to study?
		Is the course boring?
Degree of satisfaction	4.0	3.4
	Between Instructor and Students	Between Students and Students
Satisfaction with interactions		
Question	Have you talked to instructors a lot?	Have you talked to other students a lot?
Degree of satisfaction	3.3	3.5

agogical skills and methods for more effective education delivery. This finding confirms Lookatch's (1995, 11) argument that it is content and instructional strategies that motivate the learner. Another related question is how much respondents are satisfied with the frequency of interaction between students and teachers or other students. Interestingly, satisfaction about the frequency between teachers and students (3.3/5.0) is slightly lower than that about interaction between students and other students (3.5/5.0). This finding can be partially explained by the fact that most of the interaction between teachers and students is made through questions and answers. In this case, teaching assistants are in large measure in charge of responding to students' inquiries unless they are really too tricky and complex for teaching assistants to answer.

As illustrated in Table 2, students who took courses on the Internet are, however, somewhat satisfied with the quality and quantity of teaching material. Although students tend to think that more effective teaching skills are needed for motivating themselves, they seem to positively evaluate what and how much is taught. This finding directly tackles the very nature of distance learning. The ability to make your course available to anyone appears to offer an attractive way of reaching increasingly diverse groups of potential students, regardless of location. But having the potential to deliver courses is not in itself sufficient (Ryan et al. 2000). Technology says nothing about their quality in terms of the suitability of their content or pedagogical effectiveness. Therefore, the adoption of ICT in higher education does not automatically lead to improving students' learning. It needs strategies

TABLE 2

SATISFACTION WITH THE CONTENT OF TEACHING

	How Much Is Taught (quantity)?	What Is Taught (quality)?
Question	Are teaching materials sufficiently provided?	Is the content of teaching appropriate?
	Is the amount of teaching appropriate?	Are teaching materials relevant in helping you understand the course?
Degree of satisfaction	3.3	3.5

TABLE 3

SATISFACTION WITH WHAT STUDENTS LEARN

	Knowledge and Skill Acquired	Improvement of Problem-Solving Ability	Improvement of Computer Literacy	Improvement of Self-Learning Ability
Positive answers (%)	63	55	65	55
Degree of satisfaction	3.8	3.6	3.6	3.4

relevant to the changing context. What, then, matters is to understand what students expect from learning on the Web before more detailed strategies are made. The findings of this study expect to provide a case for such fact-based understanding.

As for what students think they learn from the courses on the Web, they show somewhat positive evaluations. As shown in Table 3, students are satisfied with acquiring and/or improving substantive knowledge, practical problem-solving capacity, the capability to search and use the Internet, and the ability to study on one's own. This finding is at least a good indicator that distance learning is making things happen, though the result is not up to our full expectations. This tendency naturally leads to students' overall evaluation of learning on the Web. That is, about 70 percent of the students think that eLearning is beneficial and productive. Likewise, 61 percent of the students also think that taking courses on the Internet also helped them improve communication skills on the Web. This finding is similar to other studies (Bothun and Kevan 1996; Cox 1996; Hiltz 1994), implying that despite the up and down sides of eLearning, students generally show a positive evaluation of the potential of eLearning as a new learning mechanism. Once again, the bottom line concern is not whether eLearning is productive or beneficial vis-à-vis classroom learning but how we can make eLearning helpful and effective.

TABLE 4
AWARENESS OF ELEARNING (OVERALL AND BY EDUCATION)

	Frequency	Percentage
Overall		
Yes	937	93.2
No	68	6.8
Total	1,005	100.0

	Yes		No		Total	
Education	Frequency	Percentage	Frequency	Percentage	Frequency	Percentage
By education						
Middle school	39	84.8	7	15.2	46	100.0
High school	226	90.8	23	9.2	249	100.0
College/university	598	94.2	37	5.8	635	100.0
Graduate school	74	98.7	1	1.3	75	100.0

$\chi^2 = 12.015$, $df = 3$, $p < .01$.

A survey on the general public's perception/awareness of Web-based teaching and learning

A survey was conducted during August 2001 to see how adults between ages twenty and fifty perceive distance learning. This was a telephone survey with 1,005 adults selected from all adults in Korea through a clustering sampling method. Respondents were, for example, asked about their perception/awareness of Web-based education, their interest/preference to take courses on the Internet, needs of eLearning, prospect for distance learning, and so forth (for complete detail, see Korea Research Institute for Vocational Education and Training 2001). As in the case of the students' survey mentioned above, only those parts of the survey related to the theme of this article will be discussed below.

Overall, this analysis of Korean adults' perception/awareness of distance learning shows that Korean adults are generally well aware of distance learning and express both high expectations of it and a strong willingness to take part in it. At the same time, most individual respondents have optimistic prospects for the future of Web-based teaching and learning and expect it to expand steadily in the future.

As illustrated in Table 4, most of the respondents are aware of Internet-based learning. Furthermore, this finding holds irrespective of age, location, and sex. This indicates that Web-based learning has now become a well-known phenomenon in Korea no matter how old one is, where one lives, and whether one is male or female. Interestingly, this so-called universal phenomenon, however, varies with education. That is, the more one is educated, the more one is aware of distance learning. Noteworthy is the fact that those whose education is less than middle school turn out to compose the group that needs more assistance and attention.

TABLE 5
REASONS FOR TAKING WEB-BASED COURSES

	Frequency	Percentage
Time flexibility	634	69.4
Place flexibility	204	22.3
Low cost	48	5.3
Personal curiosity	27	3.0
Total	913	100.0

The high overall awareness of distance learning is also reflected in a high willingness to take part in distance learning. That is, most of the respondents say very positively that they would take courses on the Internet (see Table 4). This finding does not vary across age, location, and sex.

About 58 percent of the respondents say yes to the question of whether they can obtain a degree (e.g., B.A.) by taking courses on the Internet. On the other hand, however, the rest of the respondents (42 percent) seem to know little about the possibility that they can get a degree from Web-based learning programs. This finding indicates that although people (i.e., Korean adults) are aware of the fact that teaching and learning are available on the Internet, they are relatively little aware of benefits such as obtaining degrees by taking courses on the Web. More aggressive public relations efforts are thus needed to get the full facts about eLearning known to the general public.

As for the reason they want to take eLearning, 69.4 percent of the respondents say they would like to take distance learning because they can take courses when they want. Of the respondents, 22.3 percent say so because they can take courses where they want. Contrary to some expectations, only 5.3 percent and 3.0 percent go for low tuition and curiosity (see Table 5). This finding clearly shows the very nature of Web-based learning. That is, the functional convenience is the major reason people prefer eLearning over traditional classroom learning (see Porter 1997). Interestingly, tuition seems not to be the main factor for considering distance learning. This is somewhat contrary to the general argument that low tuition of distance learning can induce more people to take courses on the Internet (see Garson 2000).

Another related question is about the reasons, if any, why respondents do not want to take distance courses. As illustrated in Table 6, 40.2 percent and 37 percent of the respondents suggest that distance learning is not a big help and they are not familiar with the way teaching and learning take place on the Internet. In addition, lack of knowledge about how to use computers and how to enroll in courses of distance learning are also nonnegligible factors. These findings suggest that we need to emphasize computer and the Internet literacy as the sufficient condition for successful eLearning (also see Rosenberg 2001), and more investments are thus needed to improve individual capability to use computers and gain access to the Internet.

TABLE 6
REASONS FOR NOT TAKING WEB-BASED COURSES

	Frequently	Percentage
Little help for learning	37	40.2
Lack of computer literacy	11	12.0
No knowledge about taking courses on the Internet	10	10.9
Unfamiliar with eLearning	34	37.0
Total	92	100.0

Concluding Remarks and Suggestions

As with many of the policies and standard operating procedures in public administration, most core elements of higher education, I believe, remain relatively stable over the medium run, despite other changes and revolutions in structures and processes of universities and colleges. However, the activities of teaching and learning are powerfully driven by ICT. Moreover, students increasingly rely on ICT to gather information, to complete their homework, and to communicate with others. From the management perspective, complex challenges are generated in supporting students who must cope with this more information-rich and depersonalized virtual learning environment.

Given the remarkable advances in ICT, the importance to higher education of technological resources has increased dramatically, relative to the importance of traditional resources (e.g., manual operations or classroom teaching, etc). Yet, even if a truly virtual university were to emerge, the management of teaching and learning will remain a critical strategic component of educational success.

It is less clear whether the practice of eLearning can evolve in a manner ensuring that the primacy of the quality of education will be either improved or at least sustained. In the surveys briefly mentioned above, most respondents expected ICT or eLearning to play a key role in shaping the form of future education. At the same time, the surveys revealed several real or potential problems facing students in taking courses on the Internet. Most important, students' needs and demands are treated as less important than other aspects (e.g., technological access to the system) in designing courses on the Internet. Simply put, a so-called user friendly environment is critical to ensuring the success of distance learning.

Traditional concepts and operations will not fit into changing the learning environment. New ways of motivation, assessment, reward, and communication have to be found. One of the new ways of thinking is to consider students as a critical factor in designing the content and process of eLearning. In saying so, I do not mean that students' needs or demands are the only factors to be considered. Rather, instructors or administrators involved in eLearning should be aware of what students expect from it. Universities and colleges should foster successful learning experiences for students as clients. The substantial and continuing investments in costly ICTs are best justified when their productivity is maximized through their utilization by students who are knowledgeable ICT end users. In short, client orientation is the key mode of operation in the information age.

Theoretically, there are still many questions to be answered if the application of ICT in higher education is to be managed effectively: How will the automation of computer-based operation be balanced with administrative staff's autonomy and discretion, if any? What information privacy rights of instructors, students, and staff will be ensured? How should adequate training and assistance with ICT-based learning be provided? More specifically, what knowledge will help instructors provide successful learning experiences for students? What techniques are needed for successful implementation of learning at distance? In virtual relationships, how will the positive affective bonds between participants in not only administrative work but also the learning process be maintained? These are just a few examples.

However, practically speaking, many participants in the learning process of the current higher education seem to take limited advantage of the powerful ICT tools available to them. Not only are their ICT-related training and support inadequate, but the interfaces between instructors and students or between students themselves are also problematic, not to mention the level of skills, techniques, and attitudinal aspects germane to effective eLearning. Given the depth of ICT penetration into universities and colleges, we cannot just drop the idea of learning on the Internet. Thus, a more realistic goal would be how to improve, if possible, the current state of eLearning. With so many stakeholders in the mix, a more strategic approach is necessary to ensure that eLearning has the best possible chance to succeed (for a general strategic foundation of eLearning, see Rosenberg 2001). The following are just a few suggestions based on the results of the surveys mentioned above.

First, instructors need to develop courses on the Internet by strategically designing instructions. Most universities in the above survey are at the initial stage of adopting eLearning, but they have already developed several courses tailored for eLearning. Many courses, however, are not developed through scientific and strategic design (e.g., needs analysis, considering changes in technology, prospects for future trend, etc.) relevant for courses on the Internet but from general perspectives and issues of classroom teaching. Therefore, more attention and efforts are required to develop courses to appropriately meet the new environment of eLearning. No doubt, part of such a new environment is the learner's needs and wants.

Second, more cognitive interaction between instructors and students is needed. In general, students' learning in Web-based courses takes place with teaching material, and students are evaluated based on a few tests. This phenomenon unfortunately confines students' participation in the learning process to just reading or looking at the teaching material on the Web, subsequently ignoring interaction between instructors and students. Although there are a few ways (e.g., e-mail, virtual conference, etc.) offered for facilitating interactions between instructors and students or between students and other students, what is needed is instructors' strong commitment to encourage interactions, particularly between instructors and students. In so doing, instructors can understand what students want and expect, resulting in a possible adjustment of courses to clients' (i.e., students') needs. This adjustment is crucial to the success of eLearning, considering the separation by time and place. Thus, just reiterating the teaching material of offline classrooms in eLearning courses without listening to students' voices will eventually overshadow the future of eLearning.

Finally, despite instructors' preparation, students' satisfaction with the courses they took on the Internet is not high, as shown in the survey results. This indicates that instructors need to be more aggressive in articulating strategies for course management, especially motivating students to get involved in the courses. Interestingly, students enrolled in online courses across regions or nations may be less likely to feel that they indeed belong to a school. Therefore, making strategies for effective course management should be a cooperative work by both instructors and universities/colleges. Most universities expect to play a role in building friendly environments for otherwise isolated students by sufficiently providing such services as computer-related education (both online and offline), proper infrastructure (e.g., digital library), and financial assistance.

References

Barclay, Kathleen H. 2001. *Humanizing learning-at-distance*. San Francisco: Saybrook Institute.

Biggs, J. B. 1987. *Student approaches to learning and studying*. Melbourne, Australia: ACER.

Bothun, G., and S. D. Kevan. 1996. Networked physics in undergraduate instruction. Available from http://zebu.oregon.edu/special/cip.html.

Cardenas, Karen. 1998. Technology in today's classroom. *Academe* 84 (3): 27-29.

CNN.com. 2000. What technological advances can you expect to see in 2025? Retrieved 14 January 2000 from http://www.cnn.com/2000/TECH/computing/01/14/tech.2025.idg/index.html.

Cox, B. 1996. Evolving a distributed learning community. In *Wired together: The online K-12 classroom*, edited by Z. Berger and M. Collins. New Jersey: Hampton.

Cravener, P. A. 1999. Faculty experiences with providing online courses. *Computers and Nursing* 17:42-47.

Denning, Peter. 1997. Skewer the stereotype. *Educom Review* 33 (3): 30-34.

Eddy, John, John Burnett, Donald Spaulding, and Stan Murphy. 1997. Technology assisted education. *Education* 117 (3): 478-81.

Edelson, D., Roy Pea, and L. Gomez. 1996. Constructivism in the collaboratory. In *Constructivists learning environment*, edited by B. G. Wilson. Englewood Cliffs, NJ: Educational Technology.

Etzioni, Amitai. 1964. *Modern organizations*. Englewood Cliffs, NJ: Prentice Hall.

Farrington, Gregory C. 1999. The new technology and the future of residential undergraduate education. *Educom Review* 34 (4): 38-44.

Fiske, Edmond, and Bruce Hammond. 1997. Identifying quality in American colleges and universities. *Planning for Higher Education* 26 (1): 8-15.

Frissen, Paul. 1996. The virtual reality of informatization in public administration. *Informatization and the Public Sector* 2 (3/4): 265-94.

———. 1998. Public administration in cyberspace. In *Public administration in an information age*, edited by I. M. Snellen and W. B. van de Donk, 33-46. Amsterdam, the Netherlands: IOC Press.

Garson, G. David. 2000. The role of information technology in quality education. In *Social dimensions of information technology*, edited by David Garson, 177-97. Hershey, PA: Idea Group.

G-7 government on-line project. 1996. Retrieved 17 July 1006 from http://www.open.gov.uk/govline/10120_2.html.

Guernsey, Lisa. 1998. Distance education for the not-so-distant. *Chronicle of Higher Education* 44 (29): A29-A30.

Heeks, Richard, ed. 1999. *Reinventing government in the information age*. New York: Routledge.

Hillesheim, Gwen. 1998. The search for quality standards in distance learning. Paper presented at the Annual Conference on Distance Teaching and Learning, 5-7 August, Madison, WI.

Hiltz, Starr Roxanne. 1994. *The virtual classroom: Learning without limits via computer networks*. Norwood, NJ: Ablex.

Holmberg, B. 1998. What is new and what is important in distance education. *Open Praxis* 1:31-33.

Johnston, Sally M., and Barbara Krauth. 1996. Balancing equity and access: Some principles of good practice for the virtual university. *Change* 28 (2): 38-41.

Kauver, Gerald. 1998. Electronic government: Concept, visions, and strategies. Paper presented at the International Symposium on Electronic Government, 17 October, Seoul, Korea.

Kearney, Richard, and Evan M. Berman, eds. 1999. *Public sector performance: Management, motivation and measurement*. Boulder, CO: Westview.

Kearsley, Greg. 2000. *Online education*. Belmont, CA: Wadsworth.

Keegan, Desmond. 1986. *The foundations of distance education*. London: Croom Helm.

Keider, Robert. 1995. *Seeing organizational patterns*. California: Berrett-Koehler.

Kettl, Donald. 1994. *Reinventing government?* Washington, DC: Brookings Institution.

Korea Research Institute for Vocational Education and Training. 2001. *A scheme to promote Web-based education and training for human resource development*. Seoul: Korea Research Institute for Vocational Education and Training.

Korean Ministry of Education and Human Resources. 2001. *A study of the current state of distance learning and improving strategies*. Seoul, Korea: Ministry of Education and Human Resources.

Kroeker, Brian. 2000. Changing roles in information dissemination and education. In *Social dimensions of information technology*, edited by David Garson, 141-59. Hershey, PA: Idea Group.

Lookatch, R. P. 1995. The strange but true story of multimedia and the Type I error. *Technos* 4 (2): 10-13.

Lucas, Henry. 1998. *T-form organization*. San Francisco: Jossey-Bass.

Merrill Lynch. 2000. *Knowledge web*. New York: Merrill Lynch.

Mingle, James R., and Larry Gold. 1996. Should distance learning be rationed? *Educom Review* 31 (4): 48-50.

National Council for Open and Distance Education. 2002. Definitions, glossaries and terms. Retrieved 11 March 2002 from http://cedir.uow.edu.au/NCODE/info/definitions/html.

Norman, Donald A., and James C. Spohrer. 1996. Learner-centered education. *Communications of the ACM* 39 (4): 24-27.

Oh, Cheol H. 2001. eGovernment: A critical review. *Journal of Public Policy* 9 (1): 52-86.

————. In press. Knowledge utilization: Retrospect and prospect. In *Encyclopedia of public administration and policy*, edited by Jack Rabin. New York: Marcel Dekker.

Porter, Lynnette R. 1997. *Creating the virtual classroom: Distance learning with the Internet*. New York: John Wiley.

Postman, Neil. 1992. *Technology: The surrender of culture to technology*. New York: Knopf.

Rapp, Charles, and John Poertner. 1992. *Social administration: A client-centered approach*. New York: Longman.

Rosenberg, Marc. 2001. *E-learning*. New York: McGraw-Hill.

Rosenberg, R. 1997. *The social impact of computers*. 2d ed. San Diego, CA: Academic Press.

Roth, Brenda F., and Denisha Sanders. 1996. Instructional technology to enhance teaching. *New Directions for Higher Education* 94:21-32.

Ruberg, L. F., C. D. Taylor, and D. M. Moore. 1996. Student participation and interaction on-line: A case study of two college classes. *International Journal of Educational Telecommunications* 2 (1): 69-92.

Ryan, Steve, Bernard Scott, Howard Freeman, and Daxa Patel. 2000. *The virtual university*. London: Kogan Page.

Shields, Mark. 2000. Technological change, virtual learning, and higher education. In *Social dimensions of information technology*, edited by David Garson, 160-76. Hershey, PA: Idea Group.

Slevin, James. 2000. *The Internet and society*. Cambridge, UK: Polity.

Taylor, Charles Lewis. 2000. Teaching on line and on campus simultaneously. Paper presented at the meeting of the International Political Science Association, 1-5 August, Quebec, Canada.

van Dusen, Gerald C. 1997. *The virtual campus: Technology and reform in higher education*. ASHE-ERIC higher education report 25, no. 5. Washington, DC: George Washington University, Graduate School of Education and Human Development.

Wulf, W. A. 1995. Warning: Information technology will transform the university. *Issues in Science Technology* summer: 46-52.

Young, Kimberly. 1998. *Caught in the net*. New York: John Wiley.

Zittel, Thomas. 2000. Electronic government: A blue-print for 21st century democracy? Paper presented at the World Congress of the International Political Science Association, 1-5 August, Quebec, Canada.

The Social Context of Applied Science: A Model Undergraduate Program

By
MING IVORY

This article justifies the inclusion of social context in innovative undergraduate applied science programs. It proposes a model social context program, distinguishing it from two inferior strategies that expose students to a range of social disciplines at too elementary a level or rely on unsystematic, anecdotal work experience of science faculty confronting regulatory events. The article describes stresses associated with implementing the model program. Finally, it discusses the relationship of the model program to trends in higher education. A social context curriculum should explore the tensions between knowledge and power and give students practice in institutional design. It should encourage both engagement and skepticism. Graded case studies, simulations, senior projects, and experiential elements should be used to introduce a typology of institutional designs and progressively develop students' individual design repertoires. Implementation stresses come from debates over content, interdisciplinarity, university and departmental governance, and the reform of higher education, generally.

M ost innovative applied science programs within universities have adopted various kinds of social or contextual material as a necessary or desirable adjunct to the science taught within the major. This is true within conventional engineering schools as well as within more

Ming Ivory is an associate professor in the integrated science and technology department of James Madison University and the coordinator for policy and standards for the Commonwealth Information Security Center. An expert on science and technology policy in the United States and developing countries, Dr. Ivory has a Ph.D. in political science (Massachusetts Institute of Technology, 1986), an M.A. in the history and sociology of science (University of Pennsylvania, 1973), and a B.S. in mathematics and French (Tufts University, 1971). Dr. Ivory has been designing programs and teaching the social context of science and technology for more than twenty-five years, including time at Hampshire College (School of Natural Science) and Creighton University (Political Science Department) and under contract to the International Law Institute. For seven years a project manager for the Office of Forestry, Environment and Natural Resources of the U.S. Agency for International Development, Dr. Ivory has experience at several other federal science agencies and the World Bank.

DOI: 10.1177/0002716202238573

ANNALS, AAPSS, 585, January 2003

innovative niche programs.[1] While such programs were designed at different historical periods and differ greatly in the ideology motivating them, most attempt to provide a scientific or technical education of a different stripe, one that avoids descending into mere technical training or evolving back toward mere theory. Applied science programs differentiate themselves both from basic science education that focuses too narrowly on debates internal to a discipline as it prepares students for graduate school and original research and from discipline-based engineering schools. Some programs are specifically designed to build strong connections between academic study and private-sector employment or at least to bring commercial realities into academic classrooms. But whatever the motivation, applied science programs try to produce graduates having certain desirable characteristics: they can operate effectively within rapidly changing complex contexts that demand computer literacy; they have had relevant, hands-on, nonclassroom experiences going beyond book learning; they are more broadly educated in the sciences and, as a result, more flexible and creative when confronting complex human problems requiring the interaction of more than one field.

Applied science programs at universities may have to accentuate their difference from traditional academe to attract new sources of financial and practical support or to escape the counterproductive traditions of some institutions. They may tinker with the look and feel of university lifestyle, offer new kinds of work arrangements to attract knowledgeable people from industry, use new teaching technologies, and provide new kinds of incentives to reward new kinds of academic behavior. They will focus on objects, employ instruments, and attract the kinds of students not usually seen in traditional science programs. Even so, they are in the same game: attempting to train sophisticated and creative thinkers, the movers and shakers of the next generation, and should not lose sight of their responsibility for intellectual quality control. Applied science programs must get students functioning at a higher level of analytical sophistication than is possible outside the walls of the university. They need not denigrate deep thought to produce active decision makers. They should avoid suggesting that the two cultures of corporation and academia are incommensurable and irreconcilable, and they should not sell out to a kind of corporatism that cannot be critical of its patrons. Thought and action must be effectively linked together by seeking a gold standard in both. Typically, university-based programs in applied science endorse multidisciplinary and integrated approaches and include social context material as part of the requirements of the major.

In this article, I will

1. justify the inclusion of social context content within applied science programs;
2. propose a model social context curriculum for an applied science program, distinguish it from two existing alternative strategies, and discuss the concepts emphasized within it;[2]
3. discuss some of the conceptual and institutional challenges expected during implementation of the model program; and
4. suggest the relationship of this effort to trends in higher education.

Justifications for Social Context Curricula within Applied Science Programs

Within applied science programs, social context contents may be lucky to account for as much as a one-quarter of a student's time during a four-year course of study. They are likely to account for much less. For this reason, the topics covered must be chosen with great parsimony and care. They cannot be merely a haphazard list of interesting issues. There are three fundamental justifications for including social context within applied science.

Justification 1: Technical solutions must be mediated through human institutions[3]

The strongest motivation for including social scientific or other nontechnical contents within an applied science program is that real solutions to human problems are found only in the space defined by the complex dance of knowledge and power.[4] Knowledge alone, such as of basic science and engineering principles, must be joined to the power of political consensus and legitimacy to effect real-time solutions likely to be understood, accepted, and financially supported by the society in the long run.[5] Many technically elegant solutions fail to be adopted in real systems because political, economic, and social parameters have more legitimacy and salience than technical data or scientific equivocation. Many inferior technical solutions are adopted because of the disproportionate access their advocates have to political or economic power. Solutions to heartbreaking problems are delayed because of misconceptions about what constitutes knowledge or how to assess risks. Self-confident scientists and engineers armed with methodological conviction are as political an animal as any interest group when they compete for the scarce resources of public support, visibility, and trust.[6] Lay publics, completely ignorant of any science, and perhaps devoid of any discernable logic, still have legitimate authority within democratic systems. They can and should be able to override scientific consensus. To achieve the goals of most applied science programs, the social context curriculum elements should focus on giving students the tools that enable them to understand these truths and to design appropriate syntheses between knowledge and power.

Justification 2: Applied scientists need to understand and be understood by the wider society

While sharing fundamental critical-thinking skills with the social sciences, applied science students are subject to certain preferences and habits that grow from their socialization into scientific or engineering mindsets or their troubles with social or literary ones. At a minimum, it is important to counteract some very bad habits of mind common to incoming students that can be inadvertently reinforced in their science courses or by an applied science program's informal culture, esprit de corps, or departmental style.

In the real world, decisions must be made without benefit of scientific certainty. While students profess faith in the power of science, they tend to believe that social decision making is dominated by nonscientists. This belief explains some of their cynicism about politics. Scientific training can reinforce both a "wait until all the evidence is in" kind of passivity and a "those who know the most about it should make the decision" kind of authoritarianism. Applied science students find it hard to celebrate democratic decisions that result in bad science or to respect the structure of the social system while regretting the outcomes. A sense of irony is foreign to them. Some are quite authoritarian despite their patriotism. They are convinced that science is so powerful a force that its products are unavoidable and cannot be questioned. They believe its practitioners should be given maximum autonomy, special privileges, and unusual exemptions from the market, from ethical behaviors, or from social solidarity. Scientists are exemplars of rationality, technologists the source of innovation. In contrast, the political system seems irrational, upsetting the application of scientific knowledge and retarding the progress of useful technology. The distinction between politicians and political scientists is often lost.

Many students come to applied science programs holding a mutually contradictory set of assumptions. "Science is a powerful force," yet "I cannot shape where technology is going." "Progress is inevitable," but "Bad things are always happening." "Science leads to wealth and to truth," but "Money is the root of all evil." "Government regulations impede innovation in the marketplace," yet "The government should protect us from risk and ensure the survival and profits of high-tech firms." "If a new product is popular, it is the better technology," yet "People are afraid of new technologies." "Democratic choices are best expressed by 'voting' in the marketplace," but "Mass culture knows nothing about what it's doing."

Despite having passed or even excelled in their American history courses in high school, some students have only the vaguest notion about how the U.S. political process really works. They underestimate the extent of government intrusion into free markets and do not understand that competition means some businesses fail. They have naïve notions of profit making, research and development, the stock market, and regulation. The structural details of their own society seem like so many arbitrary rules inherited from an irrelevant past. They are quick to condemn all other systems as inferior—less scientific or too socialist—and their proponents as ignorant. Although they recognize that things do go wrong in the United States, students too easily assume that some criminal needs to be arrested rather than that the system itself could be at fault. They are systems thinkers when it comes to physical or biological phenomena but are unable to apply systems logic to social thinking. Too many students employ various numerological shortcuts to social reasoning. They believe all debates have two sides and that social dilemmas can be resolved by splitting the difference, doing a little bit of everything, letting everyone make up their own mind, or letting the majority rule. Some assume the social-contextual world is simpler and easier than the scientific. Others dismiss it as hopelessly complex and unpredictable. They attack all problems sequentially, adopting conventional corporate-managerial approaches, forcing decisions by brute authority or crude majority rule. They are contemptuous of artists, activists, and academics and impatient with open-ended inquiry or a maturing consensus. They believe short-term advantages will inevitably accumulate into long-term benefits. Finally, they believe that taking no action is a neutral position or that it can protect one from being accused of anything. All of these notions are not shared by all of the students, of course. But even by their own reckoning, they feel the least prepared in the social sciences (James Madison University 1998).

Such misconceptions are part of the contextual baggage many students and some faculty members bring with them to applied science programs. If they are not corrected, they can become an entrenched part of a student's self-image, or worse, markers of membership in the program itself, which can eventually hamper a program's ability to recruit more broadly capable students.[7] If we are to protect our highly educated students from sounding like rubes when they interact with other educated groups, a bit of social context is surely salutary in giving them the professional polish they need to succeed in highly competitive contexts.

Justification 3: The study of social context reinforces scientific and technical concepts

Finally, the motivation for social context contents in applied science programs is identical to the motivation for the sciences—to produce good analysis and problem-solving skills. Proponents of the critical thinking movement within general education have known this for some time (Ruggiero 1990). The hallmark of educated students in any field is skill in pattern recognition, the ability to recognize familiar forms even when the context changes radically. Science students must understand conservation of energy in many guises. They need to be able to recognize exponential patterns in complex data sets or recognize what part of an equation reveals its behavior. Social scientific contents reinforce these analytical skills by applying logical reasoning, rules of evidence, statistical inferences, and so forth to a new (and possibly strange) set of phenomena, to institutions and social structures, and to relationships of authority and power.

Social Context Curricula in Applied Science Programs: Prevailing Strategies

In designing a model social context curriculum, I have tried to avoid some of the problems associated with two more common strategies. These are the appreciation strategy, which provides systematic yet elementary content in a formal way, and the supplement strategy, which provides unsystematic and idiosyncratic contents in an informal way.

Appreciation strategy

The appreciation strategy seeks to expose students to a range of ancillary disciplines, usually some combination of economics, political science, history of science, sociology of science, business, philosophy, and ethics, to give them an appreciation of the wider context in which their scientific skills are applied. Typically, a course or courses are required either at the beginning or at the end of a student's four-year program. This strategy correctly identifies the broader range of contents relevant to science-based problem solving, but it typically addresses them only at the most elementary level. It is more a challenge to students' short-term memory than to their capacity for integration and synthesis. For these courses to be useful, students should be able to abstract and analogize as they move through their scientific training, yet they typically learn these things either too early, when they are not developmentally ready, or too late for them to enlighten their science courses. Programs often overload beginning students with too many mutually inconsistent systems of terms. The jargon overload can alienate students since they cannot easily see the connections they are supposed to make to their developing technical skills. Social context can seem a distraction, an interruption, even when they enjoy the subject, activities, or faculty member teaching it.

The appreciation strategy also motivated the science, technology, and society, or science and technology studies, movement. Science, technology, and society programs are designed to work in parallel to science and technology programs, often having their own students, majors, and minors, but offering elective courses for the enrichment of science or engineering students. Courses in history of science, philosophy of science, public policy, ethics, and other courses bring humanities and social science perspectives into the discussion of science and technology's impacts on society. But applied science students are expected to be consumers, but not practitioners, of social context. They are meant to, at best, appreciate how difficult the finding of real solutions is or has been and, at worst, appreciate how badly the political system has messed things up, and the subject matter rarely comes into their science courses.

Supplement strategy

The supplement strategy captures social context by providing brief modules within the science courses themselves. The strategy is used in programs lacking specialized social context faculty members but having a well-motivated science faculty with somewhat broader interests or experiences. This strategy may be nothing more than the telling of personal war stories by scientists who have served on political advisory committees or suffered through the regulatory maze.[8] Class discussions of interesting ethical dilemmas or current events are typical of the supplement strategy. A biotechnology class can take a brief excursion from lab techniques to discuss the ethics of cloning or the government regulation of field releases. Students struggling with the thermodynamics of energy production can take time to discuss deregulation of electric utilities. Occasionally, modules are used to discuss controversial issues from current events; to teach specific techniques such as cost-benefit analysis, human factors in Web design, or technology assessment; to introduce regulatory procedures; or to learn software tools used by the private sector such as project management, information retrieval, or decision support programs.

But while having much to commend it, this strategy too has its drawbacks. Anecdotes of encounters with the political system, while unique, intriguing, and entertaining for students, are not case studies. They are dependent on moments of opportunity suggested by the natural course of the science contents or the specific experiences of the science faculty, and the lessons to be drawn from them lack systematic and theoretical weight. The supplement strategy identifies social problems without providing any systematic insight to solve them since time limits the discussion and the module inevitably ends where the issue becomes complex. Sometimes the personal knowledge of the professor cannot even take the case to its ultimate resolution, or it reinforces the message that social context inevitably obstructs technological progress.

Furthermore, it is difficult for students to carry the information provided in these modules from one scientific field to another. The opportunistic nature of the supplement strategy makes it nearly impossible to design appropriate sequences of increasing complexity and sophistication in the social context contents. There is little if any quality control. Some things students get several times over, but at the same shallow level; others they miss entirely, depending on their particular science concentrations or faculty. Software tools rapidly obsolesce, often before the student really gains enough facility with it, and most industries are quite happy to train their own workers in local tools and procedures.[9]

The supplement strategy also tends to reinforce the discipline-specific elements of social context as opposed to generic ones, contributing to the loss of integration. Integration is difficult enough to sustain as an interdisciplinary program expands and evolves. At its best, some students can eventually emerge with skills in social context, but many others are lost as to why the material was included at all. At its worst, this strategy reinforces the notion that social context is filler, comic relief, soft, or unimportant or is pursued only by irrational (unscientific) politicians. Dependent on the whim of the scientific faculty, it can become a participatory opinion fest, a break from the grind in which no thought, evidence, or argument is really required of the students, so long as they all have something to say.

Outline of the Model Program[10]

The model proposed here addresses the shortcomings of the appreciation and supplement strategies. Social context contents strategically important to the scientific or technological concentrations of the major are parsimoniously selected and sequenced across the four-year major course of study to give students cases of increasing sophistication and complexity within whatever proportion of the student credit hours the particular program allows. The model program focuses on three goals:

Model program goal 1—Increased understanding of the essential tension between knowledge and power: The program of study should give students practice in identifying, understanding, and describing the structures of power, authority, and influence that link the corporations, government agencies, scientific laboratories, and so forth with which and in which they will be working.

Model program goal 2—Development and practice of skills in institutional design: The program of study should introduce students to a typology of institutional dilemmas typical of what will confront them in the high-tech world, provide them with a progressively complex repertoire of creative solutions to these dilemmas, and give them practice in the design of new and innovative solutions to the dilemmas they may face in the future.

Model program goal 3—Commitment to a life of engagement and skepticism: The program of study should give students the confidence to question the assumptions of the institutions in which they work and encourage them toward developing a commitment to creative reform and social conscience.

Designing specific elements to express these goals cannot happen if social context is discussed in isolation from the program as a whole. It is necessary to understand how any piece (modules within science courses, stand-alone courses, or other nonclassroom experiences) reinforces the general plan of the applied science program itself and of the social context content within it. It requires strategic sequencing of social context contents, so that increasing complexity is possible. Each applied science program will have its own set of constraints that affect particular choices, but this model program proposes a kind of systems analysis in which the basic objects of inquiry are institutions and their arrangements or relationships. Students are taught to accurately observe the behavior of the social system and infer the relationships among its constituent institutions. They also get practice in predicting system behaviors when they know what institutions and relationships exist. All of this is conveyed to them in class through carefully selected, rich case studies and simulations and reinforced outside of class by a broad range of field trips, visiting speakers, bulletin boards, informal meetings, structured internships, special events, and possibly reflection on the program and the university itself.

The essential tension between knowledge and power (goal 1)

By essential tension, I mean a kind of creative resonance between two somewhat contradictory forces. Scientists and technologists may produce knowledge, but they have no special power[11] over the scientifically illiterate within a democracy. Democratic institutions are given authority, but they may act with or without knowledge. A progressive society must value both. Citizens should not ignore the benefits that science and technology bring to sound decision making, but neither should they shift decision making to nonelected experts or be intimidated from taking responsibility for their own futures. The market may richly reward the originators of scientific knowledge or the designers of new technology, but this is no guarantee that the technology serves human needs or causes no harm. How to balance and manage these essential contradictions is the subject matter of the model program. To address this content in a rigorous way, students must acquire basic skills in institutional analysis.

All solutions to human problems are mediated through institutions. I mean here both specific institutions of brick, mortar, and mortals and more abstract institutions like the institution of marriage, competitive markets, or a free press. We are interested in institutions having authority to frame the question (Environmental Protection Agency, mayor of New York City); institutions providing ethical guidance (churches, religious traditions, philosophy); and institutions having the resources to support research or development (Department of Energy, Merck Corporation), mobilize voluntary action (Red Cross, Computer Professionals for Social Responsibility), provide infrastructure, equipment, and tools (public works departments, National Guard, the air traffic control system), and implement or enforce solutions (city of Harrisonburg, Nuclear Regulatory Commission, courts). I also include institutions that publicize effective or ineffective attempts at problem solving (the press, corporate public relations departments) or analyze what went wrong and how to fix it (think tanks, task forces, foundations, universities). Finally, I also include institutions that motivate human actors to carry out new kinds of tasks (television, advertising, families) or inspire them to reflect on the new conditions created by new solutions (theatre, the arts).

The focus is of course on the institutions of the political and economic systems and more specifically on subsystems relevant to the behaviors of interest to applied scientists and technologists. For example, political parties and electoral politics stand toward the outer periphery of our interest, while science policy and regulatory issues, the politics of intellectual property, new drug introduction, environmental protection, and so forth are at the center. The stock market is at the periphery, but basic market forces and trade economics are more central. We would seek examples from those 7 percent of all businesses that have some kind of research and development budget rather than small entrepreneurs in the restaurant business. We are less concerned with personal morality than with social ethics. Case studies are more likely to deal with issues such as reproductive rights, toxic waste disposal, or wireless technology than issues of child abuse, immigration, or gun control.

Throughout the program, the emphasis is on structures and behaviors. The consistent message is that relationships among research institutions, high-tech corporations, regulatory bodies, international standards-setting groups, and scientific lobbyists are structured; that is, their relative authority, influence, and power are predictable. These more or less predictable structures determine the behaviors of institutions, as well as actors in them, and affect the outcomes of events in reasonably regular ways. Furthermore, citizens design institutions and their relationships. They are not natural, accidental, traditional, God given, or inevitable. Their behaviors are understandable in terms of their parts, the authority given them, and procedures they develop. Citizens make choices about how to design these objects, and the design parameters make a difference. Students are expected to know the regulations relevant to their concentration—who is in charge, what the process is, and so forth—but these are not the goal; to some extent, they are easily learned on the job. Rather, graduates of the model program should be guided toward seeing the specific institutional arrangements in their field as mere instances of more generic objects common across all scientific fields, having ever increasing variations on a few themes.

Applied science students are not used to dealing with either the vocabulary or the concepts of institutional analysis. Scientific and technological events are mediated through a great variety of institutions, but they reflect common dilemmas (such as integrating new information, ensuring access and participation, and maintaining long-term support) that arise again and again. Real-life problem solving takes place in a field between two forces, the ideal (the best science and the fairest institutions) and the real (incomplete knowledge and imperfectly designed or inherited structures). The education students get should not be so ideal that they could never apply the principles in real space. This is often the failure of basic science education. Neither should it be so in conformity with or contingent on unique conditions and existing institutional players that they have no vision of what is really possible, no guide to what they can and should challenge, and no design skills to use even if they were inclined to address institutional problems. This is typically the failure of corporate and professional education. The program should give students criteria for knowing how to move in the right direction, some idea of the trade-offs, costs, and risks, a ready toolkit of structural models from which to draw. They will, as a result, be skilled problem solvers but not necessarily docile employees. They will be whistle blowers, mediators, and creative designers, able to interpolate between the ideal and the real, not passively succumb to the status quo. They will not only be able to recognize the ethical values expressed by the institutions with which they choose to work but be able to conceptualize institutional arrangements that would better express those values or bring better sets of values into their institutions. They will have the fortitude to persist in the quest for better institutional designs, concurrent with their scientific and technical roles.

Institutional design skills (goal 2)

The skills learned in the social context model program are analogous to those of a civil engineer who develops a repertoire of standard mechanisms with which he or she can face a variety of novel mechanical challenges. Since we hope students will find employment in these same institutions, they should be ready not only to understand the motivations, the opportunities, and the limitations of the structures in which they will be embedded but to improve them or design better ones. Students need to be comfortable in a biotechnology lab, but they also need to know how to improve regulation in a way that protects wider social values, not merely the special interests of biotechnology firms or the experimental discretion of scientists.

They should not have any special antipathy to the special interest of biotechnology firms, but they should be aware that there are choices to be made and that each option has somewhat predictable liabilities and benefits, supporters and opponents. The outcome we should fear is that students adopt the interests of their employer uncritically, without reflection, unaware of the existence of other interests that they well may believe they share. To be good designers, students must become familiar enough with a range of models from which they can draw so that they are empowered to act, not just to appreciate or recognize. By the end of four years, they should have a rich repertoire of model solutions. If general relationships between goals and structures are understood, the repertoire then becomes a platform on which the students can construct the new institutional solutions that will inevitably be required.

In their science training, most students begin to concentrate on one field or another.[12] It is therefore inevitable that the particular institutions with which each student becomes familiar will differ. Students concentrating in biotechnology, information science, manufacturing, environment, or energy may well come into contact with different agencies and institutions, but they all should know whether and how those institutions are typical or unique. When approaching a new area, they can quickly identify what institutions they would expect to see and which are missing from the discussion. For biotechnology students, the Asilomar Conference then becomes an instance of one institutional design option (scientific self-regulation) within a whole repertoire of solutions to social risk management and oversight rather than a lesson about the superiority of scientific discretion over regulation. Furthermore, students expect and can find additional instances in many fields—in medical research (informed consent rules), nuclear power (regulatory commissions), or manufacturing (OSHA, insurance systems).

Engagement and skepticism (goal 3)

Finally, the study of social context in an applied science program should give students the confidence to question the assumptions of the institutions in which they work and encourage them toward developing their own social conscience and commitment to creative reform. For applied scientists in industry, there is often a tension between being a team player and being skeptical, between going along and being proactive or a change agent. Successful innovators do question received wisdom, and applied science education should include a healthy ability to question everyday assumptions that drive one's home institution. In debates about the model program, it is easy to underestimate the radical antipathy many corporate scientists and engineers have to the term "activist." They hold it in the same contempt as "politician." Users of the term are accused of advocating socialism, fomenting obstructionism and mindless protest. But if technically skilled citizens can see the gaps between the ideal and the real, but are neither motivated to bridge the gap nor skilled enough to build better institutions, we shall have failed in our mission to provide them with a meaningful education. We intend to produce neither contemplative dreamers nor destructive terrorists, but neither do we want to

graduate students who are easily seduced by high salaries to abandon their commitments to the global community or become complacent tools of mediocrity.
They must believe in their own efficacy to both design institutions that fully express
their most deeply held convictions and reform the institutions in which they find
themselves, to more closely approach their own ethical values. We might also reasonably expect graduates to become expert witnesses, environmental advocates,
science writers, regulators, and technical experts in government. Some will be
motivated to work for underserved populations and underfinanced causes,
increasing those causes' understanding of and access to scientific information.
They may end up good spokespeople for their employer's point of view, or they
might be innovators within the corporation, ones who experiment and achieve new
ways of solving both technical and institutional reform issues. They might suggest
ways a corporation might be more sensitive to the environmental impacts of what it
does or be an advocate for less hierarchical, more participatory workplaces. They
might suggest new ways of sharing information at all levels or interacting with the
neighborhood. This makes them allies of the most innovative corporations, not the
apologists for the mainstream. While the program should be dedicated to assisting
students to express their own values and take hold of their own futures, rather than
enlisting them in those of the faculty, it is also true that engagement must be modeled; it cannot be merely taught. This requires a self-consciously reflective faculty
who expect to explain their choices and commitments to their students. Whatever
their eventual role, we would hope that our graduates are actively engaged in making the world a better place and that they see clearly how their education empowers
them within a world composed of institutions. We hope they are lifetime learners
who remain skeptical of the claims of governments, corporations, and scientists
and are not easily swayed by advertising hype or lured into intolerance or compli-
ance by weak and reckless reasoning or by apathy.

Implementation of the Model Program

Delivering the model social context curriculum in a program of applied science
is of course constrained by the limited time available in which to develop complex
ideas remote from the student's own propensities and skills. It is necessary to be
quick yet comprehensive and deep. What follows are some practical considerations
for implementing such a program.

Typology, repertoire, and graded case studies

The program of study should give beginning students practice in identifying,
understanding and describing the structures of power, authority, and influence
that link the corporations, government agencies, and science laboratories through
carefully chosen case studies. Case studies are an essential tool since they can operate at two or three levels at once, both explicitly and tacitly (Polanyi 1964), and can
be tailored to introduce or reinforce scientific contents, too. As a set, the case stud-

ies students encounter during their four years constitute a typology of institutional dilemmas typical of what will confront them in the high-tech world. Each year, students see cases of increasing complexity, which provide them with a repetition of the familiar themes while introducing new material. The aim is to build a rich repertoire of creative solutions to typical science and technological policy dilemmas. This repertoire should grow from a strategically selected set of cases kept current through continous revision, somewhat in the manner that business schools do with entrepreneurial strategizing. Finally, assignments give students practice in the design of new and innovative solutions to dilemmas they may face in the future.

Students gradually transform the typology of designs into their own repertoire, and in turn, their repertoire becomes a template for their own creative designs, in senior projects or on the job. Having an institutional repertoire from which to draw guides students toward expressing their ethical values in concrete forms and thus encourages them to maintain engagement in civic life and commitment to the values they hold or adopt as a result of ethical reasoning, alongside their scientific and technological work. For the faculty, the repertoire provides the frame in which curriculum materials can evolve in response to changing technology and emerging issues. When it is clear what each case study used in the program must accomplish for the curriculum as a whole, it becomes easier to manage change in an intelligent way, and meaningless jumping from hot topic to hot topic is avoided.

Students should see institutional design cases across the whole range from the organizational to the international. At the organizational end, they might deal with the creation of an ombudsman to field client complaints in a governmental agency, the invention of design-build teams in manufacturing, or just-in-time inventory systems. Dick Sclove (1995) and the Loka Institute have pioneered the discussion of how to express democratic values within science at a local level, through the concept of science shops and community research. Linking with a public research interest group[13] is another local-level example. Students will deal with state and national institutional designs, such as regulatory and advisory boards or governor's commissions. Finally, at the international end, they will look at treaties, protocols, declarations, and trade conventions. To the extent possible, the program should allow students to engage the political process in real time by contributing to city council debates, rule making, and public forums concerning the technological systems of the community: water, sewers, roads, or power plants.

This kind of training will complement the students' ability to design technological systems. To design good social elements—such as regulations, public access, and so forth—they must appreciate the legitimacy of democratic decision making regarding scientific issues of public import and understand the fragile tension among scientific knowledge, public authority, and private interest. Thus, there is a great deal of continuity between what students do in social context and what they do in the sciences. Social decision making is presented not as a frustration of scientific and technological progress but rather as a series of political experiments, as contingent and provisional as scientific knowledge itself. To reinforce this experimentalism, it sometimes helps to choose cases as far away from familiar political territory as possible. Interesting but unfamiliar cases that can raise fundamental political dilemmas are useful because students do not know what the solution is supposed to be. This gets them out of the habit of relying on memorized facts and conventional assumptions. Many of the cases occasioned by new technology will have the requisite novelty, but historical and foreign cases, such as the design of information infrastructure in China, can be used to good effect. This is similar to but different from the supplement strategy. Scientists, with all their good intentions, are nevertheless an interested party when it comes to presenting the cases in which they are personally involved. They have been frustrated by shortsighted regulations, blindsided by political machinations, or have triumphed over the unwashed masses and lived to see the rationality of scientists prevail. But such personal stories are often poor history, not objective institutional research. They are anecdotal and do not reinforce the same level of evidentiary logic and inferential rigor for social context as the faculty would expect to see for the science contents. This sends the wrong message.

In the beginning, the cases are simple ones. They give students practice in identifying relevant players and describing their interests. They illustrate how institutional designs flow from attempts to reconcile conflicting demands but are also contingent on who has the power to affect the outcome. Consider the case of smoking and health. While in a crude way, scientific research about the dangers of smoking helps to explain why we have regulations regarding smoking, it is not sufficient to explain the waxing and waning of smoking rates, the decisions of courts, the long time it took, or the variety of institutions we have created. Students should begin by learning to identify the different interests at work (tobacco companies, growers, congresspersons, governors, patients, and the Medicare system) and the real political power they had to overrule or ignore scientific information and delay action. It illustrates the use of formal and informal authority from the taxing power of the legislature to the persuasive power of such institutions as the Office of the Surgeon General or Action in Smoking and Health. This well-documented case illustrates incompleteness or compromising of institutional designs, as when the tobacco industry is able to get an exemption from food and drug regulation. It illustrates how solutions are not eternal and are revisited again and again, each generation facing them anew. It illustrates the different paths issues have for getting on the agenda, from the adjudication of individual civil suits to presidential leadership and congressional initiative, and it illustrates how scientific knowledge is imperfectly inserted into the public debate through logrolling. It shows how many solutions are possible (law suits, negotiated settlements, taxation, licensing, local ordinances, advertising restrictions). It raises ethical issues over addictive products in the market or the assignment of responsibility. It illustrates actors at their socially responsible best and at their self-interested worst.

The cases should be chosen for their relevance to the social context of science and technology, the intrinsic importance of the institutions and processes involved in them, and their accessibility to students and faculty. In addition, cases should be graded so as to demand progressively more sophisticated analyses from students as they move through their program. Simple cases appropriate to freshman year will introduce students to institutional analysis per se, and more complex cases in sophomore and junior years will illustrate additional subtleties and ambiguities. In their senior projects, students are able to handle issues with some originality, mastery, and confidence. An important element is that the cases be developed and perfected within the program itself, to the extent possible, for they must carry some of the burden of introducing scientific contents or reinforcing scientific learning to be perceived by students as truly integrated. The following is a possible grading schema for social context cases:

Level A (freshman year) cases

- Involve one or two major federal regulatory agencies, in program-relevant technologies.
- Involve simple constitutional principles, for example, free speech, commerce clause, or due process.
- Involve elementary scientific principles, for example, statistical inferences, simple manufacturing processes, or well-known chemical/biological systems.
- Illustrate the typical stages of the policy process.
- Involve well-organized interest groups with clearly articulated ethical positions.

Level B (sophomore and junior year) cases

- Involve more than one government agency with different mandates or overlapping or conflicting jurisdictions.
- Involve more sophisticated science or emerging technology.
- Involve groups that are not well organized or interests that are ill defined.
- Illustrate a policy process with missing stages or multiple iterations.

Level C (junior and senior year) cases

- Involve government agencies at the federal, state and/or local level or both U.S. and foreign governments.
- Involve ambiguous or complex scientific grounds.
- Add corruption and extrinsic political interests, for example, geopolitical strategies or unique public events and crises.
- Illustrate institutional interaction on both informal and formal levels.

On the selection of cases: The role of history

The use of history in conventional science, technology, and society programs, or in what I call the appreciation approach, can be of high quality but is often discredited in two ways. Neither historically sophisticated stories whose fundamental lessons do not translate easily into contemporary debates students are apt to face nor amateur uses of history to socialize students into their scientific roles are desirable. Historical cases can start out being entirely understood in their true complexity but devolve toward a socialization project by the stresses of using nonexpert faculties. An example is the way in which poor history tends to tell a story about progress when retold by nonhistorians, reinforcing the notion that new science inevitably corrects the ignorance and naiveté of past science. Better theories supplant inferior ones. More powerful technologies replace the weaker. In the telling, science is always in danger of being abstracted almost entirely from its social context and seen merely as a progression of logical inferences from data, resulting in ever more comprehensive theory building. While this serves some purpose in the socialization of science students into their epistemological tasks and scientific methodology, it does not give a true understanding of social context. In this amateur history, institutional context is largely irrelevant. It is a history of disembodied ideas divorced from real people and institutions.

Another use for the inclusion of historical cases, equally to be avoided, is to reinforce the legitimacy of scientific expertise within democratic processes, by exhibiting the grand social benefits emerging from research and how many more people were saved from disease, ignorance, labor, and so forth. In this telling, the scientific class is bathed in the mythology of manifest destiny, assailed by the forces of political philistines, and legitimated in its quest for autonomy and public support more effectively than the lobbying efforts of the American Association for the Advancement of Science and professional societies combined!

These are inferior uses of history, and indeed often result from inferior history, especially when historical papers are abridged or interpreted by historical amateurs. Yet history can be used without doing violence to either the historian's craft or the goals of the model program. Historical cases can give students practice in abstracting institutional designs out of the chaos of lived reality. The value of a well-selected and -presented historical case is that the specifics are so foreign to them, and the interests of the players so largely unassumed, that they must see these things with unbiased eyes. Rich, complex histories of technological systems, such as Bjiker, Hughes, and Pinch (1987), Bjiker (1995), and Hughes (1998), recount institutional dilemmas in the past that are still recognizably relevant. Historical cases come at students relatively free of the assumption of technological necessity or institutional inevitability, which clouds their judgment when considering contemporary aspects of, say, the Internet. Science students are typically taught to deal with facts in isolation from history. They are comfortable with the way in which mathematical equations stand outside history and do not depend on verbal interpretation. On the other hand, the appreciation of, say, Marxism as a reasonable option depends on the understanding of the historical context in which it was given birth. Without it, students are merely seeing it as a dead issue, an extinct species irrelevant to preparing themselves for the future. On the other hand, as a design issue, it is as contemporary as the fall of Enron Corporation or the responsibilities of the government toward the steel industry.

Students focusing on the hardware and software of telecommunications have a hard time understanding the scope of institutional options that face them today in a rapidly mutating economic context. Richard John's (1988) historical account of the postal, telegraph, and telephone networks in the American context makes the structural significance of the choice of public subsidization or private competition more accessible to students because it is freed from contemporary ideological associations of Democrat and Republican preferences. Students can apply its lessons to the contemporary field of telecommunications, to explore what is really at stake in such issues as deregulation, monopolistic competition, antitrust, auctions and leases, universal access, and so forth. With that as a background, they can then examine the claims of AOL/Time Warner with a more precise and critical approach.

Tacit learning of complex systems: Simulations

Inevitably, what we want to teach is very complex. We want students to understand why it is that rational human beings would chose socialist forms of government, use taxes to insure private citizens from health costs, or bail out an airline from bankruptcy, because these are institutional solutions, part of the typology. We want to do it in such a way that we do not destroy our credibility with students who are not very sophisticated in distinguishing between presentation of an idea and advocacy of it. To be sensitive to other cultures is to understand in a profound a way as possible the culture's fullness and richness and possibility as a natural thing, not just as a bunch of exotica to be committed to memory. This kind of understanding involves the imagination. Students need to imagine believing, even if briefly, in other values and perspectives wholeheartedly, as if they could be their most ardent defender and advocate. When they can invent in this other world, they have understood it. Students learning a foreign language at first copy sentence patterns, but when they master it, they can create new utterances. For this reason, role-play simulations are particularly useful, especially if they are not abbreviated to fit into short classes. Real life simply does not happen that fast. At James Madison University, we are experimenting with a complex international simulation that takes the better part of a semester to accomplish, in several iterations.[14]

Social context in the senior project

Many applied science programs require students to work on a senior project in which, ideally, all their education comes together. By its very nature, there are a number of tensions inherent in senior projects. It is a time when seniors begin to act relatively independently of their mentors. Yet students can be under a great deal of pressure to be models of what the program itself is about since senior project symposiums can be a showcase to potential employers and program funders. So while there is motivation to allow seniors maximum freedom, there is also a temptation to get them working on worthy projects that express the faculty's concept of rigorous and intensive work. Supervising senior projects is so labor intensive that there is often implicit preference for students to form teams rather than work alone, and finally, there is tension over the kinds of end product expected. Are students expected to demonstrate analytical and integrative skills through writing, or is creating something enough? The senior project is also bound to be another battleground over social context. Many students and faculty of applied science would like the freedom to work narrowly and deeply, leaving aside aspects of an issue that do not interest them. Some would like to build things, others to perfect their lab skills under the direction of a well-liked professor or potential employer. Some want to demonstrate their skills at pure laboratory research to get into graduate school. Some want to work for a sponsor cum potential employer who has rather specific parameters in mind, for which the student can fill a gap. And some see it as requiring students to be creative and innovative from the ground up, with the faculty acting as consultants. Dealing with the social context elements has to be explicitly mentioned and reinforced as a requirement in order that it systematically or generally appear in senior projects.[15]

Extracurricular elements and experiential pedagogy

Just as the best laboratory for student learning in applied technology may be in industrial contexts, the laboratory, or hands-on social context experiential learning, is possible through a student's interaction with government agencies and policy-making institutions. One of the most underutilized resources in this regard is the university itself, which typically manages many complex technological systems (energy, computing, water, health care, communications). Given an administration attuned to the educational role it might play, these processes can become visible. Many James Madison University staff persons have been willing to give their time and energy to assist our students in understanding the technical systems around them. Examples of institutional power relationships, however, are less frequently accessible. Administrators tend to want to insulate the university or departmental politics from curriculum decisions and are even reluctant to share funding strategies, technological change decisions, and the like with faculty, let alone students. What better examples could be found, if only the internal process of the university itself—such as the competition between departments for resources—were laid open to students and disclosure were the rule rather than the exception? The same might be said for corporate partners, but this is even less likely to be possible.[16]

To develop skills in the design of solutions that work in a political/social context, students can also be actively involved in real technical policy issues affecting their local communities, for example, through electricity boards, cable franchises, city and county councils, and planning boards. Classroom assignments such as interviewing experts, guided observations, preparation of advocacy papers, and simulations of various kinds can reinforce both the content goals and the practice of sharp, clear, and sufficiently deep analysis.

The concept of a design contest, well known in engineering schools, might well be extended to include regulatory or legal proposals. Of course, the program should sponsor speakers—theologians, economists, politicians—on major scientific controversies. Finally, programs tend to underestimate the importance of seemingly trivial reinforcements such as installing a student accessible cable TV or a wall-sized world map in a common area, so that students can capitalize on the teaching moments provided by current events. This kind of thing may work against misplaced notions of making education space look professional, through the imposition of what amounts to rigid dress codes for walls and common areas, which is expected to be devoid of the art, controversy, or general messiness of the truly interdisciplinary process. Applied science programs should to the extent possible see themselves in continuity with the rest of the campus, in its life and debate, not as some isolated island of corporate purism, walled off from political and artistic debate.

Stresses of Implementation

Finally, implementation of the model program is likely to face difficulties as it is transformed into real modules and courses with real faculty. The stress has at least four sources: content issues, interdisciplinarity, departmental governance, and the corporatization of higher education. It is clear that the model program does not explicitly address some contents that may seem important: professional ethics, communications skills, (such as technical writing and public presentations), library research, or project management[17] and career skills (such as job hunting, resume preparation, management, or teamwork). These are worthy things for students to know, but they are the responsibility of the department or program as a whole and can be addressed in many ways.

Interdisciplinarity also causes stress over what it is, how to do it, and the status of those who attempt it. Commonly, scientists talk about what I call micro-interdisciplinarity, resulting from work at the conjunction of related sciences or from the application of a particular tool used in one discipline to problems in another discipline. On the other hand, applied science programs attempting to integrate social context with real-world technological problems involve macro-interdisciplinarity, or the integration of knowledge (science) with action. Solutions fail because of the inability of technical teams to understand political pressures and resist them or because technical teams are unaccountable to the public or private interests that support them.[18]

A faculty of a new macro-interdisciplinary program typically will pass through three stages. In the first stage, faculty members see the usefulness of enlisting the expertise of multiple disciplines and engage in juxtapositional interdisciplinarity. They form teams, institutes, or programs and hire people with differing backgrounds. Fields are still compartmentalized, though each discipline gets a whack at the problem.[19] Juxtaposition may engender the use of one field's jargon to explain phenomena in another. For example, the persistence or demise of individual businesses in a competitive free market may usefully be described as business ecology, or the attribution of large effects to relatively small causes can be referred to as chaos theory. But these kinds of semantic images are superficial, and there are no common notions of depth and rigor. Integrational interdisciplinarity begins once the faculty undertakes the difficult task of translation and forges common values and definitions. They phrase concepts from one discipline in terms of others. The difficulty of this work is often underestimated. The search for integrational interdisciplinarity often engenders conflict and debate, misunderstanding and hurt feelings. Faculty members prematurely labeled as lacking in team spirit or as insubordinate may in fact be very loyal to the interdisciplinary ideals but unable to use the jargon common to the majority, and if true integration is expected, the majority should expect to give some ground, too. The final stage is synthetic interdisciplinarity. When enough time has been spent in the trenches, translating and reconceptualizing, the grains of really unique things can sometimes arise. All parties to the collaboration feel equally at sea, but armed with navigational equipment they have forged together through a long, hard stage 2, they no longer describe what they do in the same terms as before. A new language has been created.

Another source of stress is governance issues related to career path inequality and unfairness. Applied science programs are populated primarily with applied scientists from engineering schools and industry. Inevitably, social science faculty members face uphill battles as they attempt to design an effective program in social context and seek career advancement too. A few colleagues will assume that social context takes valuable time away from the sciences or will never abide social context faculty members achieving authority over the curriculum as a whole through usual career channels. If the chair holds these attitudes or fails to take proactive measures, it can mean unfair containment of the nonscientific faculty in disenfranchised, miscellaneous divisions that undermine the credibility of social context elements within the program and impose on faculty members a second-class status.

Even supportive faculty members can sometimes make implementation difficult. Qualified social science faculty members hired into applied science programs are likely to have a strong interest in science and to have studied a great deal of it. Often, they are expected to pinch hit in some of the science courses. Science faculty members, on the other hand, are less likely to have formally studied social science. Typically, their interest in and knowledge about social context comes through work experience. Often, social context cannot enter into upper-division curriculum space except through permission granted them by science faculty members in the form of short modules. This works only if all the modules, when added together, constitute a coherent, graduated progression in skills of the social sciences necessary to achieving the goals, but they often do not. Scientific concepts (such as conservation of energy) have multiple contexts depending on the discipline, and so do political or economic concepts. When science faculty provide the examples and lead the discussion, the students can end up with only an episodic or anecdotal appreciation of the concepts, rather than with a more fundamental—and applications-independent—understanding. Experts can more readily separate the archetypes from the special cases. It does make a difference what topics are discussed and how the pieces are sequenced. It is a challenge to encourage science faculty participation without allowing their disciplinary preference and greater numbers to completely dilute and confuse the overall plan for social context. It is especially challenging to conceptualize how linkages will be made from one social context module within one scientific course to the next module in some other concentration. It requires delicate balancing between integration (which assumes negotiation among equals) and academic freedom (which traditionally assigns courses to a single instructor). The model program may demand that scientific content be reshaped in the interests of making social context contents more accessible and logical, just as it is assumed that social context contents will have to work around the scientific curriculum.

Teaching social context is also too easily confused with advocacy. Social context faculty members are likely to be highly motivated to see that scientific knowledge is more frequently and more correctly applied in making societies' decisions about its problems. Yet one of their essential and most difficult goals is to get science students to recognize the legitimacy of the contrary outcome. To colleagues and students, this may seem an antiscience position, but it is not. Students' reasoning about social forces is enhanced by engaging in critical analysis of the claims of science and technology itself. Too often, reflection on the institutional arrangements closest at hand can seem threatening. The organizational power distribution in the department or university, however, is often a rich and excellent illustration of similar processes at other levels more remote from student experience. Furthermore, one way for social context faculty to quickly gauge how well their curricular concepts are understood and reinforced by their scientific colleagues is to hear them discuss the institutional issues (such as the distribution of power) within the department. Yet analysis of departmental politics often meets with extreme reaction, as if it were gratuitous troublemaking rather than intellectual exploration.

Applied science programs usually promote the concept of teamwork, but there are many interpretations of "well-functioning teams," often mutually contradictory. Corporate middle managers coming into a university context sometimes bring with them a very narrow definition of teaming, more similar to chain of command notions in military organizations than to the open-ended, cooperating groups of equals with which a university is more familiar. In the zeal to remake university education on a corporate model, programs may lose sight of some very traditional values that are worth preserving. Hierarchy may not be the enemy, but neither is creative anarchy. In any case, the social context curriculum is trying to give students a broader range of organizational options, and this lesson can be completely undone by the tacit assumptions underlying faculty teams.

Teaming is also an important experience for the students, but some forms of teamwork (groupthink, not-invented-here syndrome, and similar pathologies) are tyrannies that creative organizations justifiably avoid. Most workers seek discretion and autonomy and are attracted to corporations offering them advancement into positions of greater latitude, increasing span of control and wider perspectives and demanding their creativity. The joy of teamwork is in the special knowledge of several collaborators that results in unexpected synergies. How to reproduce this experience for undergraduates is a challenge, but it has something to do with a diversity of preparation and allowing groups to form around difficult and sufficiently complex problems rather than with forcing students into work groups of four merely to make grading less tedious.

Finally, the creation of applied science programs is tied to waves of educational reform. As the political center has become more conservative and individualistic, the consensus about the public support of research universities has broken down, and the innovative paradigms of the 1960s and 1970s have run their course.[20]

Funds have shrunk for basic research and expanded for applied projects. University administrations have professionalized. Increasingly, college presidents are described not as scholars but as CEOs (Greenberg 2000), and students as consumers, or worse, the product. Universities now routinely manage venture capital and the intellectual property of their faculty (Melcher 2000). The rapid conversion of research into profit typical of biotechnology has become the model rather than an exception, yet faculty members assume they are not seduced by money. In many states, the preponderance of new support for higher education is now linked to the development of joint programs with industry. It used to be assumed, even at the best engineering schools, that lucrative fields subsidized less lucrative ones so that education could remain broad, integrative, and critical. But increasingly, management mentality equates relevance to short-term gain in market contexts. Not only is the university's corporate structure obscured from students, and its faculty increasingly managed as employees, but students see their scientific problems almost entirely from the perspective of the United States and of management. In many applied science programs, partnerships with industry have a very antiunion, promanagement flavor, in which the university is hard put to remain neutral and critical.[21] Applied science programs should be responsive to societal need and, in the case of public universities, accountable to the citizens who support them. They are right to break down barriers between the academy and the business world to ensure the relevance of their curriculum and to secure access to corporate internships. But just as they seek to avoid the narrow-mindedness of traditional discipline-based science education, they should also avoid falling into a kind of blind boosterism for industry. Resurgent community colleges and online, nonresidential distance learning will surely fill that vocational body shop or subcontracting niche with a broad range of focused, practical, and flexible-schedule training opportunities (Jones 1996).

The corporatization of higher education has also been described as a shift in power between the institution and its students. As tuition rises, students demand more visible return on their investment, one that can be measured in immediate market terms: employability and postgraduate salaries. Student empowerment puts pressure on the faculty to address short-term goals. The result can be grade inflation, litigation-fearful letters of recommendation, and student assessments of teaching in terms of entertainment or production values. At the same time, requiring individual departments to be fiscally self-sustaining undermines the ability of students to get experience and training in ancillary disciplines, even if they were inspired to do so.[22] Departments shut their doors to all but majoring students to preserve their control over faculty-student ratios and workload. For all these reasons, there is already a backlash against the corporatization of the university (Soley 1995).

All these stresses can profoundly affect the social context curriculum of an applied science program. If there is any value added by a university education over and above that provided by corporate in-house training or apprenticeship programs, it surely lies in the very traditional marks of the university graduate: better than average training in analysis, broader understanding of complexity, skepticism about conventional assumptions, and the creativity and flexibility to innovate. Such graduates can apply their knowledge to unprecedented dilemmas and will not be limited by the prevailing assumptions of economics or politics: the bottom line or the party line. They will be proactive and technically skilled innovators for tomorrow's jobs, with the practical street smarts and initiative to make things happen.

Conclusion: Educational Codes

One of the most difficult concepts to deal with is power. It is difficult despite the widespread acceptance of the idea that knowledge is power and that for students and faculty alike, an applied science program's goals are to empower its students into the competitive world by virtue of their mastery of technologies. Would that it were so easy! Basil Bernstein (1971), a British sociologist of education, said, "How a society selects, classifies, distributes, transmits and evaluates the educational knowledge it considers to be public, reflects both the distribution of power and the principles of social control" (p. 47). In the early days of Hampshire College, Bernstein's work was used as a model for thinking about the institution-building project on which it was engaged, and it still seems enormously relevant. According to Bernstein,

> formal educational knowledge can be considered to be realized through three message systems: curriculum, pedagogy and evaluation. Curriculum defines what counts as valid knowledge, pedagogy defines what counts as a valid transmission of knowledge, and evaluation defines what counts as a valid realization of this knowledge on the part of the taught. (P. 47)

Bernstein defined two different kinds of curricula, "collection" type and "integration" type:

> if contents stand in a *closed* relation to each other, that is, if the contents are clearly bounded and insulated from each other, I shall call such a curriculum a *collection* type. Here the learner has to collect a group of favored contents in order to satisfy some criteria of evaluation. There may of course be some underlying concept to a collection: the gentleman, the educated man, the skilled man, the non-vocational man.
>   Now I want to juxtapose against the collection type, a curriculum where the various contents do not go their own separate ways, but where the contents are in an *open* relation to each other. I shall call such a curriculum an *integrated* type. Now we can have various types of collection, and various degrees and types of integration. (P. 49)

The prevailing styles or combinations of approaches to these three systems (curriculum, pedagogy, and evaluation) constitute a society's educational code. Just as the notion of the strength of the boundary between contents distinguishes the integrated curricula from the collection type, Bernstein (1971) employed the concepts of classification and framing to generalize this notion to the educational code as a whole. Integrated curricula result from educational codes where classification is weak. The boundaries between contents are loose, or blurred, such as in applied science and interdisciplinary programs. Framing, on the other hand, is the dimension used to describe pedagogy, "the form of the context in which knowledge is transmitted and received . . . the relationship of teacher and taught."

> Where framing is strong, there is a sharp boundary, where framing is weak, a blurred boundary, between what may and may not be transmitted. Frame refers to the range of options available to teacher and taught in the *control* of what is transmitted and received in the context of the pedagogical relationship. Strong framing entails reduced options; weak framing entails a range of options. *This frame refers to the degree of control teacher and pupil possess over the selection, organization and pacing of the knowledge transmitted and received in the pedagogical relationship.* (P. 50)

In the American lexicon, we might identify the classification scheme as how the different areas of the canon relate to one another. Traditionally, classification was strong, and putting together a general education formula as often as not respected the boundaries between contents, specifying lists of stand-alone courses that the students could select that would constitute the requisite collection-type education. This is sometimes referred to as the smorgasbord approach. Recently, James Madison University has tried to redesign more integrated curricula by encouraging its faculty to develop new courses linking several disciplines, thus, in Bernstein's (1971) term, encouraging weaker "classification." At the same time, it has felt necessary to narrow the range of options available to the student by specifying a limited number of sequences. Bernstein too predicted that weakening classification was compensated for by a stronger specification of what constitutes valid pedagogy, or stronger framing. This is consistent with the society's call for education to move back to basics.

Bernstein (1971) successfully deconstructed the strong classification codes of traditional, discipline-based university education, discussing how students are socialized into these strong classification codes through a long apprenticeship: "For the many, socialization into knowledge is socialization into order, the existing order, into the experience that the world's educational knowledge is impermeable" (p. 57). At the doctorate level,

> the ultimate mystery of the subject is not coherence, but incoherence, not order but disorder, not the known but the unknown. As this mystery, under collection codes, is revealed very late in the educational life—then only to a select few who have shown the signs of successful socialization—then only the few experience in their bones the notion that knowledge is permeable, that its orderings are provisional, that the dialectic of knowledge is closure and openness. (P. 57)[23]

Bernstein (1971) also recognized that integrated codes that are single teacher based are easier to introduce than one in which the integrated code involves the relationships among several teachers. For this reason, he also predicted that pressures for "a common pedagogy and common evaluation system" will generally mean a reduction in teacher discretion in integrated codes but an increase in student discretion, which of course is a radical shift in the balance of power. Clearly, interdisciplinary, undergraduate-applied science programs with social-context goals are integrated-type curricula, motivated by the idea that strong classification is not optimal. Many experiments have resulted in the pursuit of integrated curriculum codes. Here again, Bernstein is instructive for he clearly stated that

> because one subject uses the theories of another subject, this type of intellectual interrelationship does not constitute integration. Such intellectual interrelation may well be part of a collection code at some point in the development of knowledge. Integration, as it is used here, refers minimally to the *subordination* of previously insulated subjects *or* course to some *relational* idea, which blurs the boundaries between the subjects. (P. 53)

Recognizing and developing the appropriate relational idea that binds together all of the elements of an interdisciplinary program is an intellectually challenging proposition but is crucial for applied science programs trying to integrate social context elements.

Notes

1. I am personally acquainted with three: the School of Natural Science at Hampshire College, where I taught science policy, the Energy Management and Power Program at the University of Pennsylvania (no longer existing), and the Integrated Science and Technology Program at James Madison University. I also am somewhat acquainted with a variety of other interdisciplinary programs involving applied science and social context in varying proportions: the history and sociology of science department at the University of Pennsylvania; the science and society programs at Cornell, the Massachusetts Institute of Technology, Rensselaer, and Washington University; the George Washington University Space Policy Program; and many others.

2. While the model program described here has been shaped by my experiences within the Integrated Science and Technology Program at James Madison University, it is not descriptive of that program. My views are my own and should not be taken as representing the official policy of the Integrated Science and Technology Program or of James Madison University.

3. The word "technical" here is meant very broadly to indicate those parameters of problems that involve a primarily scientific knowledge base, not limited to a single discipline and including various kinds of technological knowledge. It is not used in the narrow sense of a highly specialized or abstruse reality or in the sense of "a mere technicality." I use the term in preference to "scientific" because I firmly believe that both social context experts (e.g., political scientists, sociologists, psychologists, economists, and so forth) can and should operate within the same scientific tradition of empirically based and logically sophisticated reasoning. So within a generally scientific approach, there are technical and contextual aspects.

4. Well expressed by the Left, for example, Foucault (1980) and Habermas (1970).

5. This article primarily deals with problem solving within the United States and similar high-tech, developed economies having democratic polities.

6. There is a long history of the politics of science and scientific communities, see Ben-David (1971), Bernal (1967), Dickson (1984), Feenberg and Hannay (1995), Gilpin and Wright (1964), Greenberg (1967), Haberer (1969), Nelkin (1977), Noble (1977), Penick et al. ([1965] 1972), Price (1956), and Skolnikoff (1967).

7. In fact, many applied science programs, including the Integrated Science and Technology Program at James Madison University, have specific mandates to attract new kinds of students: minorities, women, and so forth. One theory of doing so is to rid the program of stereotypical attitudes that are off-putting to these populations, and these kinds of misconceptions definitely frustrate these diversity goals.

8. One of the best in this genre is "Mr. Feynman Goes to Washington: Investigating the Space Shuttle Challenger Disaster" (Feynman 1988, pp. 113-237). See also Dörner (1996), Piller (1991), and Schlager (1995).

9. This has been a consistent and clear message from the industrial patrons of the James Madison University Integrated Science and Technology Program.

10. While this program has been informed by my experiences in several programs, it does not represent any of them. It is an ideal toward which I would like to move. Furthermore, this is an abbreviated description of the model program. Interested readers are encouraged to contact me directly for more information at ivorymx@jmu.edu.

11. Political scientists usually distinguish between physical power (the capacity to threaten physically, or coerce) and authority (the publicly recognized ability to impose obligations on a group). Having one does not necessarily confer the other. In science and technology areas, we are primarily concerned with authority, although we are often drawn into discussions of (military) technology and therefore raw physical power. Other kinds of power can also be identified, such as influence and loyalty, which are, strictly speaking, neither physical power nor authority but may be just as important. We also speak of commercial power, or the power of money, which can feel as coercive as any other but is neither physical threat nor legal authority. Finally, some theorists speak of organizational power, group solidarity, and community. Religious groups and street theatre often refer to the power of witness; the expression of new metaphors or examples. It is with these permutations that students must become familiar.

12. The Integrated Science and Technology Program offers concentrations in energy, environment, telecommunications, information science, biotechnology, health systems, and manufacturing.

13. See the Public Interest Research Group Web site at http://www.pirg.org.

14. The simulation is available on my personal Web site, http://www.isat.jmu.edu/faculty.htm.

15. The James Madison University program has attempted to assess how well social context elements are integrated into senior projects, but the methodology is not yet perfected and few strategies have been developed to encourage it across the board.

16. I am working with a corporate partner to convert one of its technological market decisions into a case study. The first thing they wanted was a nondisclosure agreement.

17. The insights of Herbert Simon (1955) on satisficing would be one useful example.

18. The space shuttle disaster hinged on this element. The brittleness of the materials in the o-rings at low temperatures was, after all, a known technical fact. That it led to a failure of the system had to do with how poorly technical expertise and economic/political decision making were integrated. This is another well-documented case.

19. Programs that use only adjunct faculty or borrow faculty are often endangered. This was the fate as I understand it of the University of Pennsylvania's program in energy management and power. The Cornell program looks a bit this way, as do programs in engineering schools.

20. From a conservative perspective, Gaff (1991) identified "content, coherence, commonality and comprehensiveness" as the issues in earlier debates. See also Bush ([1945] 1960), Patterson and Longsworth (1966), Bloom (1987), Bennett (1984), Hirsch (1987), and American Association for the Advancement of Science (1990).

21. These labor issues are explored from different perspectives by Sclove (1995) and Chawla and Renesch (1995).

22. The University of Rhode Island, for example, tried to downsize by fiscal formula: the ratio relating tuition dollars generated by the department to the dollars required to sustain it (Roush 1995). James Engell (cited in Marlantes 2000) of Harvard observed, "Either the area promises . . . higher than average lifetime earnings, or the area itself studies money; or receives money from outside giants. . . . If it has not, it has suffered."

23. Bernstein (1971) also remarked that

[specialization codes] tend to abhor mixed categories and blurred identities, for they represent a potential openness, an ambiguity, which makes the consequences of previous socialization problematic. Mixed categories such as bio-physicist or psycholinguist are only permitted to develop after long socialization into a subject loyalty. . . . Any attempt to weaken or change classification strength may be felt as a threat to one's identity, and may be experienced as a pollution endangering the sacred. Here we have one source of the resistance to change of educational code.

References

American Association for the Advancement of Science. 1990. *The liberal art of science*. Washington, DC: American Association for the Advancement of Science.

Ben-David, Joseph. 1971. *The scientist's role in society: A comparative study*. Englewood Cliffs, NJ: Prentice Hall.

Bennett, W. J. 1984. *To reclaim a legacy*. Washington, DC: National Endowment for the Humanities.

Bernal, J. D. 1967. *The social function of science*. Cambridge, MA: MIT Press.

Bernstein, Basil. 1971. On the classification and framing of educational knowledge. In *Knowledge and control: New directions for the sociology of education*, edited by Michael F. D. Young. London: Collier Macmillan.

Bjiker, Wiebe E. 1995. *Of bicycles, bakelites, and bulbs: Toward a theory of sociotechnical change*. Cambridge, MA: MIT Press.

Bjiker, Wiebe E., Thomas P. Hughes, and Trevor Pinch, eds. 1987. *The social construction of technological systems*. Cambridge, MA: MIT Press.

Bloom, Allan. 1987. *Closing of the American mind*. New York: Simon & Schuster.

Bush, Vannevar. [1945] 1960. *Science the endless frontier: A report to the president on a program for postwar scientific research*. Washington, DC: National Science Foundation.

Chawla, Sarita, and John Renesch. 1995. *Learning organizations: Developing cultures for tomorrow's workplace*. Portland, OR: Productivity Press.

Dörner, Dietrich. 1996. *The logic of failure: Why things go wrong and what we can do to make them right*. New York: Henry Holt.

Dickson, David. 1984. *The new politics of science*. New York: Pantheon.

Feenberg, Andrew, and Alasta Hannay. 1995. *Technology and the politics of knowledge*. Bloomington: Indiana University Press.

Feynman, Richard P. 1988. *"What do you care what other people think?" Further adventures of a curious character*. New York: Norton.

Foucault, Michael. 1980. *Power/knowledge: Selected interviews and other writings 1972-1977*. New York: Pantheon.

Gaff, Jerry G. 1991. *New life for the college curriculum*. San Francisco: Jossey-Bass.

Gilpin, Robert, and Christopher Wright, eds. 1964. *Scientists and national policy-making*. New York: Columbia University Press.

Greenberg, Daniel. 1967. *The politics of pure science*. New York: New American Library.

Greenberg, David. 2000. The shrinking college president. *New Republic*, 1 June.

Haberer, Joseph. 1969. *Politics and the community of science*. New York: Van Nostrand Reinhold.

Habermas, Jurgen. 1970. *Toward a rational society: Student protest, science and politics*. Boston: Beacon.

Hirsch, E. D. 1987. *Cultural literacy*. Boston: Houghton Mifflin.

Hughes, Thomas Parke. 1998. *Rescuing Prometheus: Four monumental projects that changed the modern world*. New York: Random House Vintage.

James Madison University. 1998. *ISAT student survey*. Harrisonburg, VA: James Madison University.

John, Richard R. 1988. The politics of innovation. *Daedalus* fall: 187-214.

Jones, Glen R. 1996. *Cyberschools: An educational renaissance*. Englewood, CO: Cyber.

Marlantes, Liz. 2000. What ivory tower? A consumer mentality is boldly reshaping the college experience. *Christian Science Monitor*, 25 January, 17.

Melcher, Richard. 2000. Theory-oriented research universities adapt to keep pace with market demands. *Business Week*, 31 August.

Nelkin, Dorothy. 1977. *Technological decisions and democracy*. Beverly Hills, CA: Sage.

Noble, David F. 1977. *America by design: Science, technology and the rise of corporate capitalism*. New York: Knopf.

Patterson, Franklin, and Charles R. Longsworth. 1966. *The making of a college: Plans for a new departure in higher education*. Cambridge, MA: MIT Press.

Penick, James L., Jr., Carroll W. Pursell Jr., Morgan B. Sherwood, and Donald C. Swain, eds. [1965] 1972. *The politics of American science: 1939 to the present*. Cambridge, MA: MIT Press.

Piller, Charles. 1991. *The fail-safe society: Community defiance and the end of American technological optimism*. New York: Harper.

Polanyi, Michael. 1964. *Personal knowledge: Towards a post-critical philosophy*. New York: Harper & Row.

Price, Don K. 1956. *The scientific estate*. Cambridge, MA: Harvard University Press.

Roush, Wade. 1995. URI tries downsizing by formula. *Science* 272:342-44.

Ruggiero, Vincent Ryan. 1990. *Beyond feelings: A guide to critical thinking*. Mountain View, CA: Mayfield.

Schlager, Neil. 1995. *Breakdown: Deadly technological disasters*. Detroit, MI: Visible Ink Press.

Sclove, Richard E. 1995. *Democracy and technology*. New York: Guilford.

Simon, Herbert A. 1955. A behavioral model of rational choice. *Quarterly Journal of Economics* 69:174-83.

Skolnikoff, Eugene B. 1967. *Science, technology and American foreign policy*. Cambridge, MA: MIT Press.

Soley, Lawrence C. 1995. *Leasing the ivory tower: The corporate takeover of academia*. Boston: South End.

Integrating Tertiary Education in Europe

By
HEATHER FIELD

There have been recent steps toward the integration of tertiary education in the EU and Europe more widely. The intergovernmental Bologna Agreement has resulted in the adoption of an Anglo-Saxon three-year undergraduate degree and two-year postgraduate degree as a European standard. Course credits are to be common and transferable. In spite of fears of a loss of standards, the new arrangements are being widely adopted. The Maastricht Treaty gave the EU's common institutions specific but limited responsibilities with regard to education. They have established and run schemes to promote the mobility of students, teachers, and workers in their education. These schemes, and the integration of tertiary education, are being extended to Central and Eastern Europe, but not Russia as yet. Major difficulties in educational integration include the existence of conflicting interpretations of history and definitions of an appropriate research process as well as perspectives on the development of culture and identity. Specific regional challenges await the extension of the process to Southeastern Europe.

In North America, there is a considerable range of tertiary institutions in terms of cost and quality of education offered, yet admission tests and the structure of undergraduate and postgraduate degrees are highly standardized. In contrast to this, in Europe and the EU, tertiary institutions and education are mostly funded by the state, but there are considerable variations in the structure of courses and qualifications and in some cases in the content.

Heather Field is a senior lecturer in contemporary European studies at Griffith University in Brisbane, Australia. She has published in areas including EU enlargement, cultural and education policy, and politics, as well as on causes and outcomes of war in former Yugoslavia. She has been a visiting professor at the University of Aalborg in Denmark and has taught at associate professor level at Bond University in Surfers Paradise. Her qualifications include a doctorate in politics from the University of New England and postgraduate degrees from the Australian National University, La Trobe University, and the University of Amsterdam, as well as a first degree from Loughborough University of Technology.

DOI: 10.1177/0002716202238574

The integration of education in the EU and Europe more widely gained momentum with the signing in 1999 of the Bologna declaration by ministers from twenty-nine European countries to eliminate some of the obstacles to increased mobility of students and graduates in obtaining employment. The declaration involves agreed aims to move to a European Higher Education Area over ten years by ironing out some of the least compatible characteristics of national university systems. It represents a further step toward integration of tertiary education following the 1998 Sorbonne declaration. Common cycles have been agreed on as the basis of a common European system of tertiary education, consisting of a first or bachelor's degree of at least three years' duration and of a second postgraduate master's or doctoral degree. France and Italy are already introducing new, shorter degrees in line with the declarations (Jobbins 1999). These moves reflect the situation described by Mitchell (1998, 1-2), that many of the traditional "borders" that have impinged on education are breaking down or being redefined. These changes are part of a wider globalization of education.

In the EU, the greatest progress has been undertaken on an intergovernmental basis rather than being managed by common institutions such as the European Commission. This was first through the Sorbonne Declaration of 25 May 1998, which stressed the key role of universities for the development of a European "cultural dimension" (Einem 2000, 1). Second, the 19 June 1999 Bologna Declaration of European education ministers took matters further by setting out the basis of a common tertiary system consisting of undergraduate and graduate cycles. The Declaration was signed by a gathering of twenty-eight European education ministers and followed more than a year's preparatory work by the ministers for education of the four largest EU member states, Germany, France, the United Kingdom, and Italy. It will result in the establishment of a common course credit system based on the present European Credit Transfer Systems one. The declaration is intended to lead to a common European Tertiary Educational Space, which covers all of Europe and not just the territory of the EU. The new arrangements should increase the range of study options available to students and allow for formal recognition for academics and administrators of periods spent in research, teaching, or training in other countries (Einem 2000, 2).

Educational integration is also being furthered by, for example, the European Thematic Network on Political Science and a specific project regarding a core curriculum on European integration studies being undertaken under the direction of Wolfgang Wessels, Jean Monnet Chair at the University of Cologne (Wessels, Linsemann, and Haegele 2000). This will rely on what Wessels, Linsemann, and Haegele (2000, 4) described as the "Anglo-American 3-level model of university studies," which has an undergraduate cycle and a postgraduate one of master's degree and Ph.D. This is the same as that specified as a general model under the Bologna Declaration.

One motivation behind moves toward harmonization of European tertiary education has been the desire to counter the increasing popularity of the United States's tertiary education in both global and European terms and to reduce the extent to which its English-language basis, large home student base, and use of modern technologies such as the Internet give it an advantage over European and other systems. France in particular has been critical of the United States, with former education minister Claude Allegre accusing it of trying to foist its educational system on Europe, with the possible result of a privatization of tertiary education and a greater uniformity of teaching. He denounced the "hegemonic power" of the United States in *Le Monde* on the basis that it was seeking to establish American universities in Europe and has also proposed that education be included among services to be covered by the World Trade Organization. However, he considered it "absolutely desirable" for French students to undertake some of their study in another country, and his own proposed higher education reforms included new degrees based on three, five, and eight years of postbaccalaureate study on the U.S. and eventual European model (Marshall 2000).

On a critical basis, it might be argued that integration of tertiary education in Europe is part of a wider "McDonaldization" of education as part of globalization. This process has been strongly criticized. It has been feared that trade liberalization in the area could lead to pressures for a removal of state funding of tertiary education (McIlvenny, Lassen, and Raudaskoski 2002, 4). The United Kingdom is put forward as an example of a country within which there has been substantial privatization of tertiary education, with reductions in subsidies and the introduction of loans and fees. However, the vast majority of tertiary education is still provided by institutions that are mainly state funded, although there are many private tertiary institutions, including offshoots of overseas institutions. Even in Finland, there has been some privatization in the sense that two branches of Preston University, a for-profit organization from the U.S. state of Wyoming, have opened there (McIlvenny, Lassen, and Raudaskoski 2002, 6).

The new post–Bologna Agreement arrangements aim to fuse degree structures across Europe into a system that encourages greater student mobility and is understood by employers (Field 2000b). They are intended to promote greater movement of labor in line with general principles and aims of economic integration in Europe and the 1992 Agreement, which removed many of the further barriers to trade in services and so forth by the target date of 1992. The desire to standardize and integrate education arises partly because of the need to have comparability of training and qualifications to allow freeing up of the movement of workers between countries. Different degree structures and educational systems had meant that it was difficult, for example, for doctors and architects to move freely between countries because the requirements for qualification and the training provided differed between EU member states.

The new arrangements are attractive to those EU member states, which have become concerned about the length of their degrees and the problems of maintaining access to their tertiary systems while reducing the level of overcrowding. Overcrowding has become a particular problem in France, where all students who obtain the school-leaving qualification or baccalaureate have the right to take up a place at university. In Germany, the problem has been instead one of long completion periods and high dropout rates among students taking degrees. Ten countries already comply with the new arrangements in some way, and Austria has indicated that it will join these.

In Italy, the new system was readily embraced, in spite of some opposition from academics who thought that it would lower standards (Bompard 2000). A transition to the new European three-year degree followed by the two-year specialization postgraduate degree on the European model was commenced in 2001-2002.

In France, a new postgraduate degree of *mastaire* is to be introduced and a credit system aimed at increasing student mobility. One conclusion from an inquiry by the National Council for Higher Education and Research is that the new degrees must have "clear European equivalence" (Marshall 2000).

The new shorter degrees have already proven very popular in Germany, taking four years instead of the traditional seven. Some three hundred are already being offered, and this is expected to grow to more than a thousand. The University of Bochum in the Ruhr has gone over totally to the new system. An accreditation agency has been established for quality control of the new degrees. The decision on whether to introduce the new shorter degrees rests with the individual states of *Laender* that control and fund tertiary education in Germany. However, they have a vested interest in changes, which will reduce the dropout and failure rate in tertiary education and the very long periods that students often require to complete their seven-year degrees.

European students have been seeking some involvement in the integration process, and the National Unions of Students in Europe received assistance from French education minister Jack Lang in having its manifesto on education issues raised at a meeting of the EU's council of education ministers. The manifesto deals with issues of student mobility, access, welfare, recognition of qualifications, and quality assurance (Marshall 2000).

The new degree structures will make it easier for students to undertake different parts of their education in different European countries. This can be in terms of a first undergraduate degree in one country and a postgraduate degree in another or parts of the courses for these being undertaken in different countries. They do represent greater standardization and a loss of some of the educational and cultural distinctiveness of individual countries, but in return, there are benefits for individuals and for business and industry. The process is part of both globalization and regionalization in Europe.

Integration and harmonization of tertiary education is taking place to some extent on a Europe-wide rather than just an EU basis. This is because the ten prospective member states in Central and Eastern Europe and the applicant Mediterranean states of Cyprus and Malta are also involved in moves toward standardization and integration of education, as well as some other countries in Central and Eastern Europe. Involvement in such a process will help Central and Eastern Europe universities to upgrade to Western standards, having been held back by membership of the Soviet bloc in most cases up to 1990.

European education ministers have agreed to include the Central and Eastern Europe applicant countries—the Czech Republic, Estonia, Latvia, Lithuania,

Hungary, Poland, Slovenia, Slovakia, Romania, and Bulgaria—for membership in the education convergence process. These countries already have the opportunity to participate in the European Community Action Scheme for the Mobility of University Students (ERASMUS) educational mobility scheme and to participate in the research and postgraduate training activities of the European University Institute (EUI) in Florence. Croatia, Cyprus, Turkey, Serbia, Macedonia, Bosnia-Herzegovina, and Albania were offered the chance of joining the education convergence process in the near future at the Prague summit of education ministers in May 2001. Serbia's deputy minister of education Srbijanka Turajlic said it would be a powerful psychological boost and would signal the country's return to the wider European fold (Holdsworth 2001).

However, Russia is not at present adopting the new European system but sticking to its five-year degrees. The introduction of the new system will hence create two Europes, with Central and Eastern Europe following the EU, and Russia remaining apart and different in educational terms. This will add to the major division that is eventuating in Europe and that will become very visible once the Central and Eastern European applicant countries join the EU and their easternmost borders become the eastern border of the EU.

The integration of tertiary education on a voluntary intergovernmental basis in the EU and Central and Eastern Europe follows attempts by the EU to facilitate integration through educational initiatives at different levels and support for the movement of students, teachers, young workers, and others. A green paper (Commission of the European Communities 1993) was put forward to stimulate discussion on possible EU action in the area of education. This suggested a number of major areas for prospective action. Schools were considered to be a possible area for the introduction of a "European dimension into education so that young people feel that they are citizens of Europe as well as of their own countries" (Background report 1993, 2). School and student exchanges and language training were seen as a means of achieving this.

Programs such as the ERASMUS tertiary exchange program, the Program for the Promotion of Foreign Languages Knowledge in the EC language training scheme, Community Program in Education and Training for Technology technological training scheme, and the Action Program for the Development of Continuing Vocational Training in the EC vocational training scheme were seen to have already succeeded in demonstrating the benefits of such exchange education and training programs. The Education Information Network in the European Community information network on European Commission (now EU) education was also seen as playing a prospective supporting role.

By 1996, ERASMUS and related schemes had financed the mobility of some 250,000 EU students and young workers since 1987 (Laffan 1996, 97). These mobility schemes can be seen as attempts to bring wider European, or at least EU, influences to bear on the culture and identity of elites, as well as providing them with some positive benefits from political integration. The ERASMUS scheme has been partly aimed at developing a shared sense of identity among students from different member states (Kleinman and Piachaud 1993). More than 200,000 students participated in 1999, with Germany supplying the greatest proportion. The scheme assists students to spend up to three months of their degree in another EU country. However, there have been difficulties of imbalance with ERASMUS, with about 10,000 British students each year wanting to study in other EU countries with its assistance, but double that number wishing to come from other EU countries to the United Kingdom.[1]

The United Kingdom sought special EU assistance to cope with the excess of students, but this was refused, and EU member states were urged instead to seek a better balance on arrivals and departures under the ERASMUS scheme. This has proven unrealistic for the United Kingdom since many EU students wish to come and undertake part of their tertiary education in English as it will improve their career opportunities. The same level of benefits does not appear to accrue to U.K. students undertaking part of their course in, say, France or Germany and the language of that country. The United Kingdom has also had more experience teaching foreign students and is more flexible to their needs compared to some continental European countries. Safety may also be a concern.

Only 5 percent of Nordic students choose other Nordic states when studying abroad, most choosing to go the United States or United Kingdom. In an attempt to balance the ERASMUS and tertiary student movement books, more tertiary courses are being provided in English there. However, high Scandinavian living costs tend to mean that it is also necessary to subsidize living and study costs to attract students from other countries.

Although ERASMUS and related schemes have had some success in promoting the mobility of students and young people in Europe, they have only met objectives to a limited extent. An initial ERASMUS aim had been to get 10 percent of students participating, but the level achieved has been only about 1 percent. Only about half of the annual 180,000 places in the scheme are taken up at all. Two-thirds of participating students' parents are employed in managerial, professional, or technical jobs, and more than half of participants assess their parents' incomes as about average. More than half the students participating have said that they had faced financial difficulties during their time abroad (European Voice 2000). The scheme aims to cover only a part of the living costs of students.

In addition to these programs, the Jean Monnet scheme of assistance for course initiatives and professorial chairs in European integration has been established to facilitate the standardization and Europeanization of European integration courses and curricula through the interaction of appointees. By 2000, the scheme had resulted in the creation of more than 1,722 new university courses or projects, including 409 professorial chairs (Shore 2000, 28).

A further initiative intended to support study and research on the reality and theory of European integration has been the establishment of the EUI in Florence. It is financed by the higher education ministries of the EU member states, with the four largest member states meeting some 20 percent of the cost each. It is a postgraduate research and teaching institution and has been criticized for its high costs per student and its failure to become a stronger support for academic and research work in its area of operation. In 1997-1998, its high student suicide rate was also considered problematic, with four of its student body of three hundred taking their own lives. In its early years of operation, much of the research work undertaken had at best a tenuous link with European integration. In 1994, the deputy general secretary of the Alexander von Humboldt foundation, which funds much research in Germany, was critical of the Europeanization of research on the basis that the EUI and other centers were too expensive, much of their work was inefficient, and it only duplicated other research (Gardner 1994). They had not succeeded in becoming leading centers of research into European integration.

The EUI has been widening its admissions arrangements to take in candidates from the applicant countries for EU membership and has signed special agreements with Hungary and Poland to facilitate this. In 2001, the current president, Patrick Masterson, said that the institute had importance as "an independent intellectual resource for Europe" (Worldwatch 2001). In recent years, it has had more success in attracting a number of specialists on European integration to take up fellowships and research chairs there. It now has an academic community numbering about 1,000, some 850 of whom are researchers, doctoral students, or academics. About eighty doctoral theses are submitted and defended there each year, the completion rate for doctoral candidates being 76 percent.

The College of Europe in Bruges is another EU-funded and -run teaching and research institution, with the specific goal that it would provide training for young people who go on to become public servants in the EU's common institutions. It has been less controversial than the EUI, perhaps because it has had a clearer mission and more readily visible results.

The Maastricht Treaty came into force in 1993, giving the EU's political institutions new competencies or legal powers in the field of education and allowing the scope of common programs to be expanded. Article 126 of the treaty sets out the aims of community action in the area of education as follows (Background report 1993):

- developing the European dimension in education, particularly through the teaching and dissemination of the languages of the Member States;
- encouraging the mobility of students and teachers, inter alia by encouraging the academic recognition of diplomas and periods of study;
- promoting co-operation between educational establishments;
- developing exchanges of information and experience on issues common to the education systems of the Member States;
- encouraging the development of youth exchanges and of exchanges of socio-educational instructors; and
- encouraging the development of distance education. (P. 1)

Dardanelli (1999) argued that EU national governments should "use their exclusive control over the education systems that socialize Europe's citizens to raise their political identification with the Union" (p. 12). In support of this, he pointed out that "in the last four years over 80 per cent of Europeans supported an EU dimension of the education curricula" (p. 12). However, Eurobarometer 51 data (European Commission 1999, 54) indicate that of eighteen policy areas, education is the one that has the lowest level of support for joint national and EU decision making. Only 29 percent support it becoming a joint area of decision making, and 66 percent want it to remain national. While 84 percent of respondents supported the statement that how the EU works should be taught in schools, and only 6 percent opposed it, less than a third wanted to see a partial transfer of decision making over education to the EU's common political institutions.

The integration of tertiary education on an intergovernmental basis conflicts with the view that a closer management of and involvement in education, including tertiary education, by the European Commission is what is needed to assist integration in Europe. This view is supported by, for example, Corbett (1999), who argued that "it is the commission that has developed the know-how on almost every Bologna issue" and that "the EU, unlike the intergovernmental organizations, has a good record on policy outcomes."

It is probably true that harmonization of tertiary education might be more swiftly and efficiently achieved if it were undertaken by the European Commission than by national authorities and universities acting in concert but retaining their essential independence. However, there is the possibility of such a move representing a threat to academic independence and to the freedom universities have at least in some member states to set course content and choose research areas and issues. Also, as the "guardian" of the EU's treaties with the role of promoter of integration, the commission might be expected to place a high priority on the role of tertiary education as a means of Europeanizing elites (Field 2000a). National priorities may reflect instead concerns about, for example, widening or maintaining access to tertiary education for all social groups or the adequacy of the numbers training for less lucrative professions such as teaching and nursing. Such priorities are important in, for example, Sweden and the United Kingdom (Goddard 2000; De Laine 2000).

The Culture, Youth and Education Committee of the European Parliament has adopted a report that calls for the promotion of "training modules that meet the quality requirements of students and teachers at every university in every member state" (Nuthall, Warden, and Jobbins 2002). However, such Europeanized modules are likely to fail to meet the needs of students and teachers in specific member states. The European University Association supports quality control procedures but has resolutely opposed a centrally imposed quality assurance mechanism that would reduce university autonomy.

The current European Commission, headed by Romano Prodi, has chosen to integrate its responsibilities with regard to education with those for culture, instead of with employment where they might have been used to play a more instrumental role. This might be said to be linked to the situation that the European Commission Treaty (article 149 [4] TEC) forbids attempts by the common political institutions to harmonize national curricula or legal instruments in the field of education, educational policy still being seen as closely linked to national identity (Wessels, Linsemann, and Haegele 2000, 5). There are still many differences within the EU where perspectives and curricula on European integration are concerned (Field 1999, 2001).

One of the difficulties in attempting to unify or integrate education in Europe is that there are different views or perspectives on history, which are very much in conflict with one another. An example of this is provided by conflicts that arose with respect to the planning of a Museum for Europe to be sponsored or at least approved by the European Commission. The Greek government wanted an emphasis in the museum on the European origin of the democratic idea and, by implication, ancient Greece. However, the museum's planners wanted the history emphasized in the museum to commence in the early Middle Ages or Dark Ages with Charlemagne's empire and Latin Christendom (Kaye 2000).

A Holy Roman Empire approach and emphasis on Charlemagne are contrary to the historical instincts of Scandinavians, Greeks, and the British. For example, *An Illustrated History of Denmark* (Deleuran 1993) depicts Charlemagne as the man who persecuted the Saxon neighbors and allies of the Danes. Part 5 of the *History* describes how he beheaded 4,500 Saxon hostages and drove the Saxons from their lands north of the Elbe and replaced them with pagan Aboditrians. Part 6 stresses the earlier history of Denmark as part of the empire of Attila, the ruler of the Huns. Sagas such as that of Sigurd (the German Siegfried) are seen as being set in the context of the empire of the Huns rather than being European as such.

Pavkovic (2000, 126-27) suggested that the heroes of the battle of Chalons-sur-Marne in France, "where Europe was saved from Attila's hordes," could be viewed as the "gloriously fallen" (p. 129) in an attempt to construct a common European myth and identity. However, Deleuran's (1993, part 5) history shows that the battle between the forces of the Roman general Aetius and those of Attila, overlord of the Huns, cannot be seen as a simple tale of European defense against Asiatic hordes. It was a conflict in which there were West Goths, Alans, and Burgundians, among others, on Aetius's side and East Goths, Heruls, Gepids, Huns, and others on that of Attila. Also, Aetius was a personal friend of Attila from his earlier days as a hostage with the Huns, and when the West Goths had the possibility of winning the day by storming Attila's position, he ordered them not to.

Another example of such differences in perspectives is that the five hundredth birthday in 2000 of Charles V, Holy Roman Emperor and ruler of the Netherlands, Spain, Naples, Sicily, and the German Reich, including its then greatest kingdom, Austria, and its Hungarian possessions, was commemorated with the intention of giving people encouragement to "reflect on the foundations of European identity," according to its organizer, Professor Wim Blockmans (The empire strikes back 1998). However, Protestant, French, British, and some other Northern European reflections might well be that 1555, when Charles V abdicated and retired to a monastery to mend clocks, would be a more appropriate date to commemorate. It ended some of the pressures for involuntary unity.

In France, in an attempt to more closely fit education to Europeanization and European integration, the traditional history course is being replaced with a compulsory yearlong study of Western civilization from ancient Greece to the Romantics. However, the teaching of history in British schools has been criticized as being too narrowly based. It focuses on the Nazi period in Germany, to a lesser extent Soviet Russia, and early modern British history dealing with rule by the Tudors and the Stuarts. It has been argued that the emphasis on these areas reflects a preference for "feelgood history," which can make the British feel good about themselves while neglecting changes since the end of the cold war (Achtung! 2001).

Another area of prospective conflict for a common European curriculum is how far it should eulogize the official founding fathers yet leave out those who have achieved change by challenging this system or whistle blowing. No one could seriously challenge the need to include former League of Nations bureaucrat and visionary on Europe Jean Monnet, former French foreign minister Robert Schuman, or former German chancellor Konrad Adenauer among these founding fathers. Former commission president Jacques Delors must also deserve a place here because of his selfless devotion to integration and the management of the EU.

However, it might be argued that acknowledgment of the founding fathers should extend to those who did what they felt was the right thing and lost or jeopardized their careers as a result. These include whistle blower Paul Van Buitenen, to whom Cris Shore's (2000) book *Building Europe* is partly dedicated, and Bernard Connolly (1995) who lost his commission position after publishing the relatively technical and innocuous economic text *The Rotten Heart of Europe*. Van Buitenen refused to overlook the financial and other irregularities that led to the resignation of the then European Commission in 1999, and he had serious difficulties created for him as a result.

Efforts are also being made to more closely integrate the European research effort. Proposals for a European Research Area were discussed at the European Council summit in Lisbon in March 2000. One consideration is the perceived need to establish more mobility of researchers. Others include the number of people employed in research in relation to the workforce, the participation of people from foreign countries, the participation of women, and the age of the parties involved. A European Commission paper on a proposed research area was criticized for mentioning universities only once in connection with the proposed area. The president of the research group at the Confederation of Rectors' Conferences, Luc Weber, also said that networking of institutions was a superior option to that of the commission's proposed "centers of excellence" (Swain 2000).

There is a major difference between Anglo-Saxon research practice and that of some continental European countries with regard to the admissibility of sources. It is not totally unrelated to the debate over the academic status of cultural studies. In Anglo-Saxon practice, newspapers and indeed any sources are considered appropriate for academic research so long as there is an adequate critical appreciation of the reliability of that source and of any bias in it. Much U.S. research in areas such as international relations is heavily reliant on U.S. and foreign newspapers, or Web versions of newspapers, as a source of data.

The continental European tradition has been, in some countries at least, that using such sources meant that the research was journalism and not academic work. In this view, appropriate sources are government reports, archival material and statistics, books, and journal articles. The danger in such a limited and narrow approach is that research then becomes overreliant on establishment views such as those of government and other academics.

Another difference in approaches relates to the understanding of the creation of identity. In one view, identity is created in a grassroots upwards manner, with popular culture being overwhelmingly important. In the other, the top downward approach, identity is readily created or influenced by the actions of governments and other institutions to influence the masses. Where cultural studies has been accepted as an academic discipline, for example, in the United Kingdom and in Scandinavia, it has encouraged a grassroots perspective to the construction of culture and identity (McNeil 1998; Alasuutari 1999; Gripsrud 1998; Kallionemi 1998).

Cultural studies has not been so readily accepted as a discipline or perspective in Germany or Austria (Horak 1999). It has been accepted more in terms of journalistic discourse, not academic debate or research (Marchant 2000).

A major reason behind the failure of cultural studies to be widely adopted in Germany and Austria appears to be the Frankfurt School's critique of popular culture. Members of the school saw it as a form of mass deception by the culture industry (Shattuc 1995, 86). Horak (1999, 112) saw the Frankfurt School as having stymied the reception of cultural studies in Germany. He saw it as having created the notion of a passive consumer who is helplessly trapped in the entertainment industry's flood of cheap products. However, he noted that critics of the Frankfurt School also have a disdain or fear of popular culture and that such opposition therefore has to be understood in the context of particular intellectual traditions that see, for example, even sociology as *undeutsch* (not in the German tradition) and lacking emotion.

Given the importance of culture and identity for European integration, it is important that a wider perspective is adopted in the teaching of such issues and that the gulf between the two traditions or approaches can be overcome. To some extent, the Scandinavian tradition bridges that divide. For example, in *Signs of Nations*, Hedetoft (1995) stressed both popular grassroots sources of culture and the influence of national governments through, for example, education and the place of music and song within it. Both are seen as having an influence on culture and identity.

Integrating education in Europe will also mean that specific problems will have to be faced and dealt with. In Serbia, for example, students recently drafted a policy paper that highlighted the need to cut down on corruption. This was identified as arising from payment or favors for grades, students sitting exams for others, forging of documents needed for grants or dormitory rights, and staff remaining silent about corruption instead of reporting it (Holdsworth 2002).

Another specific problem facing integration of tertiary education in Europe is in Macedonia, where the EU last year agreed to give an additional €5 million to the Albanian-, Macedonian-, and English-taught University of South East Europe. Germany agreed to give it DM1 million. This institution has been organized in Tetovo under the supervision of the Organization for Security and Co-operation in Europe. However, the university had only 850 students, Albanians and Slavs, while the unofficial Albanian-language University of Tetovo within sight of it had 13,000.

The reason for the duplication is an attempt by the international community to provide the Albanian minority in Macedonia with own-language tertiary education, in the face of the refusal of the Macedonian government to grant official status or funding to the University of Tetovo and to bring it into the public system. Nevertheless, the establishment of the new university, a deal brokered by the party representing ethnic Albanians in the governing coalition in Macedonia, has not been considered an adequate substitute by the ethnic Albanian National Liberation Army. The lack of official status and funding for the University of Tetovo was one of the grievances that lay behind the ethnic Albanian insurgency in Macedonia in 2001 (Raxhimi 2001). Since the university's unofficial establishment in 1998, it had won considerable support as an area university for ethnic Albanians, including from the Kosovo Liberation Army (Schwarz 2001).

Integration of tertiary education in Europe is hence proceeding at a number of levels. A common degree framework and course credits and standards are being agreed on and implemented by national governments and institutions. At the level of the EU, schemes to support the mobility of students, teachers, and workers and the completion of part of a course of study in another EU country are being run and financed by the European Commission. The commission also manages the Jean Monnet scheme, which helps to fund the teaching of European integration and the interaction of academics as well as teaching and research institutions, which include the EUI and the College of Europe. These schemes, and entry to the EU's teaching and research institutions, are being extended to applicant countries for EU membership in Central and Eastern Europe. Countries and institutions in Southeastern Europe are being offered the prospect of eventual membership.

The impact of all these changes will be to more closely integrate Europe's elites and to increase their mobility in terms of employment. The benefits for overall populations are less evident, and it may be argued that such funding as is involved would be better targeted at the often poor educational facilities available to low-income groups. These changes will more closely integrate the EU with the United States, Canada, and Western education in general. However, as things stand, they risk widening the cultural and educational gap between Russia and the remainder of Europe.

Note

1. In 1999, slightly more than 10,000 British students participated in the European Community Action Scheme for the Mobility of University Students (ERASMUS) program, compared to nearly 12,000 in 1994-1995, and the number was expected to fall to 9,000 for 2000. Elsewhere, use of ERASMUS was expanding, for example, in France where 16,825 French students were assisted by it compared to 10,000 seven years ago; the number of Spanish participants increased from 10,841 in 1996-1997 to 16,297 in 1999-2000. The number of German participants increased to 15,715 in 1999, and that of Italians from just less than 9,000 in 1996-1997 to nearly 12,500 in 1999-2000. While 1,583 British students went to Germany, 3,922 came from there to Britain. A total of 20,436 students came to the United Kingdom. However, the number of applicants from EU countries wanting to study in the United Kingdom had fallen from 30,821 in 1997 to 23,756 in 2000, partly due to the fee situation in the United Kingdom relative to that in Ireland and Greece and the increasing relative cost of the United Kingdom.

References

Achtung! Too many Nazis. 2001. *The Economist* 3 November, 61.

Alasuutari, Pertti. 1999. Cultural studies as a construct. *European Journal of Cultural Studies* 2 (1): 91-108.

Bompard, Paul. 2000. Italians embrace credit system. *Times Higher*, 3 November, 12.

Commission of the European Communities. 1993. *Green paper on the European dimension of education.* Brussels, Belgium: Commission of the European Communities.

Connolly, Bernard. 1995. *The rotten heart of Europe.* London: Faber and Faber.

Corbett, Anne. 1999. One step forward . . . *Times Higher*, 24 September, vi.

Dardanelli, Paolo. 1999. EMU and the legitimacy of the European Union. Paper presented to the 4th UACES Research conference, 8-10 September, Sheffield, UK.

De Laine, Michael. 2000. Sweden tackles diversity problem. *Times Higher*, 23 June.

Deleuran, Claus. 1993. *Illustreret Danmarks History* (An illustrated history of Denmark). Copenhagen, Denmark: Ekstra Bladets Forlag.

Einem, Caspar. 2000. *Der Europaeische Hochschulsraum: Gemeinsame Erklaerung der Europaeischen Bildungsminister, 19. Juni 1999, Bologna* (The European university space: Collective declaration of the European Education Ministers, 19 June 1999, Bologna). Available from http://www.bmwf.gv.at/service/board/990729a.htm.

The empire strikes back. 1998. *European*, 2 March, 18.

European Commission. 1993. *Background report: Green paper on the European dimension of education.* London: Jean Monnet House.

European Commission. 1999. *Eurobarometer 51.* Brussels, Belgium: DG 10. Available from http://www.europa.eu.int/comm/dg10/epo/eb/eb51/eb_51_en.pdf.

European Voice. 2000. Bid to boost take-up of Erasmus. *European Voice*, 3 August, 7.

Field, Heather. 1999. Teaching the EU in Australia: Justification, aims and content. In *Teaching European studies in Australia: Problems and projects*, edited by Alexander Pavkovic and Catherine Welch, with Carolyn O'Brien. Melbourne: Contemporary European Studies Association of Australia.

———. 2000a. Integrating identity, education and culture: Questions, policies and processes in the European Union. Paper presented to the Nation and Identity Conference, 12-14 July, at Monash University, Clayton, Victoria, Canada.

———. 2000b. On the "Europeanization" and "internationalization" of education in Europe: Danish and other perspectives. *ECSA Review* 13 (1): 10-11.

———. 2001. European integration curricula and "Europeanization": Alternative approaches and critical appraisal. Paper presented at the European Community Studies Association seventh biennial international conference, 31 May-2 June, Madison, WI.

Gardner, Michael. 1994. How can you call yourself a European?. *Times Higher*, 30 December, 5.

Goddard, Alison. 2000. Class-ridden sector slated. *Times Higher*, 7 April, 3.

Gripsrud, Jostein. 1998. Cultural studies and intervention in television policy. *European Journal of Cultural Studies* 1 (1): 85-95.

Hedetoft, Ulf. 1995. *Signs of nations.* Dartmouth, UK: Aldershot.

Holdsworth, Nick. 2001. Balkans invited to join the Bologna bandwagon. *Times Higher*, 25 May, 56.

———. 2002. Fighting corruption top of Serb students' hitlist. *Times Higher*, 1 February, 11.

Horak, Roman. 1999. Cultural studies in Germany (and Austria). *European Journal of Cultural Studies* 2 (1): 109-15.

Jobbins, David. 1999. Europe aims for greater student mobility. *Times Higher*, 25 June, 64.

Kallionemi, Kari. 1998. Put the needle on the record and think of England. Ph.D. diss., University of Turku.

Kaye, Harvey. 2000. Send in the history platoon. *Times Higher*, 31 March, 11.

Kleinman, Mark, and David Piachaud. 1993. European social policy: Conceptions and choices. *Journal of European Social Policy* 3 (1): 1-19.

Laffan, Brigid. 1996. The politics of identity and political order in Europe. *Journal of Common Market Studies* 34 (1): 81-102.

Marchant, Oliver. 2000. Cultural studies as "popularized" science. Abstracts from the Workshop on Humanities and Cultural Studies, 29-30 June. Vienna: Internationales Forschungszentrum Kulturwissenschaften.

Marshall, Jane. 2000. European students secure Lang's backing for a role in making policy. *Times Higher*, 10 November, 13.

McIlvenny, Paul, Inger Lassen, and Pirkko Raudaskoski. 2002. McUniversity: The end of public education as we know it. *Northern Lights* March: 1-10.

McNeil, Maureen. 1998. De-centering or re-focusing cultural studies. *European Journal of Cultural Studies* 1 (1): 57-64.

Mitchell, David. 1998. New borders for education: Redefining the role and sites of education in the future. Centre for International Studies discussion paper 3/98. Aalborg, Denmark: Aalborg University.

Nuthall, Keith, Rebecca Warden, and David Jobbins. 2002. EU close to fixing quality standard. *Times Higher*, 11 March, 5.

Pavkovic, Aleksandar. 2000. Constructing a European identity: Problems of supranationalism. In *Why Europe? Problems of culture and identity*, edited by Joe Andrew, Malcolm Crook, and Michael Waller. Basingstoke, UK: Macmillan.

Raxhimi, Altin. 2001. Gaining ground. *Transitions Online*, 7 March, 1-4. Available from http://www.tol.cz.

Schwartz, Johnathan. 2001. Challenges of belonging in diaspora and exile. In *Beyond integration*, edited by Maja Povrzanovic Frykman. Stockholm: Nordic Academic Press.

Shattuc, Jane. 1995. *Television, tabloids and tears: Fassbinder and popular culture*. Minneapolis: University of Minnesota Press.

Shore, Cris. 2000. *Building Europe: The cultural politics of European integration*. London: Routledge.

Swain, Harriet. 2000. Brussels seeks state targets for research staff and output. *Times Higher*, 16 June, 5.

Wessels, Wolfgang, Ingo Linsemann, and Susanne Haegele. 2000. "A core curriculum on European integration studies": Basic assumptions and proposals. Cologne, Germany: University of Cologne.

Worldwatch. 2001. *Times Higher*, 23 March, 11.

Markets, Management, and "Reengineering" Higher Education

By
ROGER GREEN

Recent years have witnessed a variety of efforts to reengineer higher education into closer alignment with market principles and management approaches drawn from business. However, critical debates on these efforts typically fail to discern a number of significant issues. Many such reengineering efforts involve an intermingling of three distinctively different organizational paradigms: a professional paradigm characteristic of traditional higher education organization, a bureaucratic machine paradigm representative of traditional business organization, and an innovative or "adhocratic" paradigm defended by its proponents as a timely alternative to traditional bureaucratic organization. This intermingling typically is carried out in a fashion oblivious to the nuances of organizational design and with little or no attention to the conflicts likely to result. Continued neglect of these issues, however, will condemn proponents of higher education adhocracy to problems in the future.

Recent years have witnessed a variety of efforts to reengineer higher education into closer alignment with market principles and management approaches drawn from business. Proponents of such efforts, including those from educational administration, state government, and the business world, argue that traditional approaches to higher education organization and management are increasingly out of step with demographic trends, technological innovations, and the accelerating pace of change found in other sectors of society. Opponents of such efforts, meanwhile, oftentimes decry this as an ill-advised drive to "Taylorize" higher education

Roger Green received his Ph.D. in political science from the University of California, San Diego. He currently serves as an assistant professor of public affairs at Florida Gulf Coast University, a new campus in the Florida State system. He played a key role in developing the university's Political Science and Master of Public Administration programs as well as in developing the university's distance learning programs. He has served on several university task forces dealing with faculty evaluation, multiyear contracts, collective bargaining, and intellectual property rights issues.

DOI: 10.1177/0002716202238575

by transforming faculty into a contingent labor force and learning into a commodity.

However, the tendency for debates to focus on the disagreements above has the potential to obscure an understanding of other more subtle issues associated with these trends. Such reengineering efforts often entail an intermingling of three distinctively different organizational paradigms within higher education: a professional paradigm characteristic of traditional higher education organization, a bureaucratic machine paradigm representative of traditional business organization, and an innovative or "adhocratic" paradigm defended by its proponents as a timely alternative to traditional bureaucratic organization. This intermingling typically is carried out in a fashion oblivious to the nuances of organizational design and with little or no attention to the conflicts likely to result.

The ambiguities or outright problems inherent in the increasingly pervasive imposition of a machine organizational paradigm on higher education—with measures including a business approach to performance assessment and reporting, a market approach to distance learning, a more aggressive top-down managerial approach to university planning and organization, and an increasing reliance on (or even preference for) part-time or contingent faculty staffing arrangements—has been explored in recent years by a number of authors (Altbach 1999; Aronowitz 2000; Benjamin 1995; Leslie 1998; Lewis, Massey, and Smith 2001; Rhoades 1998; Slaughter 2001). By comparison, the ambiguities or potential problems associated with the introduction of an innovative organizational paradigm (or adhocracy) into higher education—with components that include a relatively flat and decentralized structure of power and authority, a flexible faculty staffing approach, and an increasing reliance on temporary cross-functional project teams and matrix management approaches—has received little in the way of scholarly attention. Perhaps this is due to its relative novelty, or perhaps it is due to the fact that it arguably offers a more subtle target for academicians concerned with the migration of business ideas into higher education, despite the fact that adhocracy has similar roots in business-sector organizational theory. Continued neglect of these ambiguities and problems, however, will condemn proponents of higher education adhocracy to problems in the future.

The Reengineering Phenomenon in Higher Education

A number of key trends point to the extent and significance of recent higher education reengineering efforts. Although their percentage of the overall faculty population began to flatten out by the 1990s, the number of part-time faculty members increased substantially during the 1970s and 1980s (Leslie 1998; U.S. Department of Education 1999). Accompanying this trend in the past decade have been efforts to characterize tenure as an anachronism obstructing the quest for organizational flexibility and efficiency, with a number of colleges and universities calling for or even carrying out a partial or complete adoption of multiyear contract systems (Baldwin and Chronister 2001). Business-style accountability mandates and performance monitoring systems for higher education institutions have been adopted by an increasing number of states, and calls for an extension of K-12-style competency testing into public universities and colleges have begun to surface in state government debates (Alexander 2000; Berdahl and McConnell 1999; Burke and Serban 1998; National Association of College and University Business Officers 1996; Ruppert 2001; Schmidt 2000). These trends also have featured the emergence of distance learning technology as a means for delivering higher education products in a more market-driven fashion, stimulated by dreams of transcending the barriers traditionally imposed by geography and time in the quest for new student-customers (Lewis, Massey, and Smith 2001; Oblinger and Rush 1997).

Several interrelated conditions have contributed to these trends. Fiscal concerns stemming from a deteriorating public tolerance for tuition increases, as well as perceptions by public universities and colleges of an increasingly precarious competitive position for state dollars, clearly have played an important role (Altbach 1999; Benjamin 1995; Munitz 1995). Fears of increasing competition from nontraditional "vendors" of higher education have contributed to these trends as well (Galan 2001).

These trends also have been influenced by an influential conservative critique of traditional educational institutions, government agencies, and other institutions responsible for the production and administration of public goods. According to this critique, such entities constitute a bureaucratic quagmire, populated by self-interested actors striving to maximize their budgets and perquisites, defying the customers (i.e., the public) they are supposed to be serving while shielding themselves from the market dynamics and labor discipline that ideally hold organizations and their workers accountable. The institution of tenure—caricatured as a guarantee of lifetime employment in the midst of ordinary workers grappling with the vagaries of downsizing and right-sizing—oftentimes is exploited as a target by proponents of such views (Gingrich 1995; Sowell 1993).

This conservative critique relies heavily on a market metaphor that diagnoses the source of the public sector's problems as the absence of the private sector's rules of the game. The prescribed remedy is to transform the public sector into a network of markets, either through the privatization of public service delivery or through an approximation of market dynamics within restructured public organizations. Included within this transformation is the enforcement of a customer service orientation among public employees, with a system of rewards and punishments designed to reorient them toward appropriate behavior. In the case of universities and colleges, this translates into a reconstitution of the student as customer, competition for educational market share between distance education vendors freed by technology from traditional spatial and temporal limitations, and rigorous productivity audits of faculty employees to measure their fidelity to the business of education.

In some cases, these trends and the arguments accompanying them are transparently problematic: attacks on tenure often are ensnared by partisan politics, and in many instances, the accountability and performance measurement practices championed by some state legislatures, boards of trustees, and organizations such as the American Council of Trustees and Alumni seem unaware of the scholarly literature on performance measurement.

However, in some instances, one can discern a trend less visible than those described above but nonetheless significant both for the influence it might come to enjoy and for its immunity to easy critical dissection. This consists of strategies for reengineering higher education in accordance with contemporary theories of learning organizations and knowledge management. These strategies are premised on an alleged need to replace rigidly hierarchical and functionally organized bureaucracies with flatter and more flexible organizations, cross-functional project teams, matrix management, and—to use a term coined in large part to strategically counter the stereotypical attributes of bureaucracy—*adhocracy*. As defended by proponents of this strategy, such efforts to reengineer higher education should not be feared as attacks on academia but should instead be viewed as a crusade to shatter the vestiges of relatively static and overly bureaucratized educational institutions and to usher in more forward-looking approaches to organization and planning.

One of the most recent and controversial examples of a higher education institution designed according to this blueprint is that of Florida Gulf Coast University, which in 1997 became the tenth campus in the Florida public university system. Prior to opening, its founding officials and boosters championed it as an institution destined to "break down boundaries" and as "a white canvas waiting for innovation" (State's newest college 1996). The university was to use distance learning and high-tech marketing to deliver its courses to a far-flung population of predominantly nontraditional students. The faculty members involved in such efforts—some of them full-time faculty and some of them part-time adjuncts drawn from regional public, private, and not-for-profit organizations—were to be deployed within a highly flexible adhocracy, with a strong emphasis on interdisciplinary teams and project management approaches. Full-time faculty members were to be hired on renewable multiyear contracts rather than on tenured or tenure-track contracts, thereby offering the university greater flexibility in its staffing of programs and initiatives (State's newest college 1996; New year to heat tenure debate 1995; Florida Gulf Coast university 1997; Florida's new school 1994).

Despite its commitment to adhocracy, however, Florida Gulf Coast University's innovations were to emerge within a state university system otherwise organized according to more traditional scholarly and business-style paradigms. Other institutions throughout the state's university system were to remain tenure based, and even though the system's faculty union ultimately dropped its bitter opposition to Florida Gulf Coast University's plans for using a multiyear contract system (after a convincing threat by Florida Gulf Coast University's backers to seek legislative authorization for extending multiyear contract systems throughout the state university system), tenured faculty members harbored suspicions that the university would ignore the evaluative procedures and distinctions of professional hierarchy that in their view are requisite features of a scholarly organization. At the same time, the state university system in which the campus was located was one subject in recent years to legislative demands for machine-style accountability, including increasingly comprehensive and detailed performance monitoring and reporting requirements (Burke and Serban 1998; Florida joins accountability movement 2001; Ruppert 2001).

The adhocracy trend in higher education exemplified by Florida Gulf Coast University still draws heavily on the language of business, with a number of important management theorists providing inspiration. Such sources, as well as many of the reform efforts in higher education that draw on them, are relatively free of the vitriol toward higher education otherwise so pervasive in contemporary public discourse. However, the inspiring language through which this style of reform typically is expressed may blind would-be reformers to an array of problems.

Bureaucracy, Adhocracy, and Higher Education

Although literature calling specifically for a postbureaucratic reengineering of higher education began to proliferate in the past decade, the business management literature on which it draws emerged several decades ago. Management guru Warren Bennis arguably represents the earliest major theorist whose works helped inspire these later efforts, doing so initially through books such as *Changing Organizations* (Bennis 1966), and later through works such as *The Temporary Society* (Bennis and Slater 1968) and *Organizing Genius* (Bennis and Biederman 1997).

An ardent proponent of postbureaucratic approaches to organizational design and management, Bennis stressed the idea that the key characteristic of the coming postbureaucratic paradigm would be that of transience: transience in terms of the mutability of organizational structures in the face of ever changing tasks as well as in terms of the relative impermanence of the personnel assignments within these structures. According to Bennis (1966), temporary organizational structures— "federations, networks, clusters, cross-functional teams, temporary systems, ad hoc task forces, lattices, modules, matrices"—would prove more adaptable than would traditional bureaucracies when faced with the abrupt shifts characteristic of the modern era. Similarly, relative strangers drawn from diverse professional and technical backgrounds, linked together by coordinators and task-evaluative specialists, assembled and disassembled in various constellations, would prove more nimble than would their bureaucratic counterparts when confronted with problems whose ambiguity defies resolution through discipline-specific means (pp. 13-14).

Bennis's earliest ideas on what he regarded as the inevitable supplanting of bureaucracy by more transient and flexible organizational forms enjoyed a wide readership among management specialists, but the broader popularization of these ideas was to be carried out several years later by futurist Alvin Toffler in his best-selling 1970 book *Future Shock*. In arguments whose fidelity to Bennis's earlier work was apparent, Toffler predicted that the relatively durable and vertically ordered organization of the industrial era was drifting toward extinction, displaced within the changing ecology of late-20th-century industrial organization by "flatter," more "kinetic," more "fluid" organizational forms. In Toffler's terminology, "bureaucracy" ultimately would find itself supplanted by "adhocracy" (Toffler 1970, 144-46).

Bennis and Toffler alike were aware of the changes this transformation would require not only in the design of organizations but also in the cognitive maps of the organizations' employees. Such changes would require the development of intellectual and attitudinal agility in the face of shifting problem sets, an ability to develop fleeting but intense relationships with temporary team members, and an ability to endure the abrupt disintegration of these relationships when a task is completed and the team is dismantled. Acknowledging the psychological toll that such transience might exact from workers, Bennis (Bennis and Slater 1968) recommended redesigning educational systems to better teach students "how to let go . . . how to enter groups and to leave them" (p. 139).

A number of conservative political thinkers—most notably Newt Gingrich— were attracted to this vision, drawing on it selectively to provide themselves with an attractively visionary idiom in their diatribes against progressive liberalism's bloated public bureaucracies. (Bennis and Toffler, it should be pointed out, envisioned that the gales of creative destruction would sweep through sclerotic organizations in both the private and public sectors.) However, the ideologically shrill manner in which such conservative thinkers borrowed from Bennis and Toffler should not divert attention from the substantial body of more serious works that followed in their wake. Many of Bennis's and Toffler's early ideas were explored in greater detail by subsequent organizational theorists during the 1980s and 1990s, especially those working on the exigencies of matrix management (one of the most frequently cited examples of an appropriately adhocratic organizational structure, especially given its potential for assembling and reassembling lateral, multidisciplinary project teams within an otherwise functionally structured organization). Writers such as Henry Mintzberg (1979, 1989), Raymond Hill (Hill and White 1979), Stanley Davis (Davis and Lawrence 1979), Walter Baber (1983), and Gifford and Elizabeth Pinchot (1993) sought to analyze not only the potential advantages of matrix organizations, cross-functional product teams, and other transient organizational forms but also the difficulties that might confront those who utilized these blindly or in less-than-hospitable organizational environments. The tendency for most of these authors' prominent illustrations, case studies, and exemplars to be high tech in nature—NASA's Apollo Project, the Navy Special Projects Office's development of the Polaris System, Hughes Aircraft, TRW, Texas Instruments, even the Manhattan Project (as a mammoth precursor)—helped to provide a psychological linkage between technology, adhocracy, and innovation in the imaginations of those gripped by postbureaucratic longings. The popularization of these ideas arguably reached its zenith during the 1990s in the work of Michael Hammer and James Champy (1993). Hammer and Champy were notable not only for their success in promoting reengineering as an attractive strategy in an uncertain and risky business environment but also for their success in achieving the status of "management gurus" for a mass business audience (Jackson 2001).

In the midst of debates on higher education's travails, this postbureaucratic enthusiasm ultimately found its way into higher education reform literature (Cross 1998; Dolence and Norris 1995; Duderstadt 2000; Frost 1998; Kliewer 1999; Oblinger and Rush 1997; Oblinger and Verville 1998; Rowley, Lujan, and Dolence 1998; Tierney 1999). In a 1998 book whose arguments are typical of others in this genre—*What Business Wants from Higher Education*—authors Diana Oblinger and Anne-Lee Verville (1998) suggested that the same societal shifts requiring workers to be increasingly comfortable with complexity, ambiguity, occupational transience, and self-management also point to the need for sweeping changes in higher education organization. Dramatically altering the content of courses, ideally even making courses time- and location-independent through distance learning technology, is critical but hardly sufficient, they argued. Instead, colleges and universities must jettison traditional approaches to higher education organization based on rigidly vertical structures of authority and power, "functional silos," and tenure and embrace newer approaches focused on cross-functional structures, self-managing teams, and more flexible faculty staffing arrangements (Oblinger and Verville 1998).

In a 1999 book often referenced in the most recent literature on higher education reforms, *Building the Responsive Campus: Creating High Performance Colleges and Universities*, William Tierney (1999), director of the Center for Higher Education Policy Analysis at the University of Southern California, expressed similar sentiments. Drawing on management theorists such as Bennis, Hammer, and Champy, Tierney urged the embrace of reengineering by colleges and universities to create "innovative and seamless processes that have an uninterrupted flow and occur in a natural order, with a natural velocity," especially through "flatter, cross-functional organizational units [that] replace hierarchical systems that operate with centralized, top-down authority" (pp. 34-35). His preferred mechanism? A "soft project structure" (essentially another name for the matrix management approach in which employees are assigned to functional or discipline-specific organizational units within which they may do much or most of their work but are frequently reassigned from these to cross-functional project teams with limited life spans).

However, the alternative organizational paradigm idealized by such thinkers has emerged within a broader environment in which more traditional organizational paradigms still exert tremendous control, thereby posing the possibility of paradigm conflicts and precluding any simple transition into the postbureaucratic future. Henry Mintzberg's analyses, although developed for the most part in the late 1970s and 1980s, still are particularly effective for illuminating some of the crucial tensions between the major organizational paradigms vying for influence within the reengineering of higher education. Three such paradigms are especially pertinent: the machine paradigm, the professional paradigm, and the innovative paradigm or adhocracy.

The machine paradigm, as exemplified by the traditional business organization, is the most familiar of these. Employees are organized in a vertically centralized structure of power and authority, with sharp distinctions between administrators and nonadministrators, as well as in a lateral division of labor based on functional groupings. Organizations based on this paradigm tend to rely on highly formalized policies and procedures governing production, measurement, and reporting; they tend to rely as well on a top-down pattern of strategy formulation, with a heavy emphasis on action planning and a sharp distinction between formulation (reserved for administrators, increasingly so as one moves toward the organization's apex) and implementation (delegated to workers at lower levels of the structure). Designed for efficient standardized production in relatively simple and stable environments, this form of organization also is well suited for environments characterized by strong external controls on the organization, where demands for accountability and performance monitoring, as well as a proliferation of externally imposed rules and explicit performance targets, create a perceived need to centralize power to standardize the organization's outputs and enforce production targets. However, according to Mintzberg (1979), this paradigm is not particularly well suited for problem solving. Its rigid division of labor, functional isolation and consequent "fragmentation" of the workforce, and sharp distinctions between administrators and nonadministrators create formidable problems of communication and coordination—severe problems if a complex and dynamic environment requires rapid innovation and adaptation (pp. 314-47).

An alternative model of organization is that constituted by the professional paradigm, as exemplified by the traditional university. As compared to organizations based on the machine paradigm, this type of organization relies on a relatively decentralized structure of power and authority. Along with this decentralization, it exhibits a less pronounced distinction between administrators and nonadministrators than does the machine paradigm and a more conditional delegation of power and authority to administrators by the professionals over whom they serve. Such organizations possess little in the way of a neatly integrated decision-making and planning processes. Instead, highly trained and professionally socialized specialists are granted considerable autonomy and self-direction over their work (in a sense, formulation and implementation alike are carried out by these self-directed professionals). To the degree that a more integrated pattern of organizational planning can be discerned, this tends to be an aggregate of projects that individual professional entrepreneurs within the organization have convinced it to undertake over time.

Whereas standards in machine organizations are generated in top-down fashion by administrators and/or technical analysts, standards in professional organizations tend to be generated from outside the structure of the organization itself, principally by the professional associations and postgraduate programs associated with the profession. The work carried out by the professionals employed by such organizations tends to be too complex to be supervised directly by managers or standardized by analysts. Instead, the professionals tend to pigeonhole the problems or tasks before them and then respond to these by drawing on a repertoire of sophisticated but standardized programs (e.g., in a university or college, large freshman course = lecture format and machine-graded exams; small graduate course = discussion format and research papers; promotion = peer-reviewed research).

The professional organization is relatively effective in complex but stable environments whose tasks lend themselves to pigeonholing and standardized professional responses. In addition, the relative autonomy enjoyed by its professionals, combined with their ability to discharge their responsibilities by drawing on a repertoire of professionally standardized responses, allows these professionals to continually upgrade their skills and hone their expertise with minimal interference. However, the professional organization is not without its shortcomings. In some cases, it exhibits a limited capacity for dealing with professionals who are either incompetent or less than conscientious. Perhaps more important, the relative autonomy of its individual professionals, in combination with their reliance on pigeonholing and the application of professionally standardized responses, often renders the professional organization ill suited for organizational-level innovations, especially ones requiring a multidisciplinary approach (Mintzberg, 1979, 348-79).

A third and significantly less familiar organizational form is that constituted by the innovative paradigm or adhocracy, with high-tech research and development firms typically idealized as the paradigm's exemplars. This paradigm relies on a highly decentralized and flat structure of power and authority. The distinction between administrators and nonadministrators tends to be blurred; managers serve as functioning members of multidisciplinary project teams, responsible primarily for facilitating interaction between team members and for serving as liaisons between teams. The organization's specialists may be grouped in functional units for routine personnel functions and professional development (with a high degree of horizontal specialization) but are typically deployed in multidisciplinary project teams.

Organizations based on this paradigm usually display relatively little in the way of formalized policies and procedures. Whereas strategy formulation in machine organizations is a top-down process, and in professional organizations is a bottom-up and highly individualized process, innovative organizations or adhocracies rarely evidence a process of strategy formulation in the classic sense (especially in terms of the conventional formulation-implementation dichotomy). Instead, goals and strategies evolve in a continuous and oftentimes disjointed fashion within the organization's multidisciplinary project teams.

The innovative organization is relatively effective at innovating within complex and dynamic environments. This is the case even though it cannot utilize either the machine organization's bureaucratic trappings (sharp divisions of labor, extensive unit differentiation, highly formalized policies and procedures, vertically ordered planning and control systems) or the professional organization's pigeonholing and repertoire of professionally standardized responses, because either of these would obstruct its efforts to break away from established patterns and to innovate. However, its advantages for innovating come with a price. As compared to both the machine and professional forms, it tends to be inefficient and somewhat awkward at completing ordinary tasks. Its relative lack of structure or clear lines of authority and power render it susceptible to a high degree of internal politics, with conflict and aggression erupting both within and between project teams. Its greater level of organizational ambiguity can take a psychological toll on workers. And finally, its reliance on the project team approach makes it prone to unbalanced workloads, forcing workers to alternately accommodate periods of overwork and inactivity (Mintzberg, 1979, 431-67).

Mintzberg was astute not only in his identification of these organizational paradigms' respective strengths and weaknesses but also in noting some of the characteristic tensions likely to develop between the machine and professional paradigms. According to Mintzberg (1989)—and illustrated principally with references to higher education—the typical response by external machine loyalists to professional organizations' inherent shortcomings is to diagnose these as resulting from the lack of external control over the professional and even his or her profession. The attempted remedy that typically follows consists of efforts to control the professionals' activities with one or more of the mechanisms characteristic of machine organizations: more direct supervision, more stringent formalization of work processes, and standardized outputs and reporting requirements. That this should happen so readily is due in part to the fact that among people whose occupational socialization occurred within traditional business environments, "the machine configuration is not just *a* structure, it *is* structure; it is not *one* way to organize, it is the *only* sensible way to organize" (Mintzberg 1989, 269). From this perspective, it should not be surprising that in an era characterized by a widespread exaltation of business as providing the appropriate template for reshaping all organizations, higher education should find itself confronted by the machine trends described earlier.

Paradigm Conflicts and Unresolved Tensions

Several gaps are apparent in the literature prescribing adhocracy as the appropriate remedy for higher education's ills. One of these gaps lies in a failure to analyze the probable consequences of not only combining the machine and professional paradigms in higher education but throwing adhocracy into the mix as well. The second gap lies in a failure to anticipate how external machine proponents are likely to react to the inherent shortcomings of adhocracy itself. The third and final gap consists of a failure to understand that the phenomenon of organizational transience carries implications for the higher education job market and disciplinary environment quite different from those evident in the high-tech world envisioned by theorists of adhocracy.

The increasingly prevalent admixture of professional, machine, and innovative paradigms within higher education harbors an enormous potential for generating personnel conflicts, managerial confusion, and a complicated array of external pressures. This is due to the fact that such an admixture will produce more than just a misalignment between different organizational structures, policies, and procedures. It is likely to trigger conflicts between the distinctively different cognitive maps guiding each paradigm's loyalists. In many instances, these loyalists will simply talk past one another and see entirely different problems when staring at the same set of conditions. In other instances, there may be a possibility for bridging two or more of the paradigms and for finding a common vernacular for discussing problems. However, in the current higher education environment, the more disquieting question is whether a rapprochement is at all possible between the increasingly pervasive and politically driven machine paradigm, on one hand, and the professional and innovative paradigms, on the other hand.

The prospects for reengineering an organization through the introduction of adhocracy depend greatly on the type of organization and the broader sociopolitical contexts in which this effort is carried out. Reengineering a business organization through the introduction of adhocracy—itself a sufficiently formidable task—is a far more secure endeavor than is the same process within a university or college. This is due primarily to the fact that business organizations are better insulated from the cross-cutting pressures of the political environment and are situated within a more hospitable order of discourse. Matters are likely to be quite different when adhocracy is introduced in a higher education environment beset by machine pressures and conservative critiques, especially in the case of public universities and colleges that are significantly more permeable to politically generated machine pressures. In such cases, it would not be surprising to find adhocracy deflected, reshaped, and fitted within the pervasive discourse on higher education's alleged failure, elitist refusal to submit to the strictures of public accountability, and need for externally imposed machine controls.

Perhaps nowhere is this problem more apparent than in the potential misalignment between the day-to-day working conditions of an adhocracy, the realities of a tight academic labor market, and the business-style preference that universities and colleges be granted the prerogative to flexibly shed faculty without cause. At Florida Gulf Coast University, championed by its proponents as having embraced the innovative paradigm, many of the new faculty soon began to fear that the cross-functional labor demands of an educational adhocracy might very well undercut their ability to sustain the levels of research and publication typical within traditional professional academic organizations (As faculty and staff leave 1999; Growing pains 1998). A 1998 study of Florida Gulf Coast University's initial multiyear contract faculty members had indicated that these faculty members' scholarly qualifications and research records compared favorably with those displayed by faculty members at peer institutions elsewhere in the Florida public university system (Chait and Trower, 1998). However, the fear expressed in this regard was a prospective one focused on faculty members' future levels of research productivity in the face of Florida Gulf Coast University's decidedly atypical working conditions and consequently their attractiveness to traditional professional institutions if the university were to subsequently refuse them a successive contract (Wilson 2000). Marketability to such institutions, it was felt, requires the currency more readily accumulated within a professional, rather than adhocratic, organizational environment. Such fears are not unfounded: Evergreen College, typically regarded as an exemplar of multiyear contract institutions and cross-functional work assignments, explains its relatively high rate of faculty retention in part by acknowledging, "We 'unfit' people for the job market" (Chait and Trower 1997, 7).

With respect to the second gap identified above—an awareness of how external parties are likely to react to the inherent shortcomings of adhocracy itself—higher education's would-be reengineers likely should anticipate a lesser tolerance for the learning mistakes that proponents of adhocracy ordinarily regard as an essential attribute of their favored paradigm. The classic business literature on postbureaucratic organizational reforms has consistently stressed the need for managers to look on mistakes as crucial learning tools and as a consequence to be tolerant of these as their project teams strive to explore and to innovate. As articulated by Warren Bennis and Patricia Biederman (1997), "leaders encourage creativity when they take the sting out of failure" (p. 21).

One of the key reasons adhocracy allegedly enjoys an advantage when it comes to organizational innovation is that when its members carry out their disjointed and generally inefficient problem-solving efforts, they can anticipate the likelihood that failed experiments will meet with a relatively high degree of managerial tolerance. However, the likelihood of this tolerance is far more suspect in a higher education environment subject to shrill denunciations of the crisis in higher education and to an increasing proliferation of machine-style performance monitoring and reporting requirements. Higher education experiments that fail may well be caricatured as further evidence that those who can, do, and those who cannot, teach. Even a higher education administrator sympathetic in principle to the notion that mistakes constitute a crucial wellspring of innovation may find himself or herself fatally pressured by the need to manage in accordance with machine pressures. Mintzberg was astute in his analysis of how machine loyalists—as well as many in the general public—likely would react over time in response to the evident inefficiencies and conflicts of the professional paradigm in higher education: diagnose these as resulting from the absence of external control over professionals, and then prescribe a remedy consisting of greater supervision, more stringent formalization of work processes, and standardized outputs and reporting requirements. Should one not anticipate a similar and perhaps even more intense machine response to the inefficiencies inherent in an educational adhocracy?

The third and final gap mentioned at the beginning of this conclusion consists of a failure to understand that organizational transience, which occupies a privileged place within the discourse on adhocracy, has very different meanings and impacts within the higher education job market and disciplinary environment than it does in the high-tech world envisioned by theorists of business adhocracy. Discussions on transience by business-oriented writers such as Bennis and Toffler focus on the exhilaration likely to be experienced by adhocracy's workers as they deal with frequent project shifts and ever changing constellations of teammates. Transience as envisioned by higher education theorists such as William Tierney appears on a shifting terrain of soft projects developed democratically by the faculty members holding presumably durable assignments within professional departments but periodically enlisted to work on a variety of soft project teams. Transience is regarded by the traditional professoriate as an intensification of the threatening vagaries previously situated at the pretenure career stage as well as a stealth maneuver for undercutting academic freedom. Finally, and most disturbingly for the future of higher education, there is the understanding of transcience shaping the efforts of higher education reformers from the business world. Organizational transience as conceived by the critics and watchdogs of higher education, their judgments shaped largely or even exclusively by a machine perspective, may very well center increasingly on a recasting of faculty members as readily interchangeable production components to be hired, fired, and reassembled at will.

References

Alexander, F. King. 2000. The changing face of accountability. *Journal of Higher Education* 71 (4): 411-31.

Altbach, Philip. 1999. Harsh realities: The professoriate faces a new century. In *American higher education in the twenty-first century: Social, political, and economic challenges*, edited by Philip Altbach, Robert Berdahl, and Patricia Gumport, 271-97. Baltimore: Johns Hopkins University Press.

Aronowitz, Stanley. 2000. *The knowledge factory: Dismantling the corporate university and creating true higher learning*. Boston: Beacon.

As faculty and staff leave FGCU, officials vow to monitor the situation. 1999. *Naples Daily News*, 31 May.

Baber, Walter. 1983. *Organizing for the future: Matrix models for the postindustrial polity*. University: University of Alabama Press.

Baldwin, Roger, and Jay Chronister. 2001. *Teaching without tenure: Policies and practices for a new era*. Baltimore: John Hopkins University Press.

Benjamin, Ernst. 1995. A faculty response to the fiscal crisis: From defense to offense. In *Higher education under fire: Politics, economics, and the crisis of the humanities*, edited by Michael Bérubé and Cary Nelson, 52-72. New York: Routledge.

Bennis, Warren. 1966. *Changing organizations: Essays on the development and evolution of human organization*. New York: McGraw-Hill.

Bennis, Warren, and Patricia Ward Biederman. 1997. *Organizing genius: The secrets of creative collaboration*. Reading, MA: Addison-Wesley.

Bennis, Warren, and Philip Slater. 1968. *The temporary society*. New York: Harper and Row.

Berdahl, Robert, and T. R. McConnell. 1999. Autonomy and accountability: Who controls academia? In *American higher education in the twenty-first century: Social, political, and economic challenges*, edited by Philip Altbach, Robert Berdahl, and Patricia Gumport, 70-88. Baltimore: Johns Hopkins University Press.

Burke, Joseph, and Andreea Serban. 1998. State synopses of performance funding programs. In *Performance funding for public higher education: Fad or trend?* New Directions in Institutional Research, no. 97. Edited by Joseph Burke and Andreea Serban, 25-48. San Francisco: Jossey-Bass.

Chait, Richard, and Ann Trower. 1997. *Where tenure does not reign: Colleges with contract systems*. Washington, DC: AAHE Pathways—Faculty Careers and Employment for the 21st Century.

———. 1998. Build it and who will come? *Change* 30 (5): 20-29.

Cross, Duane. 1998. Evolution or revolution: Creating a team-based organization. In *Using teams in higher education: Cultural foundations for productive change* New Directions in Institutional Research, no. 100. Edited by Susan Frost, 83-95. San Francisco: Jossey-Bass.

Davis, Stanley, and Paul Lawrence. 1979. Problems of matrix organizations. In *Matrix organization and project management*. No. 64. Edited by Raymond Hill and Bernard White, 134-51. Ann Arbor: Michigan Business Papers.

Dolence, Michael, and Donald Norris. 1995. *Transforming higher education: A vision for learning in the 21st century*. Ann Arbor, MI: Society for College and University Planning.

Duderstadt, James. 2000. *A university for the 21st century*. Ann Arbor: University of Michigan Press.

Florida Gulf Coast university hopes to innovate education/Florida's newest university will have a nontraditional approach to teaching. 1997. *Tallahassee Democrat*, 25 August.

Florida joins accountability movement. 2001. *Inside Academe* 6 (3): 1, 4, 5.

Florida's new school slowly takes shape. 1994. *Tampa Tribune*, 23 May.

Frost, Susan, ed. 1998. *Using teams in higher education: Cultural foundations for productive change*. New Directions in Institutional Research, no. 100. San Francisco: Jossey-Bass.

Galan, Nicholas. 2001. Throwing down the gauntlet: The rise of the for-profit education industry. In *The tower under siege: Technology, policy, and education*, edited by Brian Lewis, Christine Massey, and Richard Smith, 11-28. Montreal, Canada: McGill-Queens University Press.

Gingrich, Newt. 1995. *To renew America*. New York: HarperCollins.

Growing pains: Florida Gulf Coast University, the state's newest university, is off to a rocky start, some say. 1998. *Tampa Tribune*, 5 October.

Hammer, Michael, and James Champy. 1993. *Reengineering the corporation: A manifesto for business revolution*. New York: HarperBusiness.

Hill, Raymond, and Bernard White. 1979. *Matrix organization and project management*. Number 64. Ann Arbor: Michigan Business Papers.

Jackson, Brad. 2001. *Management gurus and management fashions*. New York: Routledge.

Kliewer, Joy Rosenszweig. 1999. *The innovative campus: Nurturing the distinctive learning environment*. Phoenix, AZ: American Council on Higher Education—Oryx Press.

Leslie, David, ed. 1998. *The growing use of part-time faculty: Understanding causes and effects*. San Francisco: Jossey-Bass.

Lewis, Brian, Christine Massey, and Richard Smith. 2001. *The tower under siege: Technology, policy, and education*. Montreal, Canada: McGill-Queens University Press.

Mintzberg, Henry. 1979. *The structuring of organizations: A synthesis of the research*. Englewood Cliffs, NJ: Prentice Hall.

——. 1989. *Mintzberg on management: Inside our strange world of organizations*. New York: Free Press.

Munitz, Barry. 1995. Managing transformation in an age of social triage. In *Reinventing the university: Managing and financing institutions of higher education*, edited by Sandra Johnson and Sean Rush, 21-48. New York: John Wiley.

National Association of College and University Business Officers. 1996. *Organizational paradigm shifts*. Washington, DC: National Association of College and University Business Officers.

New year to heat tenure debate to boil/Florida's university-system regents are about to take on one of academia's most sacred cows. 1995. *Tallahassee Democrat*, 23 December.

Oblinger, Diana, and Sean Rush. 1997. The learning revolution. In *The learning revolution: The challenge of information technology and the academy*, edited by Diana Oblinger and Sean Rush, 2-19. Bolton, MA: Anker.

Oblinger, Diana, and Ann-Lee Verville. 1998. *What business wants from higher education*. Phoenix, AZ: American Council on Education—Oryx Press.

Pinchot, Gifford, and Elizabeth Pinchot. 1993. *The end of bureaucracy and the rise of the intelligent organization*. San Francisco: Berrett-Koehler.

Rhoades, Gary. 1998. Market models, managerial institutions, and managed professionals. *International Higher Education* 13 (fall). Available from http://www.bc.edu/bc_org/avp/soe/cihe/newsletter/News13/text2.html.

Rowley, Daniel, Herman Lujan, and Michael Dolence, eds. 1998. *Strategic choices for the academy: How demand for lifelong learning will re-create higher education*. San Francisco: Jossey-Bass.

Ruppert, Sandra, ed. 2001. *Charting higher education accountability: A sourcebook on state-level performance indicators*. Washington, DC: National Center for Higher Education Management Systems.

Schmidt, Peter. 2000. Faculty outcry greets proposal for competency tests at U. of Texas. *Chronicle of Higher Education*, 6 October.

Slaughter, Sheila. 2001. Professional values and the allure of the market. *Academe* 87 (5): 22-26.

Sowell, Thomas. 1993. *Inside American education: The decline, the deception, the dogmas*. New York: Free Press.

State's newest college promotes cyber-curriculum. 1996. *Miami Herald*, 1 September.

Tierney, William. 1999. *Building the responsive campus: Creating high performance colleges and universities*. Thousand Oaks, CA: Sage.

Toffler, Alvin. 1970. *Future shock*. New York: Random House.

U.S. Department of Education. 1999. *Fall staff in postsecondary institutions, 1997*. Washington, DC: National Center for Education Statistics.

Wilson, Robin. 2000. A new campus without tenure considers what it's missing. *Chronicle of Higher Education*, 12 May.

The Literature of Higher Education

By
NORMA CONTRERAS
and
PAUL RICH

A Google Web search produces 5,280,000 site hits about universities—which Google located in .08 of a second. Education as a subject produces 65,200,000 hits, in .09 of a second. At least since William James published *Talks to Teachers* in 1899, the amount of writing specifically about aspects of university education has become almost overwhelming, and with the advent of the Web, the bibliography clearly is overwhelming.

Some indication of this and the present bibliographical problem is provided by the expansion of the Educational Resources Information Center (ERIC) archive, which added about 200,000 titles about higher education between 1978 and 1997 (Size, composition and distribution 1998). An excellent review of the ERIC system with regard to universities, along with a comprehensive bibliography, is provided by Lawrence M. Rudner (2000) in "Information Needs in the 21st Century: Will ERIC Be Ready?"

Rudner provided a succinct summary of the current bibliographical situation. He wrote,

Five years ago, ERIC was still basically the only education database. University Microfilms International (UMI) provided access to most of the journal articles in ERIC. The ERIC Document

Norma Contreras, Department of International Relations and History, University of the Americas–Puebla, Mexico is an active member of the world conference committee of Phi Beta Delta, the honor society for international scholars. She is currently the program chair and vice president of Vernacular: The International Colloquium for Vernacular, Hispanic, Historical, American, and Folklore Studies.

Paul Rich is the president of the Policy Studies Organization and of Phi Beta Delta, the international honor society. He is the Titular Professor of International Relations and History at the University of the Americas–Puebla and a visiting fellow at the Hoover Institution, Stanford University. A member of the Lasswell Award Committee of the American Political Science Association, he is the editor of the Lexington Press series on policy research.

DOI: 10.1177/0002716202238576

Reproduction Service provided access to the documents in RIE. Today, there are multiple education databases. For most people, the first preference will be high-quality materials they can get immediately. OCLC, EBSCOHost, JSTOR, CatchWord, the American Psychological Association and others are creating fee-based databases linked to the full text of peer-reviewed articles. ERIC's CIJE database has no such set of links, and UMI no longer provides reprint services. However, documents in ERIC's RIE database that were prepared in 1994 and later are now available on-demand, on-line.

As Rudner emphasized, the first source for the bibliography of higher education, as with many subjects, is now the Internet. But we are fast getting into a repeat of what happened when the conventional bibliography of a subject grew and grew, our need for specialized help. He offered the following comparison:

Of course, ten years ago, the Internet was not an option. Perhaps last year, many were content to search the Internet themselves. But the Internet has become massive and overwhelming. Using the major search engines often yields many irrelevant links. Typically, the user enters a word or two and the engines provide a crude ranking and relevancy match based on all the text appearing on each web page. Improvements in this area will be marginal at best. An alternative is a carefully constructed pathfinder that identifies, organizes and annotates resources within a given field. The Argus Corporation (www.clearinghouse.net) maintains an impressive list of such pathfinders. Many ERIC Clearinghouses have developed such tools and they are well-received. But, pathfinders must be maintained. URLs change; new resources become available; the pathfinder categories need to evolve; and resources should be continuously evaluated. Five years from now, the Clearinghouses will not be able to maintain their pathfinders as volunteer activities given increasing demand and the sheer growth in the knowledge base.

There are of course selective sites that try to filter the outpouring. One such, and a major biographical resource for higher education, is the International Association of Universities Web site maintained in cooperation with Unesco, accessible at http://www.unesco.org/iau/centre_gen.html. Another, recommended for current issues, is the Web site of the American Association of University Professors at http://www.aaup.org/Issues/index.htm.

To provide further help regarding Web sites, which of course are much easier to access from a Web site than when having to transcribe their hieroglyphics from a printed page, a Web site with more recommended higher education sites will be opened by November 2002 at http://mailweb.udlap.mx/~rich/ under "Annals and Higher Education." This list, edited by Norma Contreras, will be maintained for at least five years following publication of this special issue. It is hoped that this will cause other bibliographers to consider the impracticality of copying Web sites to printed page so they can be recopied to the computer.

However, the printed book has not met its maker, and those looking for general background reading on higher education are well advised to examine such classics as Frederick Rudolph's *American College and University* (1962), Robert Ulich's *Three Thousand Years of Educational Wisdom* (1947), and *Fundamentals of Democratic Education* (1940), all three of which are still in print after many years—a testimony to their value. A more recent book that is virtually indispensable in considering the problems of tenure, adjunct professors, and technology in the classroom is *The New Academic Generation: A Profession in Transformation* by Martin J. Finkelstein, Robert K. Seal, and Jack H. Schuster (1998, Johns Hopkins University Press). This offers an excellent bibliography.

Two journals that are important ways to keep abreast are *Change: The Magazine of Higher Learning*, which is edited by the American Association for Higher Education, and *College Teaching*. Both are published by the Helen Dwight Reid Educational Foundation. A third journal that frequently carries important articles on higher education is the *Futurist*, which is the magazine of the World Future Society.

References

Finkelstein, Martin J., Robert K. Seal, and Jack H. Schuster. 1998. *The new academic generation: A profession in transformation*. Baltimore: Johns Hopkins University Press.

James, William. [1899] 1925. *Talks to teachers on psychology and to students on some of life's ideals*. New York: Henry Holt.

Rudner, Lawrence M. 2000. Information needs in the 21st century: Will ERIC be ready? *Educational Analysis Policy Archives* 8 (44). Available from http://epaa.asu.edu/epaa/v8n44.html.

Rudolph, Frederick. 1962. *The American college and university, a history*. New York: Knopf.

Size, composition and distribution of the [university] literature. 1998. Available from www.srhe.ac.uk/cvcp/CVCP-SRHE%20seminar%20hounsell%201998.htm.

Ulrich, Robert. 1940. *Fundamentals of democratic education*. New York: American Book Company.

———. 1947. *Three thousand years of educational wisdom*. Cambridge, MA: Harvard University Press.

VISIT SAGE ONLINE AT: WWW.SAGEPUB.COM

Find what you are looking for faster!

Our advanced search engine allows you to find what you are looking for quickly and easily. Searches can be conducted by:

- Author/Editor
- Keyword/Discipline
- Product Type
- ISSN/ISBN
- Title

Payment online is secure and confidential!

Rest assured that all Web site transactions are completed on a secured server. Only you and Sage Customer Care have access to ordering information. Using your Visa, MasterCard, Discover, or American Express card, you can complete your order in just minutes.

Placing your order is easier than ever before!

Ordering online is simple using the Sage shopping cart feature. Just click on the "Buy Now!" logo next to the product, and it is automatically added to your shopping cart. When you are ready to check out, a listing of all selected products appears for confirmation before your order is completed.

WE'RE ONLINE!
Visit our Web site at: http://www.sagepub.com

F999008